HOW INFANTS KNOW MINDS

Vasudevi Reddy

How Infants Know Minds

HARVARD UNIVERSITY PRESS
Cambridge, Massachusetts, and London, England   2008

KH

Library of Congress Cataloging-in-Publication Data

Reddy, Vasudevi.
   How infants know minds / Vasudevi Reddy.
     p.   cm.
   Includes bibliographical references and index.
   ISBN-13: 978-0-674-02666-7 (alk. paper)
   ISBN-10: 0-674-02666-7 (alk. paper)
   1. Infant psychology.   2. Social perception in children.   3. Social interaction in
infants.   4. Interpersonal relations in children.   5. Other minds (Theory of knowledge)
6. Cognition in infants.   I. Title.
   BF720.S63R43   2008
   155.42'282—dc22   2007031717

8/28/09

*For Amma and Dada
and for Shamini and Rohan
of course.*

Contents

Acknowledgements   *ix*

1 A Puzzle   *1*

2 Minding the Gap   *7*

3 Engaging Minds: A Second-Person Approach   *26*

4 Making Contact: Imitation   *43*

5 Opening Conversations   *66*

6 Experiencing Attention   *90*

7 Feeling Self-Conscious   *120*

8 Playing with Intentions   *150*

9 Sharing Funniness   *183*

10 Faking in Communication   *215*

11 Other Minds and Other Cultures   *232*

Notes   *239*

Index   *267*

Acknowledgements

The process of writing this book had nearly the same impact—both on my life and on my family's—as did the birth of each of my children. Kevan, my husband, made both possible. His interest in infancy and in resolving fundamental questions of origins first drew me into this area, forced me to reckon with the theoretical arguments of the time (and in particular the controversial views of Colwyn Trevarthen), and supported me through many versions of these chapters. Without him none of this would have happened.

The book owes a lot to many people whose voices can be heard in it—my little sister Chitti (for being my very first guinea pig!); my students for listening and challenging me; Professor "Parry" Parameswaran for first inspiring me to rebel in psychology; Alan Costall for never letting me let up on the rebellion; Colwyn Trevarthen for seeing so many things that no one believed and for his courage in persisting with them. Many colleagues and friends have helped in unique ways: Doug Brandon with his poetry and feeling for words, Sue Leekam and Corina Hatzinikolau with their perceptiveness, Paul Morris, Giannis Kugiumutzakis, and Karl Nunkoosing with many conversations about psychology, Fiona Reed and Adeline Burrell with their pragmatism, and many others. My thanks to Annette Karmiloff-Smith, who first invited me to write a book on infant humour, and who, with Jerry Bruner and Elizabeth Knoll, put up with the time it took me to write it with more faith than I sometimes had in myself. My thanks also to Margaret Donaldson and Peter Hobson, whose books have been an inspiration. I owe a very special debt to Suzanne Zeedyk for her "midwifery"—she *made* me finish this book with a passion and strength that I can never thank her enough for, or forget. Above all, my thanks to all the babies in my studies—you will always remain babies to me!

HOW INFANTS KNOW MINDS

CHAPTER 1

A Puzzle

I can know another person as a person only by entering into personal relation with him. Without this I can know him only by observation and inference; only objectively.

John Macmurray, *Persons in Relation*[1]

How do babies come to understand people? Can babies be aware of others' minds? Do they perceive people as "persons," as psychological beings? I used to think babies were dull. I found them neither sweet nor interesting. Five-year-olds, on the other hand, were amazing. They did interesting things, made outrageous observations without concern for propriety, and, above all, you could hold conversations with them. But then my children were born and I was seduced by a new language. It seemed that if I let myself engage with them and learn their language, a new world was opening up for me—one which the textbooks didn't believe existed. The most striking thing my babies were telling me was that they could understand me and others as persons. They were teasing, joking, playing with our expectations and attitudes and interests, being shy, and showing off long before they were able to speak. Understanding other minds didn't seem to be a problem to them.

Yet, when I started to report studies investigating these infant abilities, I ran into a strange problem. Psychologists found the observations interesting—even amazing—but my interpretation (that these were revealing infants' awareness of other people's intentions and expectations and attentions) was seen as unacceptable. I was continually being told—like the users of British trains—to "Mind the Gap"! Infants, I was told, could perceive people's *bodies* but lacked the intellectual skills to grasp other *minds*. The idea of this gap mystified me. Why such a barrier? Why should minds be necessarily closed

1

to babies? Had I simply bumped into the fact that the modern science of understanding people fails to take seriously any knowledge that comes from inside the realm of personal relation? Or a still more powerful determination in psychology to keeping mind and body separate? In trying to answer these questions, I discovered that babies were an exciting "test case," not only for one of the most central questions in both psychology and the philosophy of mind—how we understand minds—but for the methods that the psychological sciences use to understand people.

The answer I am developing in this book—a second-person approach to knowing other minds—is part of a broader philosophy of science, something that is relevant not only to the question of how infants understand people but how adults—and people from different cultures—understand each other. It is also a part of a philosophy of personal relations: about how we could—and should—be open to each other in our adult, parental, therapeutic, educational, or working relationships. In a sense this book is an invitation to shift perspective. Things *can* be thought of differently. And we need to shift our thinking if we are to go beyond the traditional ruts and hang-ups of a psychology which holds on, surreptitiously, to dualisms it claims to have discarded and, more openly, to methods of investigation it knows are more appropriate to non-sentient subjects. I will use observations from infant lives, which may violate our experimental desires and offend our scepticism, but which are the closest we can get to engaging with infants on paper. To grasp the significance of these events in infants' lives and awareness, you may need to let down the boundaries between your life as a reader and your life as a person.

Bumblebees, Tuna Fish, and Babies: Similar Problems?

When my daughter was 9 months old, I was videotaping an ordinary family meal time to be shown in my class on pre-verbal language development. I caught an interaction on video which the family referred to confidently as "teasing." Watching it again and being impressed by what seemed my daughter's awareness of what other people wanted and expected of her, I stumbled on my first problem with the theoretical assumptions of the day. "Why talk about awareness of mental things like intentions and attention and expectations?" was the common academic response. "Why not just talk about awareness of behaviour? Why not just call them tertiary circular reactions or learning?" Similar comments followed with every new phenomenon

I presented: "Why not call it conditioning? Or reflexes? Why use the term *awareness*?" Whatever the problem was, it was deep and puzzling. Why the "just," the implied "merely"? Why was it so objectionable to argue that babies were aware of mentality and of psychological (rather than merely physical) phenomena? It seemed both unnecessary and inconsistent with other claims in psychology. All the alternatives that were offered to explain these subtle and impressive engagements that infants were managing seemed only to be aimed at explaining them *away*.

The problem could be likened to the old—and probably apocryphal—story about bumblebees not being able to fly. Involving (in some versions) Swiss scientists doing back-of-the-envelope calculations in pubs, the story goes that mathematical models of aerodynamics simply could not explain the flight of bumblebees. Their round, heavy bodies and tiny wings simply did not add up in terms of the lift needed for flight. But of course they *did* fly, at the rate of 3 metres per second! And there is a story told by Andy Clark involving the blue fin tuna.[2] In terms of muscle power they are far too weak to swim at the high speeds with the rapid pick-up and quick manoeuvring ability that they achieve. And yet they are real swimming prodigies.

Are human infants in something of a similar situation where science tells us babies can't understand people as something more than physical objects, although babies act as if they do? In the case of the bumblebee and the blue fin tuna, the theoretical problem came from a mis-assumption—from thinking of the organism's capacities separately from the environment in which it functions. The blue fin tuna swims so well because it manoeuvres its body in precise relation to the alternating clockwise and anti-clockwise vortices created by the flicking of its own tail. A similar story emerges in the case of the bumblebee. The bee manages to fly by creating vortices in the air around it through its rapid wing beats and then moving in the sea of vortices. If we talk of the abilities as lying within the fish or the bee, if we look at the organism in isolation from its environment and analyse its capacities without looking at what it does with the environment, we have to conclude that the bee can't "really" fly and the fish can't "really" swim. And that is absurd. But think of the swimming ability of the blue fin tuna and the flying ability of the bumblebee as belonging to an organism which is an active part of its environment, and we don't fall into this contradiction.

Could the problem for babies, too, be resolved by re-embedding the baby into the world of people? After all, we (in psychology) often think and talk about understanding other people as if it were a case of one completely separate person—and completely separate mind—trying to understand another. We don't tend to talk about people or minds as already intrinsically connected. But what if we did? What would this mean? What if we think of the starting point for understanding people as being, not isolation and ignorance, but an emotional relation and a psychological awareness? The idea of starting from emotional relation could powerfully change the way we approach the question of understanding minds. Rather than being belated consequences of a rationally constructed understanding, emotional engagements could be moments of intimacy, where a powerful awareness of the other is both revealed and forged. They could be similar to what Daniel Stern calls "now" moments, in which not only is there some new insight into each other, but the relation itself changes, creating new things to be understood.[3]

So, one problem leading to the puzzle might come from thinking of the baby as *dis-embedded* from other minds (and indeed from the world of objects and activities in which minds live). But is there an even deeper problem for us in talking about how babies understand minds—a problem of *dis-embodying* the mind? After all, much of psychology does think of mind as something private and opaque—something that is *hidden behind* the mask of the body, sometimes revealed in the body's behaviour but sometimes not. Indeed, many psychologists define the mental precisely in terms of its separation from the physical. Essentially, textbook psychology sees mind as bearing no fundamental concordance with the actions of the body (otherwise mind would be transparent to perception). In doing so, it seems to have dis-embodied mind. And this is where the real problem begins. If minds are indeed so hidden, then of course babies couldn't begin to grasp the first thing about them. Not having the intellectual and deductive skills of adults, when babies look at other people (given the assumption of the hidden-ness of minds), what else could they perceive except their physical movements and sounds? They would be completely denied access to others' psychological existence.

These two problems (the dis-embedding and the dis-embodying) make it really hard to build a coherent explanation of how minds can ever come to be understood—not only by babies, but also by adults or other animals or indeed by psychologists. If minds are only to be inferred, certainty becomes impossible, and psychology itself becomes a dubious, rather magical, enterprise—filled with ungrounded theorising, imaginary "Rubicons" for babies or species to cross, and, most important, an inability to take action seriously.

Very often we also end up with double standards for judging the significance of actions and interactions. Observations adequate for demonstrating mind knowledge in children become inadequate for infants because of the general belief that infants are incapable of such understanding. And the things that are the most meaningful to us in everyday life in terms of our understanding of others—the little everyday emotional engagements (the telltale glances, the knowing looks, the cheekiness of a smile, the startled pause, the surges of feelings) developed in established personal relationships—tend to get sheepishly sidelined when it comes to reporting scientifically on how we understand people. These double standards open up several questions about evidence for mind knowledge. To what extent do we need academic detachment for understanding other minds? Is detachment the way in which we understand minds in everyday life? Does understanding lie in experiencing the detail or in grasping the theory: in the doing or in the theorising? Who is the expert when it comes to understanding people—the detached scientist or the ordinary person in everyday life? Would re-embedding the baby into psychological relation with people and re-embodying minds solve the contradiction between what babies seem to understand about minds and what science thinks they don't understand? But does it matter how science conceives of babies?

Does It Matter?

Does it matter if science thinks that babies cannot understand us while parents think something else? After all, parents have been getting on with their infants and infants with their parents for millennia, entirely without the help of philosophers and psychologists and their arguments or misassumptions.

I think it matters profoundly. The views of science and philosophy influence people's actions even in something as fundamental as being with children. Pop psychology and parenting culture exchange information and values with the culture of the "experts," and the recommendations change and shift like fashions in the width of trousers. How we deal with the question of knowing other minds affects not only how we understand our children but also how we *act* towards them. If we think that infants have little in the way of thoughts and feelings and perceptions, then we will do less to look for or respond to what others might see as infants' thoughts or feelings. It was not so long ago, after all, that folk wisdom had it that human infants were born unable to see or hear, and that they were capable of little more than "mewling and puking in their nurse's arms," as Shakespeare put it. It was not so long ago either that medical science asserted (without parents being able to challenge it) that neonates cannot feel pain and thus justified a variety of intrusive practices like surgery without anaesthesia.

The implications of assuming infant ignorance about *our* minds are even more immediate: if we think infants have little access to our emotions and thoughts, we will make little effort to express them (perhaps when positive) or disguise them (perhaps when negative). We will create the kinds of interactions appropriate for an infant who *cannot* understand us—observing them, training them, keeping them happy, but not really *engaging* with them.

But engagement is vital. Its consequences are immediate in terms of affording or denying the baby the experiences that could emerge from them, and also, of course, for affording or denying the *parent* the experience of the baby that comes from those engagements. The way in which we allow ourselves to engage with others circumscribes the way in which we can know them: you might say, the more we engage with others, the more we *can* engage with them. Although this book isn't going to provide "shoulds" and "should nots" about engaging with babies, it is fundamentally based on descriptions of such engagements and on the premise that emotional engagement matters—not just for infants, but for adults, for other animals, and even for psychologists in their own quest to understand other minds. Neither infants nor adults nor other animals nor psychologists stand much chance of understanding if they stand aside from people and watch them without emotion and without engagement.

Trying to answer these questions has been more exciting than I had imagined, and you can't answer them without unpicking the philosophical assumptions we make about minds and babies and behaviour—assumptions that we cannot afford to be unaware of. So that's where I will begin in the next chapter. But for those who are less than keen on philosophical quagmires, you might want to skip ahead to Chapter 3, where I suggest an alternative approach for understanding our awareness of other minds.

CHAPTER 2

Minding the Gap

Like one who doubts an elephant,
Though seeing him stride by,
And yet believes when he has seen
The footprints left; so I.

Kaildasa, *Shakuntala*[1]

Minds are supposed to be impossible to "see"; yet we manage
to deal with them pretty easily. In this chapter I will do two things. First, I
will look at the roots of the assumption that mind is fundamentally opaque
and hard to access. Is that assumption necessary? Does the gap that I was
warned to mind really need minding? It seems to make problems not just for
explaining how babies know people, but also for how we as adults, and indeed we as psychologists, do so. Second, I will look at possible answers to the
question of how, if we think there is such a gap, we come to know minds.
Standard answers can be grouped into two kinds, proposing either a first-
person or a third-person bridge across the gap. Both, I will argue, are unsatisfactory. They assume a fundamentally bystander or spectator stance towards other people, rather than one of participation and engagement. In
different ways, both first-person and third-person approaches retain a "gap,"
the problem of the fundamental opacity of other people's minds. I will propose that there is an alternative approach, a second-person approach, which
I will elaborate in the next chapter. But first, what is this gap?

The (Impossible) Gap

When I spoke about babies revealing an understanding of minds in their
everyday engagements, I was advised to respect the gap between mind and

7

behaviour. What was this gap exactly? It seemed to be something that divided behaviour and mentality, the physical and the psychological, the surface and the depth. Babies were allowed to access the surface, the physical, the behavioural, but not the psychological, the mental, the depth. This is actually quite puzzling. Psychology in recent decades has credited very young infants with all sorts of understanding: for instance, an understanding of gravity and solidity and an understanding of number and size. So why, if babies can understand simple physics and simple mathematics, should simple psychology be so out of bounds to them? Why should the infant be dealing with us at a level of physical movements rather than mentality? Why should there be a gap that banishes minds to the realm of invisibility and inaccesibility? This was particularly puzzling coming from a psychology which had, a good half century earlier, rejected mind-body dualism.

For some theorists, the gap exists *between one mind and another:* put crudely, their problem could be glossed as "I know my own mind but yours is a problem." Piaget, arguably, took this position, as do many modern "Simulation" theorists. For others, the gap exists *between the physical and the mental:* again put crudely, their problem is "I can see your body (or mine), but I haven't got a clue that you (or I) have a mind inside." The modern "theory of mind" theorists could be said to adopt *this* starting position. But assume either kind of gap and knowing other minds becomes a problem; for both, other minds are opaque and unperceivable.

Here is a common modern way of phrasing the problem which rather blends the two types of gap and poses the profound frustration of the problem. How do infants come to realise that what they experience in themselves— their bodily feelings, the "internal" information about their own movements and discomfort, their feelings and perceptions—can also be experienced by another person of whom they can only perceive the "outside"? How do infants connect and recognise as similar the proprioceptive information they get about themselves with the distal perceptual information they get about other people? How, to put it yet another way, do they connect the direct "first-person" information they have of themselves with the very indirect "third-person" information they can get about other people? In fact, the problem is not dissimilar to that set up by Rene Descartes, the French Renaissance philosopher.

Descartes' Problem

Descartes argued that there are two kinds of substances in the world, mental and physical. The mental substance—*res cogitans*—thinks, while the physical substance—*res extensa*—essentially just takes up space. We think we can perceive physical substance (bodies, trees, tables, stars), but we could be deluded by sensory evidence—as happens in dreams and hallucinations. Our senses and our convictions about external reality are unreliable. However, when we think about this and experience this doubt, we undoubtedly experience the mental substance. So the only thing we can be certain about, Descartes argued, was this one thing: the existence of our own doubting and thinking mind. Hence his famous dictum "I think therefore I am," or *cogito ergo sum*. Given his assumptions a "QED" seemed warranted here.[2]

The problem was as follows: if minds were only open to *private* experience, how could one be sure that *other* minds even existed? The answer had to be that one couldn't. Not with any certainty. As with the existence of the world itself, one could not *know* with certainty—one could only speculate or guess. For Descartes, the mind was an isolated, unworldly, and disembodied thing, with no direct access to anything other than itself. As a consequence, individual minds (or people) were not only reaching across a profound gap for knowing or relating to other minds, but were also reaching across a gap in relation to knowing or relating to the world around them. Their relations were necessarily limited to their own—possibly hallucinatory—*ideas* about the world or other minds. How did Descartes survive in this strange world? His solution was to trust that God would not have misled him in speculating about the existence of the world around him or about the existence of other minds. But in psychological terms at least this was of course a cop-out.

Modern Mind-Behaviour Dualism

Today, no one takes this divine route to knowing other minds. And no one adheres to Descartes' idea of a mind-body dualism or separation: the seventeenth-century notion of separate mental and physical substances is banished to realms occupied by phlogiston, the life force, and other mystical concepts. And except for some extreme views, most theories of perception adopt some degree of realism: the organism, at least to some extent, is seen as picking up information about the physical world rather than constructing it all. Nonetheless, the modern rejection of mind-body dualism is not without its contradictions. While we might be passionately committed to a deep and profound connection between the body and the mind, we are likely to be equally passionately committed to the *distinction* between the terms *mind* and *body*, and even more oddly, to the opacity of one and the observability of the other. We seem to have rejected Descartes' mind-*body* dualism, but retained one of its implications—a mind-*behaviour* dualism. It is almost the first principle of student training manuals on how to observe behaviour that description must be separated from interpretation—in other words, that physical movement is separate from its psychological meaning. The behaviour of the body is seen as transparent to the observer, while its "mental" or "intentional" meaning is seen as opaque and only accessible to interpretation and inference. Only first-year undergraduates may be for-given for confounding behaviour with its "meaning."[3] A belief in the deep unreliability of the connection between behaviour and mind is often as-serted as strongly as a religious tenet.

Strangely, two diametrically opposed schools of psychology are both premised upon this distinction and this assumption. Behaviourism in the early twentieth century rejected all talk of mind and, by the very act of doing so, re-tained the dualism. And cognitivism in the late twentieth century, reacting against the behaviourist rejection and focusing on mind as its primary quest, sidelined the actions of the body—its behaviour—and therefore equally em-braced the same dualism.[4]

Even more absurdly, the two allegedly opposed camps are not only the-oretically compatible with each other, but one even *requires* the other: Cognitivism needs to stand on the shoulders of behaviourism to explain lesser phenomena. For instance, if the development of a complex cogni-tive representational ability is to be explained, what can the theorist do to explain the understanding present *before* this ability develops? The theo-rist has to offer not only a developmental explanation of how the cogni-tive representation develops, but also an explanation of what's going on before it. To do this, the cognitive representational theorist logically has to resort to explanations involving understanding of "mere" and "outward" behaviour, with the "understanding" based on association, learning, or conditioning. Deemed not to be the "real thing" in terms of under-standing, but presented as either stepping stones (direct precursors) or simply "pseudo" skills, these earlier phenomena are always described in behavioural terms. Cognitivism, it appears, necessarily presupposes a be-haviourist stage in development! In relation to understanding minds, this implies a stage during which no recognition of mind is possible, only the perception of behaviour and its regularities, a stage then overthrown by conceptual advance. This is quite explicit in some texts—the infant is seen to begin life as a behaviourist, and only in childhood to become a cognitivist. And the same analogy continues in considerations of the evolutionary development of knowledge of minds—monkeys such as macaques and baboons may be depicted graphically as "ethologists" (who just observe and describe behaviour), while the great apes are depicted as "psychologists" (who interpret behaviour in mentalistic terms). There is a meta-theory at work here, which puts behaviouristic and cognitivistic understanding on a single, sequential developmental path, whether in evolutionary terms or in terms of human development, leading to a conclusion that behaviouristic understanding is a (necessary) step towards cognitivistic understanding.[5]

This is not only a metaphysical problem (the split between "reading minds" and "reading behaviour" assumes a deep dis-embodying of mind) and a developmental problem (it is very difficult to explain convincingly the jump from simply seeing behaviour to conceiving of the presence of minds) but also a methodological problem. If the two are categorically separate, you simply cannot test one against the other—each sphere of explanation is complete unto itself. And we are left with an unsatisfactory evolutionary and developmental picture in which our representational explanations become no more than conjecture. Cartesian doubt is alive and well in the mind-behaviour dualism of modern psychology. Even when scientists are happy to describe the mind in physical terms—for example, seeing it as the software to the hardware of the brain—they nonetheless end up depicting it as ultimately inaccessible (except to informed guessing). In such models, it is implied that the user cannot read the software but only knows its effects and acts in interaction with them. However, unlike computational software, which can be directly written and read by the expert, mental software in this scheme cannot be read even by the expert—except, according to some, by a futuristic neuroscience. Where minds are concerned, both psychologists and ordinary humans are seen to be ignorant of what's in the alleged software; they can only guess at it. This modern model of the mind is therefore not different from the Cartesian one when it comes to postulating a gap between mind and behaviour, and even when rejecting the distinction in ontological terms, it steadfastly holds on to it in epistemological terms.[6] Other minds are, according to both models, invisible and inaccessible except to conjecture. But why is this a problem? I will identify three problems here: uncertainty, disembodiment, and privacy.

Problems with the Gap

The Intolerability of Uncertainty

The first problem is that of certainty. We aren't willing to accept Descartes' "out," which allowed a divine verification of our guesses about minds. Today's science is seriously empiricist, believing that knowing can only come through the experience given to us through our senses. As a consequence, being certain about other minds now becomes an insoluble problem for science. If we cannot know anything other than our experience, and if we cannot directly experience minds other than our own (or even our own, if we adopt what has come to be known as the "theory-theory"), then it follows with an inevitable logic that we have absolutely no way of knowing the experience of others. We can never with any certainty know about either the nature or the *existence* of other minds. This is the essence of what has become known as the "problem of other minds": given our assumptions, knowing other minds is impossible; but, given our social lives, knowing other minds is a fact. Descartes, it has been suggested, suffered from a truly bad dose of the problem—painstakingly writing to persuade other minds of his lack of conviction that other minds existed.[7] But you could argue that for ordinary people it doesn't matter. Ordinary people are not scientists concerned with establishing the truth about the existence and nature of other minds. Certainty isn't central to their everyday dealings with people in the same way as it is claimed to be for a philosopher or scientist. However, ordinary people, too, would not be able to survive or function with real uncertainty.

I used to teach an undergraduate course called Knowing Other Minds. The most interesting thing about this course was the frustration it unfailingly caused students in about Week Two. Most started out confidently asserting that it was never possible to be certain about the "contents" of another's mind. Yet they also, equally confidently, held two other beliefs: one, that they had no doubt at all that other people around them *did* have minds, and two, that in their own lives they sometimes *were* certain about others' thoughts and feelings. The reasons for the first belief were obvious: they thought of minds as invisible, inaccessible things whose "contents," therefore, no one else could *ever* be certain about. The reasons for the second and third beliefs were also clear: they interacted with people everyday with certainty rather than with probabilistic guesses about the existence and nature of their minds. And since you cannot both deny yourself certainty and claim certainty, their frustration came from finding no satisfactory way out of this contradiction. Although they were convinced about the unquestionable privacy of minds, they were also deeply committed to the possibility of interpersonal understanding and trust and appalled by the absurdity of having (by their own logic) to doubt that other minds existed.

Contradictory beliefs about the transparency of minds are not unusual. On the one hand, most cultures have sayings that vouch for the impenetrability of minds. Take, for instance, the Russian proverb "Another person's soul is unfathomable," or the Urdu saying "Gold, you can test by scraping it, but Man, you cannot test even by scraping him" or even Shakespeare's "There's no art to find the mind's construction in the face." And everyone knows from personal experience that deception happens all the time, and often effectively in close relationships, too. On the other hand, people deeply value knowing and being sure of other people's thoughts and feelings. There is a scene in Tolstoy's *Anna Karenina* in which the newly betrothed Lev and Kitty, standing in a formal Russian drawing room full of people, correctly guess each other's increasingly coded speech and thrill to the incredible intimacy of knowing each other's unspoken thoughts.

We conduct most of our personal lives knowing rather than doubting or guessing people's feelings and thoughts. We really would not be able to accept the implications of an ultimate inability to know the minds of those we cherish. Life wouldn't be worth living if we were so entirely alone or uncertain in our mental lives. We would be entering a grey half-world in which the world is and becomes only what we think it to be. As Ursula Le Guin puts it: "There is a bird in a poem by T. S. Eliot who says that mankind cannot bear very much reality; but the bird is mistaken. A man can endure the entire weight of the universe for eighty years. It is unreality he cannot bear."[8]

But the problem is greater than simply the unbearable loneliness of uncertainty. If we really lived within a framework of doubt we could never function, never really be open to engagement. We need, if not certainty, at least the absence of *un*certainty in order to *do* things with other minds. And we need to do things with other minds in order for them (and us) to continue to exist and develop as minds.

The Impossibility of Disembodiment

Disembodiment is the second problem with mind-behaviour dualism. *Can* observation of behaviour be separated from its interpretation? It may, in fact, be impossible to separate mentality from bodily movement. "O body swayed to music, O brightening glance, How can we know the dancer from the dance?" asks W. B. Yeats, reflecting a difficulty in separating the person from the person's actions. If we cannot separate the action as some ideal form (the dance) from the contextual manifestation of the action (the dancer), how can we separate in everyday life our mentality in its ideal and unexpressed forms (the mind) from its actual expression (the behaviour)? Is the mind ever separable from the movements of the body?

For Descartes the body was irrelevant to the business of knowing minds. He "de-souled" the body, as some put it. For other philosophers, however, such as the phenomenologists, far from being a depersonalised and unreliable machine obeying the commands of the mind, the body was itself an intentional thing. It was the intentional, expressive core of our being. And it was the connection *between* bodies which formed the basis of knowledge of other minds. As the French phenomenologist Maurice Merleau-Ponty put it, "it is precisely my body which perceives the body of another person, and discovers in that other body a miraculous prolongation of my own intentions, a familiar way of dealing with the world."[9] Modern neuroscience comes very close to closing this gap between bodies with its discovery of so-called mirror neurons (although talking about perceiving another's bodily expressions as perceiving another's mentality is still fairly taboo). For Darwin, too, interested in continuities in the evolution of mind, the body was an intentional entity in itself, and so for him the question of a separate system of interpretation for this intentionality (separate from a system of perception of bodily movements) would have been an evolutionary absurdity.[10] From this point of view, mind becomes the *way* in which a living body acts, not something separable from, hidden behind, or leading to its actions. To borrow Gilbert Ryle's phrase, mind is better seen as an adverb qualifying action than as a noun. For example, we sit anxiously, step carefully, move confidently, pause thoughtfully, look attentively, reach purposefully, and so on. The mentality in these actions is not seen as a separate process but rather as a quality of the action itself. The implication of such views about mind for knowing about them is obvious. If minds are what bodies do, they are public, not private. We don't need inference or theory or stories to get at them; they are transparent to perception. This is not to say that infants (or adults, or other animals, or psychologists for that matter) therefore *necessarily*, or always, perceive these qualities of action. In order to say that, we would need evidence of discrimination and meaningfulness. But in principle, at least, they could.

Another sense in which mind has been dis-embodied has been through portraying it, not as a kind of crypto-entity hidden behind the mask of the body, but as a purely conceptual or "mental representational" entity— something that must be inferred by an act of intelligence and thus exist in "representations." This view is common amongst some modern approaches, where mind is seen as "real" only through imagination or inference.[11] Defining the mental or the psychological as a hypothetical entity, as not real, presents its own problems for explaining how organisms with minds engage with the world. The implications for knowing about them, however, are similar: until that point in development when the non-real can be hypothesised and imagined, minds are out of bounds. Other theorists, without quite adopting this emphasis on a purely conceptual reality, focus on "representing" as the primary business of minds.[12] The child's task in understanding minds according to this emphasis is therefore to understand representation. However, while representing is one aspect of what minds do, focusing exclusively on this aspect is problematic for understanding the psychological engagements of infants and other people, in fact for understanding how even representing could come about. As we will see in some of the next chapters, it invites a misleading neglect of action.

Privacy

The third problem is commitment to the privacy of psychological phenomena. If we can perceive the mental qualities of actions in other people—a thought striking someone in mid-conversation, a smile that they are trying to suppress at someone's gaffe in a meeting, the concentration in a child's frown at a piece that won't fit in the puzzle, the joy in the smile that greets the sight of a chocolate cake, or the deceptive intent in the hurried hiding of the biscuit under the toy box—how private are minds? Certainly some mental experiences *can* be private, but are they *necessarily* and *developmentally* so? There are two serious reasons to question what we think of as the unassailable privacy of our experiences. One is developmental, and the other (fundamentally related to this) is cultural.

The developmental problem with privacy. The standard way of thinking about private and shared experiences is to think of privacy as the starting point from which communication about private mental states can occur, though never quite adequately. Developmentally speaking, however, this is not true. First, developmentally speaking, to be private is more difficult than to be public. In many ways, we know this to be true. We see an infant cry or smile or turn to look or frown, and there is no question that the distress and joy and interest are publicly available. While we could doubt them in an adult, we could not do so in an infant. And this is an important difference. Second, joint action and shared experience are developmentally prior to the communication of private experiences. Telling others about one's thoughts and feelings and perceptions and intentions happens only after a long history of engagement with each other's thoughts and feelings and perceptions and intentions. And the well-established finding that private speech can only occur after "public" speech adds further weight to this argument.[13] These developmental factors—that doubt about mental states is more appropriate later in development and that communication about mental states occurs after a prior history of sharing mental states—suggest that we could in fact turn the tables on the standard story and reverse the direction of effects. The story makes better developmental sense if we argue that it is shared experience of mentality that *allows* privacy. The "public"—sharing—is a developmental step necessary for allowing the "private"—concealment—and not the other way around. It may even be that genuine engagement—mutual psychological contact—can lead to an understanding of the self that would not have been possible without it.

The cultural problem with privacy. There is another angle that might help us to think about the question of privacy: culture and the very different cultural practices that can exist in relation to private and shared experiences. In Western and Westernised cultures, we tend to think of ourselves so much as separate individuals with separate problems and experiences and reactions that we find it hard to see this way of living as only one of a number of possible ways. In some cultures a problem, loss, difficulty, victory, doubt, indecision, or hardship never belongs to just one person; rather, it is always owned by those around the person as well. This concept may be hard to believe (and *very* hard to live with!) if your experience is totally within a Western culture. But because I have a foot in two different cultures, I am constantly struck by the difference in experiencing an event when it is not yours alone. For instance, it is fairly normal in Western cultures to express sympathy to a bereaved person by enquiring how they are feeling. However, it may be less common in more "collectivist" cultures. And to never be asked by visitors, "How are you feeling?" is profoundly telling. It lifts the responsibility for the feeling, and indeed the ownership of the grief, right off your shoulders. It makes the event, the feelings, and the responsibility for any actions unquestionably shared. The interesting thing for us here is that having everyone around you be aware of and "meddle" constantly with the events in "your" life might actually change how private or public your mental life *can* be.

Nico Frijda and Batja Mesquita conducted an unusual study on cultural differences in people's expectations about knowing what others are feeling or thinking. They found that people in more traditional cultures claim more knowledge about the feelings and mental states of others in hypothetical situations than do people in industrialised modern cultures.[14] In itself this difference might mean nothing. Presuming knowledge doesn't mean that you have it. However, these claims happened in groups which also reported high levels of expecting to do something to deal with, help with, or resolve *other* people's problems. Now the point here is this: could it be that frequent and intense action involved with other people's "situations" actually leads to less privacy of mental states in those situations? This claim may seem strange, but it is potentially powerful. When two people closely share responsibility for not only knowing about but doing something about their respective problems, when the lived situation is shared, how private can mental states actually be? Fantasies and imaginations, too, might end up being shared.

The question is not, "can privacy of experience exist?" Of course it can. Better questions are, rather, "does it always exist?" and "what conditions does it *not* exist in?" It seems that the more public a situation is in terms of being shared in joint action and responsibility, the more the mental experiences of each also become public in terms of being known by others. The more privacy of action is expected of people, the more private their mental experiences are, too. There is something about doing things together which is fundamental to knowing about each other.

This idea must be evident in differences not only between cultural groups but also in relationships. There is a lot you know about a person's thoughts and intentions and perceptual tendencies and even fantasies, if you are closely involved over a long period of time in working with that person or in jointly dealing with situations in which these things play a part. The question of deception in close relationships is often used as evidence of the irrelevance of shared lives in knowing about each other's minds. But this is a weak argument. Shared lives can vary enormously in the extent to which different aspects of life are shared. You can live with someone for fifty years but live and experience separate events separately. This is a sharing not of life events but merely of space and time. For sharing lives you need a sharing of concerns and purposes, to borrow a phrase from Margaret Donaldson.[15] Doing things together—engagement over time—can not only *reveal* "private" experiences, but actually *create* more public experiences. Privacy seems to be doubly problematic for engagement—preventing engagement on the one hand and reducing mental experience on the other.

So these are the three problems associated with the gap—uncertainty, disembodiment, and privacy. But since a gap is commonly assumed, how is it supposed to be bridged?

Views across the (Alleged) Gap

How can the infant—or child or adult or other animal (or psychologist!)—get to know other people as psychological beings across this alleged and profound gap? Standard answers to this question can take two routes.[16] There is what we can call the *first-person route,* which basically argues that other minds are known through reference to the self. Generically known in philosophy as the argument from analogy or in modern adaptations as simulation theory, the first-person route argues that you look across the gap, see another body, and recognise in that body a similarity to (or something of) yourself. Seeing yourself in the other allows you to recognise the other as a person. Another is what we might call the *third-person route,* which is known in philosophy as the best fitting hypothesis approach or in modern terms as the popular theory of mind theory. The argument here is that, looking across the void, the infant sees neither the other person nor herself but rather physical patterns in self and other. Interpreting those patterns and co-occurrences can lead to hypotheses (which can be continually revised) about the existence and nature of minds. It is through logical deduction that the infant comes to discover people as people.

What these two solutions share in common is the premise of the gap—the idea that other minds cannot be directly accessed and that a bridge is therefore necessary to cross the gap. This bridge, in order to reach the minds at both ends, must be made of mental substance or, in modern terms, must involve mental representations. The two solutions differ in two respects:

where these representations derive from (from experience within the self versus from observation of others) and *how* they develop (through reference to the self versus through hypothesis-testing). Each of these solutions offers a powerful insight into some of the ways in which we as adults understand other people and how this process of bridging the gap might occur. But there are also problems with each (both in terms of their logical adequacy and their explanation of development from infancy).

Analogy: Starting from First-Person Experience

John Stuart Mill provided what some say was the first argument from analogy. Assuming, as Descartes did, that we have direct and privileged access at least to our *own* mental states, Mill describes the process by which, for example, we understand that another person is angry: we see that person making vigorous movements with the fists and stamping movements of the foot, and we recall previous occasions when we had made the same movements and had experienced a feeling of anger. We infer, through analogy with our own experience, that other bodies must also have the same sort of mental states that we have. Understanding through analogy is familiar to us in everyday life, and that's why this solution seems so credible to us. We say, for example, that no one who has not personally experienced some trauma—a divorce, the death of a child, the loss of a parent, a child's transformation into a teenager—can possibly know what it is like. We must all have memories, on one hand, of failing to grasp what someone was feeling because our own experience was limited at that time or, on the other hand, of insights that we suddenly gained into someone's state on the basis of a realisation of its similarity to something in our own past.[17]

But is analogy really the *basis* of our knowledge of other minds? As a bridge to awareness of the existence of other minds, it seems incredibly fragile. Analogy usually works by extension from at least a few proven cases. In the case of other minds, however, if all we can ever have is the experience of our own, we are making a huge overgeneralisation from one case. If our experience really was so solipsistic, why would we even be tempted to make the generalisation that other minds existed? Furthermore, if analogy provided our only access to other minds, it would tie our knowledge of others totally to our own experience.

The philosopher Ludwig Wittgenstein offered a profound criticism of this assumption of the "privileged access to the self" as the source of mind knowledge. His argument centred around language and was aimed at rejecting the possibility of a private language; nonetheless, it is deeply relevant to this debate about minds. Wittgenstein saw the sharing of mental experiences between people as a prerequisite for, rather than a consequence of, knowing one's own mental experience. If we only ever experienced the feeling of anger in ourselves, and never either knew it in others or engaged with others about it, how would we know it *as* something? The feeling of anger would be beyond our awareness as a "something." It is only because we can share it as an aspect of engagement that it becomes an entity, one which subsequently becomes named and is further shared.

A modern version of the argument from analogy, called simulation theory, adopts more sophisticated concepts but offers an essentially similar explanation of how infants come to know other minds. Perceiving the similarity of behaviour between bodies, the individual has only to access her own mental experience usually accompanying that behaviour and use this experience as an internal model for the other's mind. Recognising situations that the other is in, the individual can run "simulations" of the experiences she would have if she were in that situation, and through these simulations she can feel or think what the other feels or thinks. Understanding the other's mind is an attribution based upon the self.

How is this similarity of body or similarity of situation actually recognised in order for the simulation to be applied? How does the infant realise that the perceptual information she has about the other is actually connected to the proprioceptive information and the (apparently) same sort of experiences she herself has? One modern answer within these premises is in terms of representations of similarity or "like-me" representations. Still preserving the psychological gap between self and other, this answer maintains that any awareness of mentality in others is the result of attribution, not perception. However, the bodily gap between self and other is abandoned. The starting point for bridging the gap is seen as the possession of the same neurological "body scheme" allowing the recognition of other people as "just like me." The next step in understanding comes through imitation of the other's body movements, which generates a subjective state in the infant. Once the infant experiences this mental state in the self, she can then attribute it to others.[18] Other versions of this recognition of similarity to self differ slightly: starting not from an immediate recognition of the similarity of actions, but from an innate propensity to identify with people "like me," the infant then attributes to other people what she has already experienced in herself. And as her knowledge of her own mental states develops, she attributes these correspondingly to others as well.[19] In fact, these modern answers are not purely "first-person" accounts: the reference to the self can even be in the form of a "third-person" account, as primitive forms of theorising or "an initial theory of action."[20]

More recently, theorists at the University of Parma, following the discovery of responsive neuronal activity, have offered a much more direct account of "experiencing" another person's state. Vittorio Gallese suggests that by means of a shared neural state realised in two different bodies and through similar sensations evoked in the observer "as if" he or she were doing the same thing, the "objectual other" becomes "another self." These theories have hit on the huge psychological significance of sharing the same body with other people.[21] This route is necessary for any bridge across the gap, but it isn't *enough* for the infant to be able to recognise other people as being the same as the self or to see "the self in the other." A perception of similarity is not enough to provide the motivation for engagement and communication or to explain the responsive emotions that fuel engagement. Something more is needed, which not only establishes the connection between bodies as this solution has done, but also, by not portraying bodies as merely data for establishing the perception of psychological similarity, establishes a route for responsiveness and relatedness.

Theory: Starting from Third-Person Observation

To overcome some problems with the idea of analogy, and to avoid the problematic assumption that we have some sort of privileged access to our own mental experience, one philosophical solution is to assume a general ignorance of all mentality, which can only be dispelled by a more solidly (i.e., broadly) based deductive process. Not restricted to special knowledge of one case, we could start with a sort of intellectual mystery about the meanings of observed behaviour, develop a hypothesis or theory that "behind" such behaviour lies something like mind, test the hypothesis in everyday life, then either abandon it or revise it, and settle eventually for the version of the hypothesis which fits the data best. Minds, according to this solution, are hypotheses—theoretical postulates—rather than the "real" and experienceable substance that Descartes and the argument from analogy assumed. Rather like scientists testing their hypotheses, and gradually rejecting those which are untenable, this solution suggests that we live with the least uncomfortable hypotheses we can find. And that is all we ever know in dealing with people—hypotheses about them.

Examples of such theorising and hypothesis-testing in everyday life are not hard to find, which shows why this account seems to make sense. Most of us have probably at some time in our lives been driven in desperation to create or seek theories about, for example, why teenagers grunt, why men avoid talking about problems, and so on. We have all probably also experienced situations when we use a sort of theory even to understand ourselves: saying, for example, "I seem to cry all the time; therefore I must be depressed," or "Maybe I don't really want to go on this holiday—I keep avoiding booking the flights." Theories lead not only to testable predictions but also to changes in practice; a theory that constant weeping indicates depression, or that avoidance indicates dislike, leads to specific actions—for instance, a reduction in the stresses one inflicts on oneself or a cancellation of the holiday one is avoiding. Theories about minds, like theories about diseases, can not only explain why people do what they do, but they can be very useful in knowing how to *act* appropriately with people (even oneself).

Since the late-twentieth-century version, this solution has taken developmental psychology by storm. Calling itself the theory of mind theory (or the theory-theory for short), it argued that children get to know minds, not only others' but also their own, through the development of a theory of mind, at about 4 years of age. There are many modern versions of the theory-theory.[22] But all of them assume that we need a rational deductive route to minds: that some abstraction (whether a concept or a hypothesis or a theory) from otherwise meaningless sense data is necessary to derive the idea of the psychological. Prior to this reflective realisation, the sense data are portrayed as a jumble: chaotic, disordered. Once transformed, this knowledge allows the recognition of minds and enables meaningful actions upon them. The theory (or other reflective realisation) is seen as a *prerequisite* for engagement with other minds and indeed for experiencing one's own. The pre-theoretical infant could neither understand other people's actions as anything other than behaviour patterns nor play with or react to others' psychological states per se.

More recently, others have argued that the infant is an observant analyst of body movements, able to detect all manner of physical contingencies but not able to grasp any *mental* qualities. The human infant, they say, does have an innate propensity for, and preparedness to engage in, affective interchanges with caregivers. However, this is seen merely as an evolutionary device which leads to the development of a social-intentional scaffold for the infant's subsequent theoretical "discovery" of minds: these affective interchanges are not in themselves seen as reflecting any awareness on the part of the infant of what the other's subjective state is, or indeed that the other experiences a subjective state at all. This a priori reluctance to describe infants as intersubjective is telling: it can only make sense within the Cartesian dualism of mind and behaviour. And yet, the dislike of the Cartesian ontology is so strong that these theories sometimes portray intersubjectivity itself as a neo-Cartesian notion. The confusion here is profound: if intersubjectivity were seen as an ascription of one's own subjectivity to others, it would indeed be a neo-Cartesian concept. However, if intersubjectivity is seen as the engagement between subjectivities, then it is profoundly non-Cartesian. Both the reluctance to acknowledge infant intersubjectivity and the assumption that it must involve privileged access to self stem from the same source: the assumption that mental qualities cannot be directly perceived in others. This is a neo-Cartesian dualism in which the infant can see behavioural patterns but not mentality; the infant is innately driven to engage with caregivers' affective behaviour but not with their affects; the infant is driven to seek and enjoy control over producing *effects* on, but not *responses* in, contingent caregiver behaviour.[23]

The reason for such distinctions is often attributed to the scientifically respectable desire for parsimony. Parsimony, however, exists only in a theoretical context: if, and only if, we accept a theory which says that perceiving the physical is simpler than perceiving the mental, is it more parsimonious to suggest that infants perceive only physical qualities. But if we reject the dualism of separating mind from body (as modern psychology has largely done), it may well be more parsimonious as well as more coherent to reject the dualism of separating the perception of the body from the perception of the mind.

However, even if infants can be said to only perceive the physical, can we really understand subjective experiences through theories about them? *Qualia*, as the philosophers call the quality of subjective experiences, can be feelings, like the feeling of redness, the feeling of a heart racing, or the feeling of the warmth of a fire seeping over one's body. How could a theory about mentality and mental experiences ever capture such feelings? First-person theorists are quite right when they insist on direct experience being the basis for knowing other minds. In this notion they differ profoundly from those who espouse theory-theory. It is only the experience of something which can let us access its feeling qualities. But, as I will discuss in Chapter 3, by presuming that the only access to other people's experiences is to feel the *same* as they do, strictly first-person approaches miss the opportunity to portray access to others' experiences through often different *responses* to them.

Unlike first-person theories, a theory-theory would have problems not only with sensations but also with emotionality. How can one theorise emotion without ever experiencing it? It would be rather like assuming that a Martian—or better still, one of *Star Trek*'s famously unemotional Vulcans—given the task of understanding human psychology—could ever do more than build a rather detached theory about human oddities, vulnerability, and excessive emotionality. Their understanding of emotion *has* to be different from—we would call it more impoverished than—ours, because it is devoid both of the experience of emotion in the self and of the experience of emotional engagements with others. At the very least, it is a different understanding: more like the understanding of a bystander than that of a participant. And any theory-theory is necessarily wedded to this type of detached understanding.

Above all, the theory-theory is a rationalist enterprise. It invites the same criticism which was levelled against Piaget when he argued that the epitome of intellectual development—whether in humans or in evolution—was the emergence of de-contextualised, abstract, scientific thought: an ethnocentrism of sorts. In the same fashion, the theory-theory is practising another culturo-centrism, epitomising the psychologist's ultimate fallacy: I am a psychologist because I observe people and understand them through detached hypothesis-testing and theories; this must therefore be how anyone does it. It seems, oddly, the perfect example of the *practice of analogy* and thus is subject to every one of the same criticisms as the argument from analogy!

So We Have a Problem: Once You Postulate the Gap You Can Never Cross It

Once we assume that one or other version of Descartes' gap exists, the routes open to bridging the gap between minds are inadequate to the task. A first-person route—through recognising the self in the other—emphasises the need for *experiencing* mind and mental states in order to know them in others. But, although it tries to close the bodily gap between people, it still sees minds as disconnected from each other. The jump to other minds is still seen as an *attribution* of some sort based on the experience of the self. And although modern versions make *action* crucial to the discovery of the similarity of self and other, a first-person approach cannot convincingly explain *inter*action or dialogic engagement. Dialogue needs more than a recognition of similarity—it needs a recognition of difference and the ability to respond as well.

A third-person route, through theorising about minds, deals with some of these problems—for example, the narrowness of such an experiential base by giving the knowledge of other minds a genuinely wide base—but it raises other more unpalatable ones. In ignoring any experiential basis for mind knowledge, the theory-theory makes itself totally attributionist, much less grounded than a simulation view and even less able to explain engagement. Because of this neglect of the role or presence of direct experience, this route is even-handed—the theories of an alien or a non-participant by-stander are as good or bad as anyone's. But, as I will show in later chapters, bystanders' theories about minds are likely to be a poor substitute for par-ticipants' experience of minds. Both routes, even when they assume that interaction is the essential source of data, run the risk of positing an ob-server and an observed, of thinking of "mind-reading" primarily as a "spec-tatorial" process.[24] Both first-person and third-person routes see the knowl-edge of other minds as an attributional process—something which requires more than just perceiving the psychological. But there is an alternative which starts from questioning the very assumption of a profound gap be-tween minds. In the next chapter I will suggest that this alternative—a second-person approach—changes the way we think about the "gap" and even suggests that psychology's methods for understanding people need to be changed. As we will see through the rest of the book, it offers a better ex-planation about what babies do with people in everyday life.

CHAPTER 3

Engaging Minds:
A Second-Person Approach

I see it feelingly.

King Lear, Act IV, Scene 6

King Lear asks the newly blinded Gloucester how he claimed to be able to see. Gloucester's powerful reply—that he saw "feelingly"—could serve as an apt metaphor for an alternative way of knowing other minds. In the first- and third-person approaches to knowing other minds, both retaining the premises of the gap, other persons are "known" either by extension of the experiences of the self or from the outside through observation, inference, and theory. There is an alternative to this view that I will call a second-person approach.[1] This approach suggests that others are experienced as *others,* in direct emotional engagement, and that this fundamentally undermines the "problem" in the "problem of other minds." In the first half of this chapter I will explore the assumptions and logic of such an approach, and in the second half I will examine the profound implications that this approach holds for the methods psychology uses.

A Second-Person Approach

There are three core features in the assumptions of a second-person approach. *First,* it rejects the "gap," the dualist assumption criticised in the last chapter, which portrays other minds as opaque to perception, only speculatively accessible through various mechanisms of inference, modeling, or theorising about behaviour. It sees minds as transparent within (and within the limits of) active, emotionally engaged perception. *Second,* it pluralises the other, rejecting the assumption of singularity in the way we sometimes talk of other minds—of "*the* other." Since we can have many different kinds of engagement with others, what we can perceive of them must vary with the degree and type of engagement. We can relate to (at least) two such kinds of "other": others whom we relate to in the second person, addressing them (and being addressed by them) as a You, and others whom we relate to in the third person, talking about them (or being talked about by them) as He or She. Engagement in the second person allows us to experience others within our emotional responses to them *as* particular others—an experiencing which is more than simply a recognition of their similarity to ourselves. *Third,* it sees this active emotional engagement between people as constituting—or creating—the minds that each comes to have and develop, not merely providing information about each to the other.

So what is the difference between the second and the third person? Imagine how you might feel when someone you love catches sight of you unexpectedly and smiles at you. The breath-catchingness and warmth in *receiving* that smile are likely to be rather different from *observing* that smile directed at someone else. Imagine your mother turning to frown at you and how you experience this frown. Then imagine watching her turning to frown at your brother. Imagine when, on catching a baby's eyes, you lean over and say hello and she bursts into tears. Then imagine observing the baby reacting that way to someone else saying hello to her. It matters powerfully whether the "other mind" that you observe is turned towards you in engagement with you or towards someone else. The expressions—the frown, the smile, the tears—may be literally the same, but the information they hold for you and your experience of them can be phenomenally different. Not only is the experience of the other person more immediate and more powerful in direct engagement, but it calls out from *you* a different way of being, an immediate responsiveness, a feeling in response, and an obligation to "answer" the person's acts.

We know the term *second person* from grammar: it is the voice that is used when talking directly to someone, speaking to them as someone who can respond and understand and who deserves recognition as a person. In some languages—Greek, for instance—this difference in voice is actually crystallised into an explicit vocative case, where even the name of the person changes (the name *Christopheros,* for example, becomes *Christophere* if used to address the person). In contrast, referring to a person as a "he" or "she" can in some contexts and some languages be less than respectful, especially if done in their presence. Illustrating this sentiment is a strange British riposte involving a sharply critical "Who's 'she,' the cat's mother?" when someone violates the politeness rule against such third-person pronouns by calling someone a "she" (or presumably a "he") in that person's presence. Use of the third-person address generally excludes the person from the engagement, pushing the person into the position of observer. This can happen, of course, even when one is addressed as a "You": you can still be treated as an object, or be addressed as a member of a category, and not really be listened to as a person. You might be spoken to as an Indian or a student or a lecturer or a rugby player in varying degrees of a distancing haze. The effects sometimes can be disconcerting, even belittling. We also know how difficult it can be to be openly observed—whether being watched while we have a serious conversation with a friend, or even while we have a "conversation" with a class of a hundred. The observer is outside the interaction, occupying a more impersonal (even if sympathetic) relation to us. Of course, at times this impersonal relation may actually be easier to bear, as when we are dealing with emotions that are too heavy to handle. And an impersonal (third-person) relation can give us advantages of distance and disengagement which a second-person relation doesn't afford. The second-person voice captures a fundamentally personal engagement going beyond the mere use of the "You" to something in the psychological regard and openness—and intimacy—of the speaker to the listener.

This difference in the second- and third-person voice is captured by the Jewish theologian Martin Buber in his now famous (if somewhat cryptic) book *Ich und Du* (usually translated as *I and Thou*). He differentiated between the *I-Thou* (or *I-You*) way of relating to and knowing another person or thing, and the *I-It* way of relating and knowing. The former involves opening ourselves directly to another person or thing, without, as in the latter, a more distant observation through the filter of reflective evaluations, anticipations, or theorising; it means being involved in the "now" of the engagement; not being a spectator, but "feeling" the other person. Buber, along with many other philosophers such as John Macmurray (on the field of the personal), Max Scheler (on empathy), and Mikhail Bakhtin (on dialogue), saw this openness between people (i.e., really seeing/hearing/feeling the other as they are in the moment) as critical for genuine dialogue (rather than mere monologue).[2] There is an inevitable circularity in the way that genuine dialogue both emerges from this recognition of the other as a person and simultaneously allows us to come to know the other as a person. But how does the perception of others as *persons* work?

Perceiving Others in Engagement

Perception is not merely observation. All perception is embedded in living and doing. In the Cartesian scheme of things, meaning emerges from putting together the basic building blocks of more disinterested perception. In contrast, for philosophers such as Martin Heidegger (according to his eminent interpreter Hubert Dreyfus) "the objects of mere staring" are the debris of what's left over when action and involvement are inhibited in everyday practical life: perceiving in a disinterested way is very far from seeing things as they really are.[3] Within this anti-Cartesian phenomenological approach, meaningful perception must therefore always involve engagement. This is crucial, of course, to the perception of persons, implying that it is only if we are actively involved with persons that we can perceive them as they are. A related point was made by Gestalt psychologists nearly a century ago—that organisms perceive in meaningful wholes rather than parts. What is meaningfully perceived has to vary between different individuals, different species, and different relations and, although they did not speak of engagement as such, with the nature of the engagement. From inside engagement things have "relevance" in a way that they don't from outside. So a frown in response to a comment would be meaningless to a creature who does not make comments or does not frown. Or if it did bear some meaning, it would be a derived and different kind of meaning (associationist and statistical, perhaps) than it holds for most of us.

But how does even interested perception work if we are looking across a gap at other minds? How do we make the psychological connection, as one modern statement of the problem of other minds goes, between first-person proprioceptive experience of our own mental states and third-person perception of other people's behaviour?[4] In a second-person approach, the key answer is that this problem is a myth: the gap between perception and proprioception is not as clear as it looks. Perception always involves proprioception, and engagement profoundly influences how perception relates to proprioception. J. J. Gibson's ecological revolution of the 1960s and 1970s brought into mainstream acceptance the idea that exteroception (or perception of the external world) always involved proprioception (or perception of the organism's internal world), and indeed the reverse—that proprioception always involves perception. The more recently coined term *ex-proprioception* captures this sense of the simultaneous awareness of self in relation to the world.[5] Our perceptual experience of another person's frown or smile or tears, therefore, must always include in it our proprioceptive experience of our own bodily state and, most importantly, our affective and motivational state. Conversely, our proprioceptive experience of our own acts and reactions and feelings always involves the perception of what relevant others are doing, saying, or feeling. As the psychologist John Shotter put it, there is a constant intertwining and intermingling of the two.[6] It follows then that the nature of our engagement with others is absolutely fundamental to our experience of them. When the "other" whom we are perceiving is someone we are engaged with in a second-person exchange, the gap between third-person perception and first-person proprioception is even more implausible. The intertwining of perceptual and proprioceptive information is looser and often qualitatively different when our perception-proprioception is a more uninvolved observation. The line between experiencing the self and perceiving the other is, therefore, at most a permeable one. Within active emotional engagement your perception of the other always involves proprioceptive experience of self-feelings-for-other, and your proprioception of the self always involves perception of other-feelings-for-self. It may be time to invent a new word to refer to this simultaneous emotional/perception/proprioception.

Psychology has traditionally preferred to see the knower as distinct from the thing known. In the domain of knowing other minds, if the "other mind" is construed as quite separate from the self as knower, the only alternative is to adopt one of the two traditional routes to understanding the other. This very Cartesian legacy in our theories of perceiving and knowing perpetuates the opposition between first-person and third-person approaches.[7] However, whenever others are perceived, and especially when within engagement, there is an emotional link between people. This link cannot but be part of that which is known. Within engagement, I know you in a way that I do not know you when I am merely watching you. When you glower at me, my grasp of the meaning of your frown involves my response of fear or threat or disturbance. My understanding of your frown is necessarily coloured and shaped by my emotional response and the situation in which we are acting. When you are addressed directly by someone's action or expression, the involvement of your affective response and your action—whether completed or incipient—is a powerful link between self and other. This link is necessarily based on your recognition of the expressive similarity of self and other which first-person approaches emphasise, but it goes beyond it to also involve your *response* to the other—a response which could be very different in form and affect from the act that you perceive. The idea of a profound gap between one mind and another disappears and is replaced by a perceptual link consisting of active emotional responsiveness. But engagement with the other does not just yield psychological ex-proprioceptive information; it also *creates* it.

The Constitutive Role of Second-Person Engagement

One summer Naomi, one of the two sheep we "adopted" from the rescue centre, died. The other one, Isis, was lonely, bleating continuously. So we brought her into the garden, where she started to explore the outhouse and even the kitchen. She started to terrorise the sheepdog by coming in to eat the dog food and standing in the doorway pawing her feet on the ground like a ferocious bull when the poor dog tried to come back in to salvage the food. For us she became interesting to play with, perhaps because her loneliness drew her into being interested in so many more things than she had been interested in before. But when we got her a new friend and she went back into the field, she was largely transformed again into looking dumb and doing nothing; we found it hard to believe that she was the same dynamic, interesting animal from a few days ago. The complexity of different social environments can clearly invite and provoke complex and intelligent actions.[8] The bullish streak in Isis may have lurked in her undiscovered had it not been for that interlude; it disappeared soon enough when her engagements with us changed.

But how does a story about a sheep help illuminate the implications of psychological engagement? Its relevance is to the question of what constitutes the "natural" in the environments we—or other animals—grow up in. It has an interesting parallel to a recent debate about the skills of human-reared chimpanzees compared to those in the wild. Some would argue that the human-reared chimps' complex abilities to understand intentions and beliefs are not really chimpanzee abilities—fostered as they are by our human-like interactions with them. But this is an absurd argument, as some primatologists have pointed out, for are human skills not also drawn out by human environments?[9] Whether we are talking of chimpanzee understanding of human intentions or human infants' understanding of human psychological phenomena, the skills and awareness in the engaging only become manifest when they are drawn out in engagement. There is a circularity here in terms of mind knowledge: what we know of minds must depend on our engagements with them, but these engagements must themselves depend on what we know of them. This is a very complete and very scary mutuality—the more you engage with other minds, the more there must be to engage with. As E. M. Forster put it in his notes on the English character, "The emotions may be endless. The more we express them, the more we may have to express."[10]

The claim made by many philosophers that being treated as a *Thou* actually allows the I to come into existence now begins to make sense. Until you are the "subject of an address," as Mikhail Bakhtin, the popular Russian philosopher puts it, you cannot begin to become a person. Hegel speaks of the need to be confirmed by other "consciousnesses" in order to become a "consciousness" yourself. You need to be recognised or acknowledged or confirmed as a person in order to become one. If we search our own histories, we can probably all find examples of ourselves flowering and developing in some way within the perception of someone else's confidence. Something about being treated as brilliant or able or attractive or kind or trustworthy can help us become so. There clearly was a limit to how much of a "person" we could have transformed Isis the sheep into: she merely became more interesting in the variety and emotionality of her responses. But there is no doubt that without the complex demands of a human environment, she would not have even transformed as much as she did.

There is a crucial implication in the insight that you have to be addressed as a subject to become one: in order for the other person's "address" to work, the addressee needs to perceive the address as an address. Infants would have to perceive the other's perception (of them as a person) in order to respond to it. Can infants do this? Do infants perceive personal relations as personal rather than merely as physical? These are the questions that need to be answered in order to evaluate the claims and arguments of a second-person approach. And so, these are the questions I will be exploring in future chapters in a range of different domains of infant engagement.

A Second-Person Methodology?

Psychology, Detachment, and Third-Person Methods

Adopting a second-person approach carries major and unavoidable methodological implications for psychology. If we accept that for ordinary people knowing others' "minds" differs depending on their engagements with them, then this *has* to affect psychology, whose central business it is to know "other minds." If knowledge comes from the relation we have to the thing we are seeking to know, and if a relation of engagement gives us more profoundly personal knowledge about other people, then psychology's traditional methods of detached observation and experimentation may be giving us very partial—and biased—answers to questions about interpersonal knowing.

Psychology never really took to introspectionism—what might be called a first-person method—but instead invested heavily in what might be called third-person methods. Psychology has often been described as courting detachment, as basing the very methodology of psychological experiments on emotional distance between the scientist and the "subject," as presuming that in order to understand the personal, the scientist must first of all be *im*personal! The official coinage of academic psychology today, as John Shotter puts it, is formalism and disengagement, not involvement. There appears to be, as was noted over a hundred years ago, an unfortunate blurring of the meanings of "experimental" with "empirical," with the empirical unnecessarily subsumed into the detachment of the experimental.[11] What then, of a second-person methodology, where the scientist would need to engage with people? The scientist would bring to the data his or her own perceptions, intuitions, feelings, and responses to the "subject's" actions precisely in order to understand them better.

This is not an easy option for modern psychology: indeed, its implications are so radical as to strike many as an unimaginable method for a science. Anthropology accepted fairly long ago that to study other cultures we must not only "get off the observational verandah" to live and work with the people we want to understand but also engage our own sympathies for them. This was Malinowski's famous achievement in the Trobriand islands. Psychology, despite its recent commitment to the terminology of "participants" rather than "subjects" and its recent espousal of qualitative methodologies, still has difficulty with participant-observation and relational knowing. However, if engagement and relation is really a powerful influence on perception and knowing—on its processes, its content, and, effectively, its ontologies—then the bullet needs to be bitten and the question needs to be asked: does psychology need to rethink its impersonality when it wants to understand the personal? Does it need additional concerns in its methods?

Second-person methodologies are not unknown in psychology—at least in clinical settings. Susan Lanzoni describes the way in which European psychiatry in the 1940s and 1950s, concerned with ways of diagnosing schizophrenia, saw the development of a controversial technique called *gefuhlsdiagnose* or "feeling diagnosis." The clinician used his or her own emotional response to the patient (what some labelled the "praecox feeling," from the term *dementia praecox*) to detect the disconnection from reality that characterises the schizophrenic.[12] Perhaps it takes clinicians, in unavoidable engagement with their clients, to acknowledge the importance of relational knowing and the use of one part of the relation—their own feelings for the patient—to understand them. The psychoanalyst and experimental psychologist Peter Hobson is another, more recent exception to the academic norm in psychology. His beautiful description of his own feelings in response to a patient's actions, his belief that "nothing is more important than the *feel*" for our understanding of autism, and his frequent development of this feeling into experimental tests suggest a way forward using the "feeling diagnosis."[13]

This discussion is as pertinent in literature as it is in psychology: how close a novelist gets to his or her characters (and therefore how close the reader gets to them) varies with the novelist's method. Despite his intimate and much quoted depictions of personal memory (the sight and taste of the *madeleines* in his childhood still sticks in mind), some would argue that Marcel Proust fails to deliver intimate knowledge of his characters precisely because he veers uncomfortably between a first-person and third-person method of description. His method has little engagement in it—nothing of response—and therefore he provides only a detached kind of knowing. When talking of characters other than himself, he is always on the outside looking in through constrained windows. And even when he is talking of himself, there is a strangely observational stance, no sense of involvement. This is in contrast to Dostoevsky, for instance, whose method is fundamentally dialogic.[14]

Disengagement Is Inevitable and Valuable

But engagement has its limits: disengagement is not only inevitable, it provides a valuable dimension to knowledge that is born within engagement. Buber, comparing the intense intimacy of the *I-Thou* way of knowing with the *I-It* way, pointed out (albeit poetically) the inevitability of the latter: genuine engagement for him was a time-limited phenomenon.

But this is the exalted melancholy of our fate, that every *Thou* in our world must become an *It*. It does not matter how exclusively present the *Thou* was in relation. As soon as the relation has been worked out or has been permeated with a means, the *Thou* becomes an object among objects—perhaps the chief, but still one of them, fixed in its size and limits.[15]

If we can see past the strangeness of Buber's language, what he is saying is that we can remain in direct engagement with no person or thing for long without switching out, disengaging from them. The sadness in his words is, I suppose, something like the sadness we might experience when realising that the complete harmony of a new love has been broken by a disturbing and unshared (or unshareable) thought or when realising that the total absorption in a 2-month-old's entrancement with you is broken by her increasing interest in looking around the room.

Disengagement is indeed inevitable. Even within the most intense mutual gaze and mutual responsiveness there are moments of looking away in order to return again. In every conversation that we hold, perhaps in direct proportion to the degree of its focus and intensity, there are moments of pause in order to rethink, reflect, restate; this is the case even in 2-month-olds sometimes tuning out from contact. Many different human skills require this mix of engagement and disengagement. Humour, for instance, is the archetypal example: it is a skill which depends on the rapid fluctuation of disengagement and engagement and which, as we shall see in Chapter 9, is practised even by babies before they are 1 year old. The grip of an engagement needs to be stretched—even if momentarily—for laughter to occur. Disengagement is also valuable in freeing us from the unwanted present. If we could not disengage, we would be caught in traps in the way that babies born with central nervous system dysfunction might be—exhausted and wanting to but unable to turn away from the stimulation in the environment. We would be helpless victims of every pain, every boredom, and every unpleasantness. We would not have the reprieve of a "temporary anaesthesia of the heart"; we could not distance ourselves from psychological pain or change things through reflective identification of what it is we want to change.[16] We simply would not be able to see big patterns. Disengagement seems, therefore, to be as necessary as engagement, for knowing about people.

But this is not detachment; it is disengagement born within, and alternating with, engagement. What psychological science needs is a balance—engagement first and disengagement second—between the two. Even babies engage in experimentation—teasing and testing boundaries, as we shall see in Chapters 8 and 9. But there is no detachment in their experiments; rather, there is merely a temporary stepping outside the frame to explore the frame better. This is in sharp contrast to the teasing done by children with developmental problems—where it is discordant with the people they tease and where they don't seem to know when or how to stop. Can psychology develop an experimental method that comes from within the knowledge it gains in engagement with its participants?

Feelings for the Organism

Too much formalism and disengagement have dangers, which psychology has itself experienced at various times. The dangers of detachment from the concerns of experimental subjects are most familiar to us from Stanley Milgram's studies. The dangers of neglecting the social psychology of the experimental situation in psychology—its fundamentally interpersonal nature—ought to be familiar from the many revisions of language and rationale that became necessary in post-Piagetian developmental psychology.

The dangers of formalism and disengagement don't just apply to psychology; they concern other, less personal sciences as well. William Bateson warned biologists in 1908 of the dangers of neglecting the unusual and the rare. "Treasure your exceptions!" he wrote. "When there are none, the work gets so dull that no one cares to carry it any further. Keep them always uncovered and in sight. Exceptions are like the rough brickwork of a growing building which tells that there is more to come and shows where the next construction is to be."[17] Experiments (whether in psychology or in any science), with their focus on averaging, can lead us to forget this lesson. And we can also fail to realise that relating to the individual participant in our studies—engaging with them—is vital for really knowing what's going on in development. Barbara McClintock, the Nobel Prize winner, claimed that it was her "feeling for the organism"—of all things, maize plants—which allowed her to be sensitive to the unusual and the different and led to her discovery of the meandering of genes.[18]

Undergraduate critical evaluations of famous theorists can be very telling of what are "culturally" acceptable methods within the community of scientific psychology. The two most common criticisms of Piaget, for instance, focus precisely on his observation of the small and unusual, and on his potential involvement with his participants. The first criticism focuses on the need for replicability and the distrust of data that comes from isolated and unanticipated examples, from the unusual and the un-averaged. Student pens hover sternly over the word "anecdotes" when discussing Piaget's observations (although as the primatologist Richard Byrne quips, the difference between my data, your observations, and his anecdotes may be pretty subjective!).[19] There may be many reasons to distrust isolated observations: they may have been badly recorded; they may simply be anomalies and should not sway the whole field; and it may be difficult to know the contextual influences surrounding them. But distrust and discomfort in the discipline goes well beyond such legitimate concerns, which, in fact, affect *all* our methods—experiments and detached observations as well as engagements. And often it is the scientist and observer's personal involvement which gives the richer field of information about contexts and typicality.

This is, at the best of times, a difficult balance to strike. But the criticism of Piaget for his involvement is ironic. Although his observations are beautiful and reveal a powerful empathy for children's intentions in relation to the physical world, he was strangely unengaged with their relations to their social world. Take the following sensitive description of Jacqueline at 10 months:

> OBS 63. At 0;10(3) J. put her nose close to her mother's cheek and then pressed against it, which forced her to breathe much more loudly. This phenomenon at once interested her, but instead of merely repeating it or varying it so as to investigate it, she quickly complicated it for the fun of it; she drew back an inch or two, screwed up her nose, sniffed and breathed out alternately very hard (as if she were blowing her nose), then again thrust her nose against her mother's cheek, laughing heartily. These actions were repeated at least once a day for more than a month, as a ritual.[20]

Piaget's observation focuses on Jacqueline's individual actions and sensory interests. They do not include reactions from others or from himself (even if they had occurred, they may have been seen as irrelevant to this phenomenon). In this particular instance, however, it is hard to believe that the mother, whose cheek was being rubbed and breathed into, and whose ears were filled with a 10-month-old daughter's hearty laughter, did not react at all. Or that on subsequent occasions, there were either no reactions from other people or that they had no impact on Jacqueline's actions and interests. His observation of Jacqueline, though containing acute perceptions of her intentionality, curiosity and playfulness, nonetheless portrays her as separated from and unengaged with himself.

And that absence matters for the science. In this particular example, the relevance of interpersonal feelings and reactions for the development and exploration of that action may have been missed completely. The amusement of the observer would have played an important role in letting the observer notice that the baby is *enjoying* amusing them; it would have sensitised the observer to notice the motivational and emotional connections of the phenomenon. Our feelings for the phenomena we observe sensitise us to observing them.

Relational knowledge is a double-edged sword: without relation we can know nothing (or at least, know what we know in very different and distorted ways). But in relation we can only know what is particular to that relation. Dewey captures this tension, which both energises and constrains our knowledge:

> One wholly indifferent to the outcome does not follow or think about what is happening at all. From this dependence of the act of thinking upon a sense of sharing in the consequences of what goes on, flows one of the chief paradoxes of thought. Born in partiality, in order to achieve its tasks it must achieve a certain detached impartiality.[21]

Relation may well be the principal "inconvenient truth" (to borrow Al Gore's phrase) that psychology has to embrace: learning to acknowledge it, use it, and manage it as central to knowing. The only adequate methodological solution may be a sustainable process of disengaging and re-engaging within relation. If we could not engage in the first place (whether as infant or psychologist or manager or therapist) no amount of observation with simulation or deduction could get us off the ground in understanding others. We would be locked into a bizarre world of irrelevance.

In my own research with babies, the starting point has almost always been my observation of events, sometimes highly emotionally charged events, which occurred within my own children's engagement with myself or other family members. If I had not been interested in my feelings about infant actions, I would never have had the courage to take them seriously or the confidence to explore my knowledge of their developmental histories. Had it not been for my feeling of being "touched" in a similar way (or for my "feeling for the organism," to use Barbara McClintock's words) I would never, for instance, have made the initial connection between the

smiling gaze aversion of 2-month-olds with the smiling gaze aversions—
commonly called coyness or self-conscious affects—of older children. If I
had not felt tricked and teased by my 9-month-old, or watched (and indeed videotaped) her tricking and fooling my husband, I would not have
taken seriously the label of teasing that everyone in the family used to describe it. Nor would I have focused on the phenomenon itself as something
intriguing, and, from the point of view of standard theory, rather anom-
alous. Remembering the many occasions where I have failed to engage,
where I was so busy "observing" that I forgot to respond, or forgot that my
observation itself was an act which the child was responding to, I know
how crucial the nature of the personal relation with the knower is to the
psychological aspects of the person who is known. Psychology as a discipline which focuses on the personal cannot sensibly ignore the personal in
order to get its data.

In the selection of data in this book, therefore, I shall mix the use of experimental findings, more detached descriptions, and observations described from within engagement. Often, these different kinds of data com-
plement each other. Each has a vital role to play in our understanding of
other people. Engaged perception, giving us a responsive experiential access
to the other, is vital, but it can be frustratingly bound to its local relations,
the very emotional relations occluding a more distant view of patterns and
trends and external relations. The challenge is to identify what each means
at different times and in different situations, and to work out just how they
relate to each other and how differences and problems in one "mode" of
knowing can affect the other. Psychology needs to play not just with *ideas*
about people but with people themselves. And to play one needs a huge
commitment to authenticity in the engagement. Play doesn't work if both
players are not really "there"!

Infants, a Second-Person Approach to People, and the Rest of the Book

But when and how does all the infant's psychological engagement with
people happen? If infants cannot perceive that they are being addressed as a
You, they cannot begin to gain from it. When do they tell the difference between second-person and third-person interactions? What do they in fact
perceive of others' perceptions of them? This is a key question for the book.
William James once wrote that the most fiendish punishment imaginable

would be to be turned loose in society but remain absolutely unnoticed. The rage and impotence that would fill us if we could get no one to turn when we entered or answered when we spoke or minded what we did would be worse than any physical torture they could inflict on us. At least, if we were being tortured, we would have achieved some sort of recognition of our existence.[22] What is it about being noticed that is important? Is it simply that when we are noticed we notice that we have an impact on the world—that we are effective? Or is there something special about being noticed by other minds? If infants were not noticed by other people what would they become? In order to understand how infants come to understand other minds, this book looks at what infants *do* with other persons, in direct engagement, whether in naturally occurring interactions or in experimental situations. It explores the question of whether, in the face of these data, infants are really blind to minds. It considers different phenomena that many think involve crucial aspects of people's minds—imitation, communication, attention, intention, humour, self-consciousness, knowledge, and deception—and asks how infant engagement with these aspects could help us to reach an understanding of mind which is not permanently closed even to adults and which is gradually accessible to infants and animals too.

In the following chapters I will explore what a second-person story about knowing other minds would mean in very different domains of infant life. If what I have said about the importance of responses to others is true, and if this is indeed a vital link with other minds, then we should be able find evidence to substantiate that claim in infants' emotional engagements with people. The evidence could come both from the chronologies of development in each domain, with experiencing psychological directedness to the self preceding other more indirect experiences, and from atypicalities of development within each domain, with problems in the experience of psychological directedness to self preceding other problems. In each of the following chapters I take one, usually currently controversial, domain where infants seem to be able to engage with people in surprisingly complex ways and where questions of awareness of mind are problematic. So in Chapter 4 we look at the troublesome phenomenon of neonatal imitation, in Chapter 5 at the conversations of the 2-month-old, in Chapter 6 at the question of the understanding of attention *before* joint attention, in Chapter 8 at infants' violations of others' intentions in teasing, in Chapters 7 and 9 at early expressions of self-conscious affectivity and humour, and in Chapter 10 at the very early appearance of deceptive communication. In each case I suggest that a second-person approach to all these phenomena is key to understanding their development and continued functioning.

It may seem surprising that this book includes no separate chapter on emotion. The omission is deliberate. Conceptualising the understanding of emotion as separate from other aspects of mind and mentality is, I think, problematic. If this were a book on the development of concepts of mind, then a chapter on the development of separate concepts of emotion would make sense. However, engaging with other minds and becoming aware of them is an emotional process from start to finish. The awareness of attention or intentions or amusement or belief has to involve awareness of emotion. *Feeling* other minds is itself an emotional process. There are some chapters where I take a more explicit look at emotions—in discussing the awareness of others' facial expressions at 2 months (in Chapter 5) and in discussing the development of self-conscious emotions (in Chapter 7). I will argue that rather than derive from conceptual developments in the second year of human infancy, these emotions exist in simple form as ways of managing the exposure of self to other from early in the first year and are crucial for shaping the infant's emerging conceptions of self and other.

There is yet another reason not to have a separate chapter on emotion: although it may be overly simplistic to speak of such a split, there is reason to believe that positive and negative emotional engagements influence the process of knowing, and this, if true, would affect how we know about *all* aspects of others' minds. Barbara Frederickson suggests that positive emotions—such as joy or love or attraction or contentment—enhance our readiness to engage with people and things, making us more attentive and open to and able to integrate the things we experience.[23] Negative emotions, on the other hand, are believed to "narrow" rather than "broaden" the individual's reactions and openness to the world. Since positive emotions, at any age but particularly in infancy, are felt most intensely within interpersonal engagements, it seems clear that the more positive emotions the infant experiences, the more open to interpersonal engagement and knowing the infant becomes. But positive emotions also increase the infant's attractiveness to others, which further increases engagement—a potential double whammy for early life when there are problems with engagement or with positive emotionality. In the following chapters I will describe different kinds of positive emotional engagements—where we have data about them—which seem to support the infant's developing awareness of different aspects of mentality.

One more note: throughout the book I will include some references to autism and to data about atypical performance in children with autism compared to typically developing infants and children. Why is this relevant? To some extent, autism has been largely responsible for the relatively recent flood of interest in the issues surrounding children's understanding of other minds. But the original theorising about the profound and sometimes shocking co-relation between differences in key abilities and categorical differences between those children with autism and those without is now somewhat passé. We can neither look at children with autism as if they were indeed members of a distinct category, nor look at their abilities as being something of an either-or kind. And yet the large amount of data we have collected over the past twenty years on differences in functioning between those within and outside the autistic spectrum are indeed interesting and sometimes striking. I refer to some of these studies not because of the value of a categorical characterisation of autism, but because this spectrum highlights a really important dimension of how we understand people: the dimension of participation. Where children with autism find it difficult to participate in ordinary everyday engagements involving various aspects of mind—whether because something is too overwhelming or too threatening or too different from how they experience things—their difficulties highlight what might be involved in more typical development: an easier engagement with other people. Developmental trajectories (like knowledge) seem fundamentally influenced by participation.

CHAPTER 4

Making Contact: Imitation

Though the *Thou* is not an *It*, it is also not "another *I*." He who
treats a person as "another *I*" does not really see that person but
only a projected image of himself. Such a relation, despite the
warmest "personal" feeling is really *I-It*.

Martin Friedman, *Martin Buber: The Life of Dialogue*[1]

I remember being struck—and very moved—while watching
the film *Gorillas in the Mist* when Sigourney Weaver, playing the intrepid
primatologist Diane Fossey, manages after months of tracking and familiari-
sation, to get close enough to her gorillas to "talk." How could she begin?
What could she possibly do? She began to imitate them. The big silverback
grunted, and she did the same; he thumped his chest, she did too; he turned
his head sideways, so did she. He relaxed, ignored her, and just sat; she did
the same. Somehow imitation worked to make contact. The gorillas began
to allow and seek more communication and interaction after that tentative
and fragile beginning.

In this chapter I will ask whether imitation is the first psychological contact we can make when we are confronted with the unknown. And if it is
such a powerful means of psychological connection, what does it actually
involve? What does it involve when even newborn infants do it? Recent
neurophysiological studies support the claim that neonatal imitation is the
first demonstration of a psychological connection between self and other.
But why do neonates imitate? The answer seems to lie in engagement—in a
blurring of lines between imitating and being imitated, in a process of conversation.

Psychological Contact with Strangers

Before I get to newborn infants, I am going to talk about imitation in two other areas: its use in communicative impairment and its use in making contact across cultures. Imitation can be successfully used by practitioners working with children and adults who have communicative impairments. Phoebe Caldwell is one such practitioner, who has helped to develop a (flexible and communicative) system of imitation for, as she puts it, "learning the language" of those who are often considered unreachable. Her success was startling enough that Pavilion Publishers and the Joseph Rowntree Foundation set her a challenge, offering to film her at work with the most difficult "case" they could find. Gabriel was a young man with extremely severe autistic spectrum disorders, who spent most of the day in concentrated flapping and noise-making, and had essentially been given up on by scores of specialists. They simply could not make psychological contact with him. Phoebe's attempts to communicate with Gabriel—all on film—lasted three days. Within 20 minutes on the very first day, imitating his small repetitive flapping movements, she tuned in to one aspect of them—his sensory interest in touching his left hand with any object that he was flapping—and she did the same herself on her own hand. Gabriel moved almost magically from the closed self-absorbed focus he habitually showed to a quieter, more outward focus, casting occasional looks at her hands while they both flapped in turn. Within two days (actually about five hours of working time) Phoebe and Gabriel were spending long moments of contact and silent mutual gaze. It was so simple it seemed unbelievable. Responding through imitation seemed to open a conversational channel with Gabriel when everything had seemed hopeless. The last day Phoebe spent with his carers, showing them how they could interact with him in a similar way.[2]

Imitation also seems to be the favourite option of explorers and travellers on meeting "primitive" peoples. Darwin's contact with the Tierra del Fuegians during his voyage on the *Beagle* is one such famous episode. Following a detailed description of their skin colour, clothing, and demeanour, Darwin writes about the first contact with one of the tribes:

> Their very attitudes were abject, and the expression of their countenances distrustful, surprised, and startled. After we had given them some scarlet cloth which they immediately tied around their necks, they became good

friends. This was shown by the old man patting our breasts and making a chuckling kind of noise, as people do when feeding chickens. . . . He then bared his bosom for me to return the compliment, which being done, he seemed highly pleased.[3]

That imitation can be a means of making contact in the absence of any common language is clear. It seems to establish something shared, some common ground on which both interactants can stand. More simply than that, it seems to be a way in which both people, if one imitates and the other accepts being imitated, can touch each other psychologically. It seems to be a psychological door through which one is immediately led into a world of intentional relations with another person.

Is this the door through which human infants become aware of other minds? Could this be the bridge across the supposed gap between people? But do newborn infants possess such abilities?

Imitation and the Newborn Human

There has been a strangely passionate debate about this question: can human neonates imitate? In the first half of the twentieth century, there were writers who reported observations of imitation in very young babies: the French psychologist Zazzo, for instance, filmed imitation in his 25-day-old son and then conducted a study with parents as observers reporting imitations of tongue protrusions in babies 7 to 15 days old. It is reported that his mentor, Henri Wallon, was aghast at Zazzo's seemingly ridiculous claim.[4] These reports were either unknown to, or ignored by, modern Anglo-American psychology. Piaget and most of empiricist psychology argued that neonatal imitation is impossible for two reasons: (1) because imitation requires quite a complex ability to grasp the similarity between self and the person or animal to be imitated, an ability presumed to be impossible at birth without considerable experience of self and others; and (2) because imitation of specific acts was presumed to require specific learning about the similarity between self and other in the parts of the body producing those acts—learning which in some cases requires access to mirrors, which the neonate cannot have had. So, for instance, if you thump your chest and I do the same, I need to grasp that you and I are similar at least in the respect that we can both do the same thing (I can see your arm and chest as well as my own). But if you stick your tongue out and I do the same, I need in addition to have seen my tongue in a mirror, preferably while I was moving it and could also feel it, in order to realise that what I can otherwise only feel in my mouth is the same as what I can only see on your face. Both of these reasons take us right back to the old questions of the gap. That is, how do we know that the other person is in some way the same as us in the first place, and how do we know that the visual (exteroceptive) information we get from the other is the same as the kinaesthetic (proprioceptive) information we get from ourselves? Without the chance for empirical learning, which neonates have not yet had, neither the traditional argument from analogy nor the theory-theory view could accommodate neonatal imitation, although modern first-person views postulating a neural connection between self and other certainly can.

Doubts about logical possibility notwithstanding, human neonates do imitate some facial and manual gestures of other humans—and not only human neonates, as we now know, but chimpanzees and even, amazingly given their much lower evolutionary status, rhesus macaques.[5] Somehow, even at birth with no previous experience of the other person and no experience at all with mirrors, newborn primates seem to match the actions of the other person with the potential actions of the self, and actively imitate human facial gestures. Ironically, the first challenge to Piaget's theory (which predicted that imitation of "invisible movements of one's own body" should only happen when the infant was around 8 months of age) came from his own institution, from a Greek postgraduate called Olga Maratos. Speaking at the Annual Conference of the British Psychological Society in 1972, she told a sceptical audience of psychologists how she had found babies in their first month protruding their tongues to her when she had done it to them. When she was in Geneva a little later, she went to discuss this with Piaget in alarm because the finding was so fundamentally out of synch with his theory. He asked to see the videotapes for himself. Together, at Pierre Mounoud's laboratory, they watched the babies in silence. At the end, Piaget simply said: "Indeed they imitate!" and his calm response to her panicked "What shall I do?" was to say that it would be up to future theorists like her to further develop his theory or another theory to embrace the new data. The grand old man had a point; but thirty years later although we have some new theories (although none as grand as his) we are still squabbling about whether the phenomenon is "real." Piaget, however, never doubted the data. He repeated his view that this was imitation and not merely an archaic reflex at Olga's public defence of her Ph.D. in Geneva where, in the audience and interested in Piaget's response to these spectacular data, was a young Andy Meltzoff who then went on famously to explore this phenomenon.[6]

To date, there have been nearly a hundred studies of neonatal imitation in humans, and there is complete acceptance that neonates can imitate tongue protrusions, considerable evidence that they can imitate mouth opening, and some evidence that they can imitate finger movements and eye blinking and even one vocal sound—an elongated "aaaa." Rather more controversially, a few studies show imitation of some facial expressions (rather than just gestures), particularly that of surprise, with its raised eyebrows and enlarged eyes. However, the debate is just as passionate as it always was, now having shifted to the question of whether we could actually call such acts "imitation." The very least we can learn from the vehemence of academic responses to data claiming to show—or not show—neonatal imitation is this: imitation, or rather its impossibility, seems to be at the heart of some pretty central beliefs in psychology.

Imitation as a Paradoxical Skill

This vehemence and ambivalence in interpreting imitation is not new. Imitation is a genuinely paradoxical skill. It is not uncommon, for instance, to say that something is "mere" imitation. After all, monkeys did it. And so did "natives." Labelling their actions as "imitation" was not meant to imply that they were doing something intelligent; indeed, it meant the exact opposite.[7] In the words of one very questionable early American ethnologist, "it turns out that everything whites can do Negroes can imitate, but they can't *do* any of these things that whites can do."[8] Darwin's wonder at the events on the beach at Tierra del Fuego in 1832 has also been seen as consolidating this equation of savagery with mimesis. Darwin suggested in fact that the mimetic faculty may derive from a sensory keenness, not something to be admired like an intellectual sharpness, but indicative instead precisely of its absence:

> They could repeat with perfect correctness each word in any sentence we addressed them, and they remembered such words for some time. Yet we Europeans all know how difficult it is to distinguish apart the sounds in a foreign language. Which of us, for instance, could follow an American Indian through a sentence of more than three words? All savages appear to

possess, to an uncommon degree, this power of mimicry. I was told, almost in the same words, of the same ludicrous habit among the Caffres: the Australians, likewise, have long been notorious for being able to imitate and describe the gait of any man, so that he may be recognised. . . . How can this (mimetic) faculty be explained? Is it a consequence of the more practised habits of perception and keener senses, common to all men in a savage state, as compared with those long civilised?[9]

A similar pejorative view of imitation can be seen in the psychoanalytic tradition in which imitation is deemed to carry either a defensive hostility towards the other or is merely "skin-deep" and indicative of "adhesive" states. This is seen as quite distinct from the deeper contact with other people's experience to be found in genuine identification. It doesn't take much to see that the distinction between "skin-deep" and "genuine" imitation parallels the dualism of behaviour versus mind of the last chapter, or that the pejorative "mere imitation" is indistinguishable from the equally pejorative "mere behaviour" with which seemingly clever interpersonal acts tend to be dismissed when done by those too young to fit the theory. We come back, therefore, to the central importance of a Cartesian problem here: is imitation "behavioural" or is it in some sense "mental"?

Today, in a post-Piagetian psychology and following the resurrection of interest in the Other Minds problem, imitation has a higher profile and status. Imitation is now serious scientific business. But the ambivalence about what it really means is still evident when imitation appears to occur when it shouldn't—for example, in neonates. Then psychology reacts with passion: sceptical and dismissive as the nineteenth-century explorers, or defensive and illogical as nineteenth-century theologians in the face of a theory of evolution.

The first of the key beliefs challenged by neonatal imitation in recent psychology is the belief in the need for some sort of intellectual bridge (a third-person stance) to connect people. If we believe imitation involves some psychological common ground between people, and if we do not believe that neonates are capable of perceiving this connection or experiencing this common ground, then how can neonates imitate? Today's alternatives to describing this as imitation are somewhat more sophisticated than a simple dismissal as "primitive": levels of imitation have been distinguished in which the superficiality or "mere behaviour"-ness of the imitative act can vary in degree (although the number of critical levels is differently estimated: some putting it at four, others at ten, and some simply specifying alternative explanations to exclude).[10] Once we have established that it is something other than accidental, of these alternative explanations, the chief contender for explaining neonatal imitation as other-than-genuine (and we have yet to work out what "genuine" would actually mean) is that it is re-flexive, a result of an innate releasing mechanism or a fixed action pattern of some kind. Are neonates seeking to make the sort of contact with the adult humans in whose company they (literally) land up, which Diane Fossey sought with her gorillas, or which the "savages" sought with the white man in Tierra del Fuego? Or is it much more simply (if unexcitingly) that these imitations are driven by some kind of reflexive power? To deal with the issues of interpreting neonatal imitation, we need to answer these questions first.

Is Neonatal Imitation Reflexive?

We know that even at birth human infants can do more than simply act re-flexively. They can track objects visually and move their heads 180 de-grees, express preferences by facial expressions and head turning, learn (for example, even particular passages of poetry in utero!), and deliber-ately suck or move their heads and arms to evoke particular effects. In an ingenious set of experiments Audrey van der Meer showed that 1-month-olds, even if they had to make a big physical effort to do so, moved their arms more in order to elicit a beam of light, or to watch their own arm movements on video.[11] Even in utero, and as early as 15 weeks gestational age, ultrasound scanning studies have revealed at least fifteen different well-co-ordinated non-reflexive movement patterns, including indepen-dent finger movements, rapid and slow mouth opening, hand movements, repetitive contacting of mouth with fingers, and by 24 weeks, evidence of finely modulated facial expressions and eye movements with open eye-lids.[12] It seems indisputable that human neonates are capable not only of intentional actions, but also of intentional actions motivated by curiosity and interest rather than merely those driven by physiological needs. But this does not mean that all the actions they engage in are of this kind and, therefore, that neonatal imitations are necessarily intentional actions. The hypothesis remains to be tested: are neonatal imitations anything more than reflexive acts?

Evidence for Innate Releasing Mechanisms?

There is evidence to suggest that they may be. Neonates not only imitate tongue protrusions, but they also "imitate" the protruding movement of a pen or a ball by protruding their tongues (though slightly less frequently than they imitate a real tongue).[13] This lack of (statistically significant) selectivity between the stimuli has been interpreted to support a "releaser" explanation. Anisfeld, the most serious exponent of the view that neonatal imitations are driven by some kind of innate releasing mechanism (IRM) rather than by any (more complex cognitive) awareness of the similarity of self and other, argues that the range of studies now available on neonatal imitation show that tongue protrusion is the only gesture for which there is reliable evidence that observation increases the frequency of subsequent performance of the act.[14] His conclusion is based on a variety of reasons: some studies (but not all) fail to show significantly greater mouth opening to adult mouth opening models than to other types of models; in general, the frequency of mouth opening (MO) is much lower—whether taken as a baseline rate or in a model condition—than for tongue protrusion. For instance, in Meltzoff and Moore's classic study in 1977, even though there were more mouth openings to the MO model than to other models, the actual number of mouth openings even to the model was lower than the tongue protrusions, and in any case, ridiculously low—no more than 8 in total between 12 babies. If it is the case that tongue protrusion is the only reliably imitated gesture, it seriously weakens the claim that neonatal imitation is driven by some more general capacity for imitation or based upon a recognition of self-other similarity. However, there are important methodological debates here; use of a responsive and infant-sensitive presentation of the actions to be imitated leads to higher frequencies of imitation than a more inflexible and disengaged procedure, both in human neonates and in chimpanzees.[15] A "second-person" method, it seems, leads to different findings across a number of studies—and species—from a "third-person" method. The arguments about the existence of the phenomenon are wrapped up with arguments about the method used to explore it.

Several investigators have claimed that neonatal imitation disappears after the first two months, only to reappear much later, towards the end of the first year much as Piaget had observed.[16] Many other newborn reflexes—for instance, neonatal "walking" (when you hold a newborn up with feet touching a surface and they make stepping movements), the palmar grasp reflex (when you put a finger in a newborn's palm and they grasp it tightly enough to carry their own weight if you lift them up), and the Moro reflex (when they react to loss of support with thrown-out arms and legs and pulling back of the neck)—disappear shortly after birth (unless they are deliberately encouraged), and reappear much later more gradually and in more controlled form. The apparent disappearance of neonatal imitation has been taken to indicate that they too are reflexive, sub-cortical phenomena, of little significance for development or for the neonate's everyday living.

Today there is doubt about the hypothesis that there is a change from sub-cortical to cortical control for any of these reflexes, given, for example, the evidence that the walking reflex survives perfectly if the infant is held under water because there is more support for the immature muscles to manage the growing skeleton.[17] More than that, there is doubt about whether imitation does in fact disappear. In a longitudinal study of imitations in natural interactions, Giannis Kugiumutzakis in Crete showed that what changes is not the *fact* of the imitation but *what* is imitated. At birth, the greatest likelihood of imitation is first that of tongue protrusions and second that of mouth opening. By the second month, the imitation of tongue and mouth declines (in a U-shaped curve), but the imitation of eye movements continues. And the imitation of vocal models starts to become systematic and to increase, suggesting that this might signal the increasing salience of vocal (rather than oral) communications with development.[18]

Other evidence suggests that neonatal imitation is indeed different from later imitation, although whether it offers support for the innate releasing mechanism (IRM) hypothesis is questionable. Mikael Heimann and Eva Ullstadius found, in another longitudinal study, that while individual differences in imitation at 3 months did relate to individual differences at 12 months, there was no relation between individual differences at birth and those that occurred at 3 or 12 months. This lack of continuity of "style" could either be a result of two quite different mechanisms controlling imitation at birth and at 3 months on, or it could be the result of situational factors (such as stress and novelty) playing a greater role at birth and overriding or distorting other differences in "style."[19] In fact, drawing on data from pathology (in which adults with specific focal lesions in the lower half of the frontal lobes appeared to be unable to inhibit imitation of gestures) George Butterworth argued that a similar absence of strong frontal lobe influence at birth might actually increase the neonate's tendency to imitate.[20] Even though imitation is not compulsive in neonates as it is in adults with frontal lesions, but appears more sustained and intentional, nonetheless, what might be developing in the first months, he suggests, is an increasing capacity to inhibit—whether imitation or any other action.

Furthermore, the imitations are not elicited by static images. Confronted with a person whose tongue is already stuck out, or whose mouth is already open, the neonate does not respond with imitation; it is only the observation of the action itself that produces imitation.[21] Could imitation in human neonates be nothing more complex than the seagull chick opening its beak every time it sees a white cylinder with a red dot? Or than a frog darting its tongue out every time it sees movement in its visual field? These animal behaviours are simple inflexible reflexes. Could neonatal imitations be nothing more than this? Several sets of evidence argue against this conclusion.

Evidence against the Reflex Interpretation

First, as Meltzoff and Moore have argued, why would humans have evolved an automatic releaser for apparently meaningless gestures like tongue protrusion? Arguments that tongue protrusion is a reflex, adapted for feeding released by the approach of a nipple-like stimulus, don't quite work: the pronounced protrusions of the tongue don't normally accompany feeding behaviour, nor have they ever been described in the context of a real approaching nipple. In any case, there appears to be no consistent releaser: not all "nipple-like" stimuli work—a forward-moving black pen elicits tongue protrusions, but a forward-moving brown cylinder doesn't.[22]

Second, imitation by newborns doesn't have the immediate and automatic character of other actions known to be reflexes or driven by innate releasers. For instance, imitation can occur after a delay. In one of Andrew Meltzoff's studies, a dummy was put in the neonate's mouth while the adult modelled a mouth or tongue movement. When the modelling was completed, the dummy was removed; neonates still produced correct imitations.[23] In a similar experiment with 6-week-olds, infants were shown a modelled face movement but were prevented from reproducing the movement; one day later the same adult visited the infant, this time with a passive face. Even after the twenty-four-hour delay, infants produced the same movement when face to face with the same adult.[24] Even without artificial attempts (like a dummy in the mouth) to stop immediate imitation, the neonates in Kugiumutzakis's studies did not always imitate immediately and compulsively. Most of them concentrated attentively on the model's face for a few seconds before producing the imitative movement. Interestingly, these delays were longer for premature babies, indicating the greater effort and processing time they required.

In a dramatic study with 1-day olds, a young Hungarian medical student called Emese Nagy showed that such delayed imitations were not simply delayed, but were actually serving as provocations for interaction. In her study, newborns produced tongue protrusions, mouth opening, and hand movements, not only in response to adults who modelled the actions, but also after a delay, when the same adults just watched them pleasantly. What made these delayed imitations "provocative" was that they were accompanied by a totally different heart rate pattern than the imitations: the heart decelerated, indicating greater preparatory attentional focus on the acts of the other, in contrast to the clear acceleration characterising imitations.[25] Reflexes, on the other hand, are usually immediate and do not begin after the withdrawal of the stimulus; they certainly do not occur twenty-four hours after the observation of the stimulus or appear to provoke a response from the other person.

Furthermore, imitation in newborns is not inevitable or even predictable. It does not always occur, either each time the action is observed by the same infant or by all infants. That is, the same infant sometimes imitates and sometimes doesn't, and a few perfectly normal and attentive infants never imitate at all.[26] It is not at all clear why this should be the case. The strong individual differences which operate right from birth in many aspects of infant behaviour and temperament, including imitation, might explain, according to Mikael Heimann, the apparent elusiveness of neonatal imitation and the "disappearance" of the phenomenon when responses are averaged out across infants.[27] Reflexes, on the other hand, are by definition predictable. If we don't blink our eyes when a light shines into them or don't gasp for air on coming out of the water or don't cry on being born, there is a neurophysiological reason for it. Not so in the case of neonatal imitation.

Third, the imitations by neonates are often effortful and creative rather than effortless. This is most clearly visible in the imitation of eye blinking (not an easy action in any case for neonates) in which the neonate's blinking is performed by an effort involving the muscles of the whole face.

Also, infants don't simply produce one easy imitation and then stop. In Kugiumutzakis's studies, newborns displayed several different patterns of imitating. Some infants produced several imitations one after another, each of which got progressively better, while other infants produced a perfect imitation the first time followed by weaker repetitions of the movement.[28] In an attempt to test the imitated actions even further, Meltzoff showed 6-week-olds a model of a tongue protruding to the side rather than forward; some infants gradually corrected their initial forward tongue protrusions, or even tried to achieve correct imitation by sticking their tongues out forward and turning their heads to the side![29] Reflexes and fixed action patterns in the animal kingdom (including those in humans) are not so complex, they are usually stereotyped, they change little with practice, and they involve little apparent effort to perform. Unlike neonatal imitations, the organism involved in a fixed action pattern does not correct itself while trying to achieve a goal.

A further intriguing explanation of the disappearance of tongue protrusion imitations is that tongue protrusion may be an attempt at oral exploration in the absence of the ability to reach and bring the object to the mouth for actual exploration with the tongue. Susan Jones has shown in her work not only that tongue protrusion occurs to some extent in response to any interesting visual display, but that the "virtual" exploration with the tongue stops as soon as infants begin to reach with their hands. She argues that neonatal "imitation" of tongue protrusion is neither reflexive nor intentional; it is simply not imitation at all.[30] If it were indeed the case that imitation were limited to tongue protrusion, then this argument would have serious weight. But it doesn't appear to be. While this explanation might indeed hold for the disappearance of tongue protrusions after the first month or so of infancy, it cannot explain the finding that other kinds of imitation do not disappear only to reappear at the end of the first year.

The arguments rage on. Perhaps the reason for the vehemence (on both sides of the debate) is that the phenomenon carries serious implications: if newborns recognise the similarity between self and other within minutes of birth, not only is the apparent gap between people non-existent, but the gap between mind and behaviour itself may become irrelevant. Barring complete reflexivity, however, we still need to explain how it can be that an infant who has never seen its own face or mouth or tongue can imitate someone's else's tongue, mouth, and face movements. But this mystery at least is well on its way to resolution.

Neonatal Imitation and the Gap

If there was indeed such a gap between self and others as philosophers and psychologists have postulated and struggled with, a gap which required extensive experience and observation of similarities to bridge, we would either not have neonatal imitation at all, or if we did, this imitation would first involve those "visible" features of the body (such as hands or legs) in which the self-other visual comparisons are more apparent. However, we do have neonatal imitation and it primarily involves the non-visible features of the body. Whether it involves reflexes or a more complex process of matching, it indicates that there is already at birth some connection across the alleged gap. But what *is* this connection exactly? And what does it say about the nature of the gap that it appears to dissolve?

Neurophysiological Bridges across the Gap?

The discovery of "mirror neurones" in monkeys was the first clear evidence of a neurophysiological basis for the recognition of self-other similarity. Rumour has it that this discovery (like penicillin before it) was an accident. A scientist in Giacomo Rizzolatti's now famous lab at the University of Parma was measuring the discharge of a specific neurone in the premotor cortex of a rhesus macaque to a goal-directed movement by the monkey. The neurone in question, linked up to an audio speaker, fired (loudly) every time the monkey picked up a peanut and brought it to its mouth. The scientist, wilting in the Italian heat, nipped out for an ice cream. As he came back and lazily licked it, the same neurone in the monkey's brain fired, although the monkey was merely watching him lift his ice cream and was not picking up a peanut itself. This happened again and again, with nothing wrong with the recording equipment. Observing an action appeared to cause the same neuronal activity as doing it—at least in monkeys. Some kind of direct "resonance" seemed to be present between action and observation, and therefore, between the actions of the self and the actions of the other. Could this be the bridge across the so-called gap?

The discovery of mirror neurones and its potential impact on psychology has been likened to the discovery of DNA in biology; the recent burgeoning of literature in neuroscience following this discovery certainly supports this view.[31] Mirror neurones, however, are likely to be red herrings for explaining neonatal imitation: the firing of mirror neurones cannot, for a start, explain delayed imitation lasting as long as twenty-four hours; nor can they explain the very active self-correction that was observed in the neonates during imitation in both Meltzoff's and Kugiumutzakis' studies, nor the provocations in Nagy's Hungarian babies and Meltzoff's American ones. Mirror neurones seem insufficient as a bridge across the so-called gap.

Two other sets of neurological and muscular findings offer a more complex story. One is the finding that the premotor system (where the mirror neurones are to be found) sometimes allows a "brief prefix of the movement" to be exhibited, one which is recognisable by and can be responded to, involuntarily, by the other. Rizzolatti and Arbib offer a complex and more process-based explanation of mutual motor attunement and the beginnings of primitive dialogue:

> This fact (the prefix of the movement) will affect both the actor and the observer. The actor will recognise an intention in the observer and the observer will notice that its involuntary response affects the behaviour of the actor. The development of the capacity of the observer to control his or her mirror system is crucial in order to emit (voluntarily) a signal. When this occurs, a primitive dialogue between the observer and actor is established. This dialogue forms the core of language.[32]

Another is the set of findings showing broader perceptual-motor links between doing something oneself and seeing it done by another. In humans, studies using magnetic imaging (deep electrodes to record the firing of specific neurones are, of course, unusable) have found evidence for a broader story about the possible unity of perceptual and motor neuronal activity. Areas of the brain which are activated during actions, namely, the motor cortex and the right and left inferior parietal lobes, are also activated during observation and even imagination of the actions.[33] Furthermore, the activity during observation of the action is not restricted to the brain; it permeates the whole motor system. Watching someone else grasp an object, for instance, leads to increased motor-evoked potentials in the watcher's hand as well as in the premotor cortex, and listening to speech increases the excitability of muscles in the tongue, findings which bear uncanny resemblance to discredited (behaviourist) predictions from the early twentieth century about vocal cord activity during thinking.[34] These findings suggest that any bridge across the so-called gap between self and other must involve bodies, not just brains.

Some Attempts to Close the Gap

Various explanations are on offer to deal with just how these neurological or broader bodily connections can be seen to close the gap between self and other. Andy Meltzoff and Keith Moore invoke a mechanism called AIM to explain how, even in utero, movements ("body babbling") provide proprioceptive feedback allowing the mapping of an "act space" (into which newer body positions can be interpolated by comparison) and which are stored "supramodally"—that is, without being tied to a specific sensory modality. This representation of proprioceptive and visual feedback in the same space is, they suggest, the bridge we need: it allows the active intermodal matching (AIM) of others' movements to one's own.[35] It not only allows the recognition of similarity between self and other, but it allows neonatal imitation; in addition, through a gradual process of learning (about the match between behaviour and mental states in the self) and reasoning (about the likely match between the same behaviour and the same mental states in others), it allows the infant to understand the relation between others' observable behaviour and their minds.

Despite its cognitive science clothing, the AIM hypothesis still leans on the argument from analogy. Intentions, within this model, are not tied to movement; they are considered to be conceptual entities, invokable through inference. Minds are thought of as essentially unobservable. Therefore, the infant's task is to grow beyond the merely behavioural, developing beyond the perception of persons as "mere dynamic bags of skin that I can imitate and which imitate me" to awareness that they are psychological beings as well.[36]

In contrast, another first-person suggestion, Vittorio Gallese's concept of a "primitive we-centric space" existing at the start of life, avoids the need for inference and develops a more compelling line of explanation.[37] The shared space could be the bridge across the self-other gap and, according to Gallese, could explain the feeling of "self-ness" we "attribute" to others. Gallese suggests that this shared space could enable the social bootstrapping of all development, providing a powerful tool for making perceptual discriminations about regularity, coherence, and predictability in the interaction and allowing emotional as well as intentional attunement. While a shared "we-centric" space is vital in a second-person explanation as well, it is not enough. It still does not offer an explanation of an "I-You" space in which the other is recognised as *different* from the self, a difference to which the infant is attracted and moved to *respond*.

Some writers link not only the perception of action with its execution,
but the action with its intention. Jean Decety, for instance, using magnetic
resonance technology, showed that, at least in adult humans, the perception of action is encoded differently depending on the perceiver's intention.
Perception with the intention to imitate showed activation patterns in the
brain that were more similar to those during actual execution of the action
than to brain patterns that are activated during mere observation. Imagined
actions too are different in their cortical activation patterns, depending on
whether they are imagined as being done by the self (more left inferior parietal lobe activation) or by another person (more right inferior parietal lobe
activation). A promising suggestion is that action may be some sort of singular phenomenon, varying in degree rather than in nature, between the
doer, the planner, the imaginer, and the observer, but supported by a
common neural substrate.[38] This sort of explanation potentially avoids dualist distinctions between intention and action, and also therefore between
self and other.[39] It could transform the gap to one of degree: the degree of
self-ness versus other-ness in an act, the degree of imagined-ness versus
perceived-ness of an act, the degree of perceived-ness versus executed-ness
of an act, and so on.

Not Similarity but Relevance

These findings and explanations serve only to explain the matching
(without confusion) of self and other; that is, we are now close to explaining self-other equivalence in neurological terms. But simply explaining
the infant's recognition of similarity between self and other is not enough.
Neonates do more than "match" to the world around them. They act appropriately in a physical world which doesn't resemble their bodies, using actions which are different from, not just similar to, actions and patterns in
the world around them.[40] For instance, neonates reach out to swipe at balls
held out to them, they turn their heads to follow moving faces, they localise
sounds in space which they have never before experienced, they suck
harder on dummies to re-elicit lights and pictures. Kevan Bundell, a student
of Colwyn Trevarthen, asks, for instance, how we actually perceive the affordances or potential for actions in the world (a question not answered
within standard Gibsonian theory) before we act in it, or how we know the
meaning of something, for example, of a graspable object, before we have
grasped the object. Using Bernstein's theory in which actions are planned

before they are executed, and in which there is no real difference between planning an act and executing it (except its bodily execution), Bundell argues (in contrast to the Meltzoff and Moore explanation) that we don't have to *do* the act to know its meaning. The body and its potential for action must be constantly represented in patterns (dynamic and analogue patterns) of neuronal firing in order for the body to be a live agent, and in the same code of neuronal firing must the perceived world also be dynamically represented. The information shared between the represented body and the represented world would allow a unity between the body's potential for action and the world's potential for being acted with or on. However, even this explanation cannot explain reciprocal actions with people. Why do we do more than match or imitate them?

When interacting with people newborn infants don't just imitate, they respond. They respond with interest or disinterest, with attention or avoidance, and at least within weeks, with reciprocal rather than imitative emotional actions. It has been argued that even imitative interactions are not merely imitative and that the actions themselves are never identical to those observed. They often involve (even in neonates as we shall see in a minute) varying degrees of approximation and varying degrees of hesitation and change: *responses to,* rather than *mimicking of,* another person. In Nagy and Molnar's and in Meltzoff's experimental studies, moreover, imitative acts seem on occasion provocative, occurring as prompts to the other. Some would argue that imitation—unless done robotically—is *always* a response. We have not yet gotten an explanation of this phenomenon: "like-me" representations and mirror neurones and analogue representations of body and world could explain *how* imitation occurs, but they don't explain *why.* Even less could they explain how neonates could respond with different—reciprocal—actions. What we need is a theory of *self-other relevance.* Relevance as a concept demands an explanation of meaningfulness and appropriateness rather than just similarity, and in doing so, immediately opens the door to explanations which ask and answer questions of motivation.

There are many puzzles of intentionality involved in understanding imitation. How, for example, does the imitator decide which aspect of an act to imitate?[41] Any successful imitation must to a large extent already occur against a shared background of meaning that allows a protruding tongue to be distinct from, for example, the turning away of a face. This common "knowing" might be yet another example of the "massive hermeneutic background" involved in language-learning in questions like "How does the toddler know that the word 'rabbit' refers to the whole animal and not just to its ears or tail?"[42] This hermeneutic background must lie not only in shared intentionality but also in the engagement in imitation itself. Imitation by definition needs two players. As Ina Uzgiris, that grande dame of Piagetian and post-Piagetian developmental psychology, argued, it might be more fruitful, given the fragility and situation dependence of imitation, to see imitation as a primarily interpersonal activity and to ask questions about motivation and function. If an interpersonal approach is adopted, it would lead us to see imitation as bi-directional (i.e., the model and the imitator blend into one another in reciprocal fusion, with an inevitable alternation of roles and influence), as relevant to the interaction rather than involving arbitrary acts, as directing the interaction down specific routes, and as, overall, a cultural activity with wider social meanings bearing upon the imitative activity. In order to understand what's going on in neonatal imitation we need to ask the motivation question: why do infants do it?

Why Do Neonates Imitate?

The acts which neonates imitate are to some extent bizarre, albeit of those aspects of the body that are specifically adapted in form and timing for communication—facial, vocal, and gestural expressions. People don't normally go around, in face-to-face conversation with anyone, sticking their tongues right out and holding for a couple of seconds, or opening their mouths wide and slow. Colwyn Trevarthen suggests that it could be precisely because these acts are awkward and odd in conversational terms that they seem to require some marked response from the infant. Unexaggerated or otherwise "understood" face-to-face acts—whether between familiar adults or between anthropologist and "savage"—must go unremarked with unexaggerated responses. It is the odd behaviour which stands out and seeks a responsive comment.

But why *imitate?* There are at the moment two explanations on offer: a rational attempt to test the other's identity and/or an attempt at conversation. Arguing that behaviour serves as gestural signatures for people, Andy Meltzoff suggests that having learned that this is what person X does, infants attempt to reproduce the act on seeing the person again as a way of testing their identity or of reinstating person-specific interactive "games" or routines. On the other hand, a more dyadic and mutualist explanation refers to the infant's and adult's contributions as part of the same conversational unit. Echoing Merleau-Ponty's argument that imitation is both a sharing of the body of the other and a completion of the other body's act, Kugiumutzakis suggests that neonatal imitation is a simple form of communication with the model. The neonate, in imitating, is responding to this communicative attempt by the other by the completion of the other's as yet incomplete interpersonal action.

There is some empirical evidence for this suggestion. In Kugiumutzakis' experiments, the model presented the to-be-imitated action a maximum of five times at the rate of about once every three seconds, but stopped presenting as soon as the infant imitated the action if the imitation was earlier. More than three quarters of the infants reacted after the fifth presentation, although they could have interrupted the presentations earlier. Combined with their evident interest and concentrated attention, Kugiumutzakis sees this timing as an important indicator of simple turn-taking; the infant responds to the adult's communicative act after the adult has stopped. Similarly, the greater success (at least in chimpanzees) of a more conversational and less rigid experimental procedure in eliciting imitations suggests that something about a face-to-face interactive setup (and not just the perception of the modelled act) is important in eliciting neonatal imitations. Further, the difference in heart rate patterns between imitative and provocative acts in neonates suggests that at least the provocative acts are initiations of some interpersonal kind—attempts at some rudimentary kind of conversation. Nagy and Molnar suggest that these two actions are a good analogue of the two components of all motivational processes known in ethology: the genetically opened and plastic appetitive (initiation) and the closed and rigid consummatory phases (imitation). A conversational or communicative answer to the motivation question may be cognitively far less demanding than an individualist "identity-testing" one. Communication seems, unavoidably, to be on the agenda in discussions about neonatal imitation. It is at the heart of the questions about the gap.

Neonatal Imitation as Interpersonal Activity?

The descriptions by Darwin and Fitzroy (captain of the *Beagle*) of what was involved in the mimicry of the "savages" and the Europeans on the *Beagle* are illuminating here. Darwin described the imitation as more or less one-directional. The sailors provoked. The "savages" mimicked. The phenomenon that was deemed to need explanation was the exceptional mimicking ability "inside" the "savages." But Fitzroy's descriptions, less meticulous but perhaps unhindered by concerns of theoretical consistency, read differently: "They expressed satisfaction or goodwill by rubbing or patting their own, and then our bodies; and were highly pleased by the antics of a man belonging to the boat's crew, who danced well and was a good mimic."[43]

As Michael Taussig puts it: Who is mimicking whom, the sailor or the "savage"? Intriguingly, the same chicken and egg problem, he argues, surfaces in children's interactions with adults:

> Adults imitate what they take to be baby talk or childish tones of voice and expression and insert themselves in what they take to be the "child's world," playing with the child, sometimes with the aim of controlling it, or teaching the child by getting it to imitate the adult's imitation—patting the dog this way, not that way, eating this way, not that that way, and so forth. . . . And the child? Does it respond to this with mimicry of mimicry? And what then was the adult imitating in the first place—a real reality, as we might like to simplistically describe the issue, such as the child's tone of voice or behaviour? Or instead was the adult imitating the child's mimicry of the adult's mimicry?[44]

We're getting into strange waters here. Circularity of modelling and response is not that unusual: mirroring of posture in conversations amongst friends, one act leading to an influence on the other and back again, or an imitation which pleases and encourages the modeller to act again, imitating the imitator. In the case of the neonate and the adult, the imitations (if occurring naturally and outside of rigidly controlled experimental conditions) also occur within an interactive context. They cannot do otherwise. As in any other interaction, the adult cannot help but be influenced by the infant's response and so on.

The French psychologist (and student of Zazzo's) Jacqueline Nadel presented a novel paradigm for exploring the effects of being imitated, which shows very vividly this complete interconnectedness of imitating and being imitated. In her videos, where she as an adult and experimenter imitated the whole-body posture and actions and movements of children with autism, the effects of being imitated are very powerful in moving the child to curiosity and communication. It soon becomes very difficult to keep the line between imitator and imitated clear. It is also difficult to establish—acontextually—criteria for which act is an imitation and which isn't. Yet, we have been thinking of it as a primarily intra-individual capacity. We ask: what is the neonate capable of? What can the neonate see? What is the neonate interested in? The "it" that we are concerned with has been largely defined as something that is going on inside the individual infant. But if we are to take the (Wittgensteinian) notion of engagement as essential to meaning, then we must ask here, "Would neonates imitate tongue protrusions outside of engagement?" and even "Would parents protrude their tongues to neonates if they weren't trying to engage them (however bizarrely)?" Kugiumutzakis and his colleagues have shown that acts of imitation between parent and infant are, as he puts it, "swimming in emotion." Smiles are often seen in both infant and adult just before, during, and after the imitative acts.[45] Smiles also appear to increase around the time of the imitative acts in imitative exchanges with older children and people with disabilities.[46] Not only does imitation appear to produce pleasure, but pleasure seems to facilitate the occurrence of imitation. Such a circularity of effects, in keeping with other research on the effects of positive emotions, can easily be seen to continue with more complexity into childhood and adulthood, influencing the reduction of opportunities for interaction and mutual understanding. Imitation as an emotional activity seems to be essentially mutual. Recent findings in studies by Teresa Farroni and her colleagues in London are illuminating here. Studying various behavioural and neurological aspects of the perception of other people's gaze direction in 2- to 5-day-old newborns, they found that from birth babies prefer to look at faces that look directly at them rather than at faces that look away. By 4 months of age, there was evidence of an enhanced neural processing of direct rather than averted gaze.[47] The idea of I-You engagement in neonatal imitation seems not at all absurd.

What Functions Does Imitation Serve?

Parents are not usually aware of the phenomenon of neonatal imitation, even though, as has been shown, neonates do imitate a little even in natural interaction. Contrary to the frequently made accusation that parents are always willing to attribute the highest levels of skill to their infants, parents can be prone to under- rather than over-interpretation, and occasional imitative acts are easily dismissed as chance. But when evidence of the phenomenon is made available to parents, imitation appears to be one of the few interpersonal exchanges that parents can use to engage and test and interact with their neonates. It is ridiculously easy to produce imitations in some infants, if not in the first hour after birth when they are still alert, then after the first two days. The infant needs, however, to be in a state of what is called quiet alertness: awake and quietly attentive to the surrounding environment rather than in an active thrashing state. And it can be fun—an opportunity for pleasure which exhausted parents dealing with a demanding and otherwise not particularly responsive infant sorely need. Berry Brazelton made a similar observation when he noted parents' reactions to his 4-week clinical checkup with infants; they watched the infants respond to his voice, turn when he called them, melt into his body when he patted them, and focus on his face when he engaged them. Parents often commented they were unable to believe that this was the same infant they had so intensively cared for in their homes for four weeks without knowing that he or she was capable of such responses and such interests.[48] Being able to engage with the infant's interest in our invitations to communicate through imitation can provide a turning point in parents' relationships with them—the first "now moments" that are possible.

In adults imitation can serve any interpersonal function that we can think of. It can be cruel, a mocking act that serves to emphasise another's weakness; it can be funny, cheeky, irritating, flattering, almost anything you wish to use it for. But in interactions between neonates and adults, its functions may be simpler, showing resonance, implicit or explicit, reflecting a tuning in to the mood of the other. Intriguingly, the psychological function of imitation may be more for the receiver than the actor; as Jacqueline Nadel puts it, being imitated is a deep compliment. It is saying to the person whom you are imitating, "I take you the way you are." Imitating may not be intended as flattery, sincere or otherwise, but it seems to be a simple and very powerful way of "confirming" the other person in the terms of Buber and Hegel discussed in the last chapter. The dramatic successes of imitation in eliciting communication in children with disabilities (of Nadel's groundbreaking method of imitating children with autism and of Caldwell's work described earlier) may be due precisely to this interpersonal confirmation, an acknowledgement of the "You." Being imitated seems to establish a powerful and immediate statement of interest, connection, and intentional relation, and, as Suzanne Zeedyk suggests, with several recent studies of its effectiveness in situations of neglect and communicative difficulty, it is *being* imitated which is crucial for intimacy.[49] For the same reason, perhaps, neonatal imitations might matter in everyday life to parents. The "function" of imitation might be its effect on the other and the interpersonal dialogue it promotes. The next chapter explores the phenomena and claims made about the earliest conversations in human infants: what have been called proto-conversations in 2-month-olds.

CHAPTER 5

Opening Conversations

The singer alone does not make a song,
there has to be someone who hears.

Rabindranath Tagore, *Broken Song*[1]

"Of all affairs," said the great educationalist and philosopher John Dewey, "communication is the most wonderful."[2] Communication and dialogue create and transform the individual and the realm of meanings, but also, intriguingly, seem to demonstrate the recognition of another being. You would not have a dialogue with someone unless you took for granted, or at least hoped, that he or she was a minded being, capable—at some level—of understanding and responding. Unless you are Shirley Valentine talking to her wall or John Cleese talking to his Mini, talk seriously to a mindless thing and you run the risk of being labelled mad. So if we generally reserve dialogue and communication for creatures with minds, they must imply a prior recognition of mentality. But what makes an exchange a dialogue? Can we have dialogue without content? Can we have conversations about nothing?

In this chapter I will look at the proto-conversations of the 2-month-old—the face-to-face "chatting" with neither words nor topic—a phenomenon which is still controversial after many years of debate and still central to claims about the early origins of intersubjectivity. I will start first, though, with the question "what is dialogue?"

What Is Dialogue?

What do *you* think of when you think of dialogue? Here are some examples that spring to mind: an Islamic genre of music in south Asia called *Qawwali*, often involving two groups of singers, each deliberately setting up musical and poetic challenges for the other, repartee building up until one of them wins; a jazz player's seamless conversations with his fellow musicians; all-night discussions about the meaning of life in a student hall of residence; Israel and Palestine sitting down for talks in Egypt while the world waits; young couples whispering endlessly into telephones about nothing much; a baby and mother face to face, each enjoying an intense wordless exchange.

What is it about these very different exchanges that makes me think of them as dialogues? In each of these examples, there is at least some mutual recognition of the consciousness of the other, some kind of openness in each partner to the acts of the other and a taking of turns in responding to them. The answer may seem obvious, but it is far from agreed upon. And it is no mere academic debate: doubts about the meaning or relevance of dialogue influence how we act, and even parents in their everyday interactions can be stricken with doubt about some exchanges.

Take, for example, the following excerpt from an observational diary we had kept after our daughter Shamini was born. I was clearly having trouble deciding what to make of her apparent responsiveness to us in the face of the books which said that she would not smile or "chat" or respond to another's affect until a dramatic shift at around 2 months.[3]

> *19th day:* . . . (the first full, social smile today) . . . A little later I picked her up 'cause she was . . . fussing, . . . spoke to her (in a sort of amazed tone saying "why are you doing that?," with a smile on my face and in my voice) and she immediately gave me another smile, . . . then her gaze wandered off very quickly. I wasn't sure what to make of it all. First time I've felt a response in her to *my* smiling. *Feels* clearly a response to my affect. But still can't trust (it) . . . she (won't be) ready for it until (another few weeks). . . .
> *Later:* (she was fussing, so I brought) her face within five inches of mine, hoping to keep her quiet so I could continue reading [ouch!]. I peered into her surprised face and said a big hullo and smiled. And she looked back at my face and smiled back—a clear smile but only half her face—on the side which was up. I was startled, chatted for a bit—still felt dubious about the personal-ness of the smile. Convinced of it being a response. But unsure whether to trust that it was the beginning of her relationship with me. Unwilling to impute too much to her.[4]

Fortunately, it seems that despite my academic self-consciousness I didn't quite believe my own doubt and, drawn in by her communicative attempts, carried on actually chatting! I was not alone in my doubt and caution. Most of developmental psychology was and still is sceptical about the possibility of genuine communication before the end of the first year. In trying to pin down communication, psychology generally focuses on language and the communication of "information," of meanings about things outside both partners. Simple exchanges of smiles and vocalisations are seen as meaningless in this sense, and often as somehow biologically driven and less than intentional.

In the sceptical atmosphere of the late 1960s and early 1970s, Mary Catherine Bateson (inspired by a film of a 9-week-old infant with mother, which she reportedly saw while she herself was pregnant) was the first to call the interactions of 2-month-olds "proto-conversations." There was a strange *zeitgeist* in the air, and the work of several independent researchers began to converge on the early communicative abilities of very young infants.[5] It was 1966, and Colwyn Trevarthen, a young biologist, had just completed his doctorate on consciousness in monkeys with the Nobel Laureate Roger Sperry and had gone to work for a year in Marseille. Two significant things followed: he had his first child and was becoming fascinated with him, and he met the dynamic and irrepressible Jerome Bruner, who was thinking of setting up a research group at Harvard to study babies. Within a year Trevarthen was at Harvard, collaborating with Bruner, Berry Brazelton, and Martin Richards. Altogether independent of these two separate labs was the work of two other key figures, Daniel Stern, on the intricate and involved games and timing of mother-infant interaction, and Hanus Papousek on communicative emotional expressions by infants involved in conditioning experiments.[6] The rest is history. It was a few years later, and after Trevarthen had moved to Edinburgh, that infant communicative skills hit the headlines. And immediately the debates were raging. Trevarthen's claim that not only were these very young infants having "conversations," but that their conversations involved an "innate intersubjectivity," or the ability to share and participate in another person's feelings and thoughts, was a serious, seemingly ludicrous challenge to mainstream views.[7] Just as ludicrous was Zazzo's claim that his newborn son could imitate face movements.

The apparent communications were dismissed as "pseudo- (rather than proto-) conversations" (again, just as Piaget and others had previously used the term *pseudo-imitation*). The dismissals were motivated by cautions and *a priori* theoretical convictions that came from a variety of traditions. The

behaviourist–social learning theory–tradition objected because its proponents sought to explain the interactions as the result of a variety of learned
associations and reinforcements. The newer cognitivist—or at least
Piagetian—tradition objected both because its idea of interpersonal understanding began with a profound childhood egocentrism and because its
proponents were beginning to require elaborate evidence of mental representational skill for countenancing any claims about communication.
Needless to say, the now familiar dualism of mind and behaviour under-
pinned both these objections. Where communication was defined as a
"mind-to-mind" process, infants of that age were seen as simply too young
to be able to grasp the idea of minds in order to communicate with them.
Where the emphasis was on a more behavioural construct of interacting
reinforcements and contingencies, the behaviour of the infants (and indeed the adults) was seen as resulting from environmental and other behavioural constraints, with no need to invoke the fancy mentalistic labels
of intersubjectivity and communication.

The strongest caution, however, came from a new tradition—social
constructionism—which resisted the individualism of Piaget and embraced
a deep sociality from the traditions of George Herbert Mead and Lev Vygotsky. The Norwegian philosopher Ragnar Rommetveit wrote in 1974 that
"intersubjectivity has to be taken for granted in order to be achieved" and
this now famous dictum was applied to infancy to mean that it is only if
mothers act "as if" their infants could understand them that the infants actually come to understand them. Intersubjectivity was seen to emerge in relation, but with an interesting twist: through a *mistaken* attribution by one
or both of the partners in the relation (in this case by the mother) about the
intentions and understanding of the other. Within this camp the theorist
could remain agnostic about what the infants in fact "understood" about the
other person, or about what the infants' actions actually "meant" before the
attributions were made.

However, Rommetveit's dictum can be interpreted another way: that in
order to *initiate* any interpersonal communication the initiator must presup-
pose intersubjectivity.[8] That is, the infant's initiation of communication is
evidence of the infant's recognition of another's subjectivity. Of course, not
only is defining what constitutes communication a controversial issue, but
even defining initiation is problematic. Our communications are deeply embedded in each others' reactions, so who is to say where an individual stops
responding and starts initiating?[9]

Nonetheless, this slant takes emphasis away from social constructionism and maternal self-fulfilling beliefs and attributions and instead puts the onus also on our descriptions of what infants do. *Do* they in fact initiate interpersonal communication? In the literature on animal communication, there is considerable evidence of young mammals calling for attention and company. In babies, however, although there is a large literature on crying, there is a strange neglect of positive calling. Mothers report that by about 3 months of age, there is a "calling" tone in infant vocalisations, used when they are not being attended to and very different from a responsive tone used when engagement is already established. Precisely what the infant is calling the other *for* remains to be established: for face-to-face attention, for physical contact, for vocal exchanges, for entertainment. Vocal initiations by infants within engagement, however, are commonplace, often picked up by parents and imitated (in the manner of Diane Fossey with her gorillas).

It is clear that in order to escape this quagmire, we need to have a good look at what conversations with 2-month-olds are actually like. But how do we do this? How can I bring the qualities of these conversations to you as a reader? Second best to getting in there and talking to a baby ourselves is watching someone else do it. Videos of babies never fail to intrigue audiences in lectures, and there is a deep significance in these audience reactions. There is one particular video I have of my son at 10 weeks, which always moves audiences. The episode feels intensely dialogic: his responses are so attuned to mine and the whole is so like a conversation that one needs to make an effort to not see it.

> Rohan, 10 weeks, lying on the settee with me leaning over him; following a series of intense face-to-face vocal exchanges between us; there is one particularly long and expressive vocalisation from him which overrides a vocal response I was beginning to make. I pause in my response until about a second after he finishes the utterance and then I ask in a quiet voice— "What?" He pauses for two seconds, still intensely watching me, and then responds with a smiling vocalisation, curving head and body away slightly. I laugh at this and ask "Are you singing?" He responds suddenly with a much larger smile—a near laugh—lifting his face upwards, eyes still on mine.

Was this really communication and dialogue? On what basis can we decide?

Structural Features of Dialogue and Communication

One way of deciding whether an interaction really is communication might be to look to the structural features generally identified as occurring in conversations between human adults (with the caution that using the criteria of a more mature version of the phenomenon carries the risk of obscuring from our view the very origins we seek). Such features include a *repertoire of communicative acts* (such as expressions, words, gestures), *self-synchrony* (the ability to produce organised and coherent actions), *interactional and affective synchrony* (the ability to relate your own actions and emotions to the other's actions and emotions), *turn-taking* (an ability to take turns in acts), *attentional co-ordination* (i.e., the ability to know when someone is attending to you and to co-ordinate your attention with the other's to a third thing), *reference* (i.e., the ability to point or verbally refer to things), *information content* (i.e., the ability to say something about these things), *symbolism* (i.e., the ability to use arbitrary symbols to stand for things), *grammatical* and *textual competence* (i.e., the ability to produce and comprehend well-formed sentences and to link sentences together to convey large amounts of information) and *socio-linguistic competence* (i.e., the ability to discriminate between the rules and needs of different situations and audiences). Over the course of the first year, infant communication develops to show at least some competence in most of these features. How does communication begin?

Trevarthen and his student, the late Penny Hubley, conducted a classic study of a baby called Tracy, following her monthly from the first month through to the end of the first year. They found several distinctive changes in her interests and her "communicative" actions with her mother over the course of the first year: most notable among these changes were the onset of intense face-to-face chatting at around 2 months, shifting to a marked interest in the environment at 3 to 4 months, leading to a period of games in the middle of the first year as the mother, fed up with the infant's wandering attention, used rhythmic games and songs to keep the baby chatting, and finally, from about 9 months to the onset of a triadic interaction between mother, baby, and the objects around them. Trevarthen distinguished between the nature of communication at 2 months, which he called primary intersubjectivity, and that at 9 to 12 months, which he called secondary intersubjectivity. These labels and the engagements they refer to have now become part of the furniture for students of developmental psychology. But the interpretation of the exchanges at 2 months is still hotly debated by theorists.

It is the first four features in the preceding list which Trevarthen highlights as particularly significant for his argument that the smiling, cooing, and "chatting" of the 2-month-old are conversational and intentionally communicative. *First,* these actions are in themselves significant precursors of adult speech movements, involving lip movements and movements of the tongue inside the mouth during and prior to vocalisations that he called pre-speech movements, that is, movements of the appropriate organs even before speech. These occur in co-ordination with smiles, vocalisations, and arm movements. In other words, 2-month-old infants are using communicative behaviours which we as adults recognise as such. *Second,* they are coherent. That is, these behaviours are not random emissions but co-occur in organised patterns. In the same way that when we turn to talk to someone we may look, smile, adjust our bodies, and say something all at the same time, the 2-month-old infant's smiles, vocalisations, and arm movements also occur together in a pattern. Various body parts are involved in vocal conversation, each often moving in different directions and at different velocities but maintaining a relationship with one another and constituting a "movement bundle," revealing what some have called "self-synchrony." *Third,* the infant behaviours occur in conversational turns, with first one partner and then the other "saying" something, rather than in a chaotic overlap. Many studies have found a minimal overlap of vocalisations between infant and mother. *Fourth,* they express emotions which are reciprocally related to the emotions of others, implying some kind of recognition of what others' emotional expressions mean. While the first two features (the presence and coherence of "communicative" behaviours) are unchallenged, the last two are controversial, and provide the key both to understanding how infant communication begins and develops and to learning how communication relates to the awareness of other minds.

Turn-Taking and Engagement

One criticism of early turn-taking comes from Kenneth Kaye, who argued that much as Fred Astaire famously danced the tango with a hat stand, mothers in fact create an illusion of coordinated response. During early feeding interactions, mothers tend to jiggle their babies between their bursts of sucking, an alternation that looks very much like a co-ordinated dialogue. Mothers believe that the jiggling helps to get the baby to start sucking again. In fact, he says, the jiggling has remarkably little effect on the infant. It serves simply to give the mother the illusion of a conversation and to set the pattern of turns for the future. In the same way, he argues, it could be that the turn-taking pattern of conversations with 2-month-olds is created by the mothers slotting their responses into the gaps between the infant's acts, rather than by the infant actively waiting for its turn. The effect could be a "pseudo-dialogue" in which the infant simply does her bit, regardless of what the mother does. That is, the co-ordination could be merely apparent, with the infant's actions not "responses" to, or dependent on, the mother's. Indeed, some argue that you *could* in fact impose this gloss on the exchanges between 2-month-olds and their mothers.[10] While the mother's acts may not really matter to the infant, the mother could be taking note of the infant's utterances and acts and, by unconscious use of the gaps, creating the illusion that the infant is responding in coherent turns. Such an illusion could be really useful—helping to shape the mother's interactive behaviour to the infant and to promote the infant's development—but ultimately it would be an illusion.

Is such turn-taking really illusory? Are the infant's responses not responses at all, but independent acts? It was to answer this sort of question that three separate labs (Trevarthen's, Hanus and Mechthilde Papousek's, and Ed Tronick's) developed what have become known as perturbation experiments. In Trevarthen's lab at the University of Edinburgh, John Tatum, in an Honours dissertation, and probably inspired by lectures from Tom Bower on the use of perturbation as a method in biological research, developed a complex device involving changes of lighting to get mothers to switch from talking to their babies to an adult instead. However, far from not noticing the switch, the babies were upset. Lynne Murray, Trevarthen's doctoral student at the time, developed from this what they called the "blank face test," a test which Ed Tronick independently and famously developed as the "still-face experiments."[11] In these experiments, all you have to do is to get a "conversation" going with a baby and in the middle of it just hold your face still in a pleasant expression, continuing to look at the baby but not talking or responding in any way. If your responses don't really matter, the baby should carry on "emitting" her acts regardless. We tried this with my daughter when she was 6 weeks old and had been charming us for about two weeks with occasional smiles and coos, and the effect was dramatic.

6 weeks: . . . During a period of good "chatty" interaction, with Shamini lying on the bed and me leaning over her, I held my face still, continuing to look at her with a pleasant expression, but totally unmoving. Her reaction to this was textbook typical, but quite shattering to experience. She continued to look at me, smiled and vocalised a bit, then sobered at not getting any response, looked away briefly, then back to me again, smiled and vocalised again, sobered, looked away and back a few times. It must have lasted all of 30 seconds but felt much longer. I couldn't stand not responding any more and broke into a smile, spoke to her and leaned forward to hug her in apology. At this her face crumpled and she began to cry. I was shocked, dismayed and immensely touched. She actually cared! This incident jolted me out of my self-consciousness and made me take her dialogues with me seriously. It was a turning point in my understanding of her.[12]

Many versions of the still-face study have now been published; this kind of distress in infants to the unresponsiveness of a partner has been demonstrated time and again. The infants' negative reaction is worse when the person holds the still face while looking at them. The infants seem to have strong and "sensible" expectancies for the other person's actions in relation to them: the mother's inaction evidently affects the infant's responses. The responses of infants whose mothers have postpartum depression, however, show little difference from "normal" conversational conditions, suggesting that their experiences may not have established these stable expectations.[13]

There is other evidence that early conversations involve genuine turn-taking: Ed Tronick and his colleagues showed that even in structural terms the interaction at 2 months is appropriately characterized as a conversation. The mother emits a large number of what are called turn-yielding signals common to adult conversation (such as changing intonation, drawling, moving the head, and occasionally the hands, at the end of a "turn"), and the infant modifies her behaviour in relation to these signals, particularly in relation to intonation changes, starting at such points to smile and vocalise more. The infant is not an equal partner in the dialogue, but does take turns and does participate actively in it. Simultaneous (or co-active and overlapping) vocalisations between infant and mother also occur, as Daniel Stern showed, but they appear to occur more during high arousal times such as during active play, when both may laugh or squeal together. The co-occurrence of such vocalisations, or of non-vocal facial and gestural expressions, does not seriously limit the ability to take in what the other is doing at the same time. It is only later, when the linguistic content of the vocal utterances becomes important, that it is necessary for the infant (or adult) to wait in complete silence while someone makes an utterance. Although it is certainly the case that adults don't always wait during conversations (as anybody who has tried to transcribe a tape of a conversation has painfully discovered) still, conversations are held and understood.

The answers from these studies showed clearly that a lack of response is noticed by, and matters to, the 2-month-old. Infants show signs of attempting to regain the mother's engagement as well as signs of distress when they fail to do so. However, what does this mean? It could be that the infant simply finds the rather odd behaviour of the mother—different from what she has been used to—upsetting. It could be the *difference* rather than the *unresponsiveness per se* that the infant dislikes. To explore this question, Lynne Murray, influenced by a visit to the Papouseks' laboratory in Munich in 1975, devised an ingenious experiment involving closed circuit television. She got 2-month-olds to interact with their mothers through television monitors. That is, the baby was looking into a monitor in which his or her mother's face could be seen, live, and the mother was, similarly, looking into a monitor that framed her infant's face. The two partners were then encouraged to interact as usual; despite the strangeness of this technological mediation, it was clear (judging by the vocalisations and facial expressions of both) that perfectly happy interactions could occur between mothers and infants. Importantly for the procedure, the behaviour that each partner displayed during these live interactions could be surreptitiously videotaped. So, once happy interaction had been established (and taped) for a while, the videotape would be surreptitiously rewound and, unbeknown to both infant and mother, replayed to them. Instead of seeing the mother live, the infant would now view the mother as she had been a few minutes earlier. The infants showed puzzlement and confusion, looking back at the video image of the mother now and then as though to check. They showed fewer smiles, looked away more, exhibited more closed-mouth expressions, and intermittently attempted to regain interaction. In short, they could detect the changes in the mother's behaviour. Even when the mother was smiling and chatting—the very same smiles and conversational offerings from the mother that had minutes previously produced happy responses in the infant—the infant looked sober and wary.

Clearly, it was not just odd behaviour by the mother which the infant disliked. A few minutes earlier, the infants had responded happily to the very same behaviour. The problem seemed to be the *inappropriateness* of the responses, the fact that the mother's behaviour was not a response to what the infant did. Interestingly, the mothers—who were unaware of what was happening—also reacted with puzzlement to their babies' behaviour. They could still see the baby live, but they did not know that the baby was no longer viewing a live image of the mothers themselves. The mothers could detect, however, that the babies were no longer engaged with them and that they were behaving oddly and unresponsively. The mothers thus also became less engaged, starting to speak and interact with less "motherese" (the typical higher pitched and exaggerated utterances most adults unthinkingly use when speaking to babies). The specific responses of the 2-month-old seemed to matter to the adult as much as the specific responses of the adult mattered to the infant.[14]

In order to perform this experiment successfully, the researcher needs first to wait for good engagement to be established between the mother and the infant. If the researcher is not sensitive to this requirement, the replay condition ends up being in no way different from the live condition: in one the interaction has not *yet* been established, and in the other the interaction *cannot* be established. This was found in an attempted replication with introduced improved controls—a second live condition after the replay—but with the switching of the condition controlled from live to replay on the basis of a fixed time schedule (after a minute) regardless of whether the infant had successfully engaged with the adult before that. This study found no difference in infant behaviour between live and replay conditions.[15] Jacqueline Nadel and her colleagues in Paris repeated this experiment with the same improved controls but with the replay condition being switched only after good interaction had been established. They found that the infant's behaviour altered in the replay condition, with fewer smiles, more looking away as well as more concentrated looks and more intensely negative reactions and then became "normal" again in the second live condition.[16]

Instances of miscommunication are not limited to experimental manipulations. As Ed Tronick and his colleagues have shown, they happen all the time in normal interaction, with periods of mis-co-ordination and repair (getting in tune again) alternating every few seconds. When infants chronically experience prolonged mis-co-ordinated interactions without the experience of the repair, they seem to regularly withdraw from the other person, showing behaviour such as turning away and exhibiting dull-looking eyes, poor postural control, much oral self-comforting (e.g., fingers in the mouth), rocking, and self-clasping. This is also the sort of reaction that has been noted in many studies of post-natal depression or in situations of neglect. Interestingly, such infants show more looking away during still-face experiments than do infants who have had more normal experience of repair of interactions. Other studies have shown that lack of experience of interactive repairs seems to lead to later problems in elaborating communicative skills and problems in the establishment of a positive "affective core" and a sense of effectiveness. These studies show us very slightly exaggerated versions of what the infant normally experiences and illustrate how much miscommunication does matter in everyday life if failure to repair it becomes chronic.[17]

Reciprocal Communication of Affects: Exploring Gergely's Myth

So the infant's interactions with adults at 2 months show clear evidence of engagement, with some evidence of turn-taking by infants. The claim that they are merely pseudo-conversations does not stand up. But what does this engagement actually say about the infant's knowledge of the (m)other's mind? According to the Hungarian researcher Gyorgy Gergely, a recent critic of the intersubjectivity argument, the infant is equipped with a capacity for contingency detection, which says nothing at all about intersubjectivity or mind knowledge. That is, just because the infant can respond in a timely fashion to the mother's actions, or detect the untimeliness of her actions, does not mean that the infant is engaging psychologically—communicating—with the other. Gergely argues that this capacity—that is, the infant's ability to detect the close temporal sequencing of events such as "I gurgle—mother smiles"—allows infants (like adults) to feel causally effective (or "empowered" to use adult jargon) and therefore positively aroused. Combined with some predispositions to engage in affective displays and interactions (the motivation for which must come from "hardwired" action patterns), contingency detection alone, he maintains, is sufficient to explain the interactive behaviour of the 2-month-old. Primary intersubjectivity, according to Gergely, is a myth. Building on John Watson's theory about the effects of experiencing different kinds of contingencies, Gergely further links contingency detection to the child's subsequent formation of theories of mind.[18]

This theory has clear assumptions. Attributing physical-temporal contingency detection to the infant is seen as acceptable, while attributing emotional-psychological feature detection is not. Attributing a rudimentary understanding of the causality of physical events is seen as acceptable, while attributing a rudimentary understanding of the psychological meaning of acts is not. The distinction is crystal clear: babies can perceive and understand physical things, but they cannot perceive mental things, which therefore can only be inferred and theorised. Mind-behaviour dualism is alive and well. However, Gergely's alternative myth raises a legitimate and seemingly empirical question: is it the case that very young infants detect *only* the temporal relations of interpersonal acts and not their emotional relations or relevance?

To answer this question, we need to look in detail at the content of the engagement, not simply at its contingent nature. Trevarthen argues that what the 2-month-old is doing is engaging in a communication of emotions. She is revealing her emotional state and is perceiving the emotional state of her partner as it relates to her. The emotional tone expressed by each partner is not identical but reciprocal. That is, some emotional states are most appropriately responded to with the same emotion—such as joy and pleasure—but others are most appropriately responded to with a different emotional tone. Anger, for instance, could more appropriately evoke a response of distress or even fear, forcefulness could evoke a response of withdrawal, and reticence a response of boldness. Ed Tronick's "mutual regulation model" argues that infants at 2 months are not only engaging in just such a reciprocal affective interaction, but are trying to influence and maintain the partner's affective state.

The evidence for infant responses to emotional expressions and emotional tone in others is still sparse and somewhat contradictory. On the one hand, there is evidence that even newborns (at 36 hours after birth) discriminate between the posed expressions of happiness, sadness, and surprise, responding to each with different but appropriate imitative actions. Infants of mothers who were depressed seemed to show less expressiveness to surprise and happy expressions.[19] Newborns respond to distress vocalisations of other infants (but not their own), played via audio equipment, with facial signs of distress and a reduction in non-nutritive sucking.[20] Two-month-olds (but interestingly not 5-month-olds) can discriminate happy from neutral expressions posed in a holographic image.[21] Young infants also seem to prefer to look more at certain facial expressions (such as joy) than at others (such as anger).[22] Different kinds of maternal expressions have a different impact on the infant: gentle, friendly approaches often lead to smiles and increased interest, while vocal and facial displays of anger lead to upset or fearful responses and displays of sadness lead to self-soothing (increased "tongueing") behaviour even in 10-week-old infants.[23] These infant emotional responses do not show a passive mirroring of whatever the adult experiences; rather they seem to show some appreciation of the other's expression in context and a response to it. Three-month-olds whose mothers report more anger during an interaction themselves express more anger, but 3-month-olds whose mothers reported more sadness express more distress.[24] In short, the 2-month-old appears to be sensitive to micro-emotional shifts in others' expressions within engagement: when maternal mood shifts downward from the positive to the slightly negative, infants in the seconds following can show a rapid decrease in "brightness" and shift in attention.[25]

On the other hand, there is evidence suggesting that although it is easy to show discrimination in 3-month-olds between different expressions of the same person in photographs, this discrimination does not clearly generalise across different faces or to different orientations of faces (for instance, upside-down faces). This has led to the conclusion that what is being discriminated may not be the expressions per se, but some features of their occurrence in the ongoing context. That is, it may be that the 2-month-old infant does not have a categorical awareness—a concept—of particular emotional expressions, and that not until after 6 or 7 months of age is there consistent evidence that the infant not only treats facial expressions as examples of a general category, but also seems to link them meaningfully to things in the outside world. The meaning of emotional expressions for the 2-month-old seems to be an *interactive* meaning rather than an *abstracted* one. That an interactive meaning is present is shown clearly by infant responses to affect in actual engagement, both when affect is experimentally simulated and when it is real.[26]

Trying to distinguish between mere contingencies and affective responsiveness, Maria Legerstee from the University of Toronto measured the extent of affective mirroring that different mothers showed in live interaction. Still using the double video paradigm and dividing mothers into high-affect mirroring and low-affect mirroring groups, she found that the 3-month-old babies of both groups of mothers were able to detect the contingency violation of the replay condition and to respond to it with greater averted gaze. However, the babies of the high-affect mirroring group not only showed greater smiling, gaze, and melodic vocalisations in the live interactions, but greater negative reactions during the replay, although in the group where the replay was shown first, they did recover their interest during the live condition, unlike the babies of the low-affect mirroring group. This complex study raises as many further questions as it addresses. It suggests, however, that affective engagement between infants and mothers is a reality which sets infants up for greater negativeness when the engagement is disrupted but also greater confidence in accepting it when it returns.[27] Moreover, even the 5-week-old babies of highly affectively attuned mothers discriminate between normal engagement (with intermittent rather than perfectly matching contingencies) and imitative (closely contingent) or non-contingent displays by the mother, while the babies of less affectively attuned mothers don't. The direction of influence in this study seems to be from affective response to contingency rather than the other way around![28]

Maternal depression provides a difficult situation through which infants experience prolonged exposure to a partner who is not always contingently responsive and shows flattened affect, more facial and vocal sadness, often more anger, and less joyfulness. Infants are rapidly affected by such interactions, themselves picking up the affective patterns and showing them even when interacting with other people. Interestingly, even the brief simulation of depression by the mother (interacting in an emotionally flat and withdrawn manner) has a negative impact on the infant's ability to engage with others, leading to more flatness of affect and withdrawal in the infant.[29] Tiffany Field suggests that these infants may learn "helplessness" and have an impaired sense of control in their engagements—a theory which can explain Legerstee's findings. However, there is room for optimism: these effects can be alleviated with appropriate interventions. Field reports the reassuring results of an intervention programme in which mothers with depression were trained in simple ways to respond contingently to their infants, to imitate them and show more positive affect. Infants and mothers improved in their communication with each other and with others.[30] Are the infants of depressed mothers learning "how to be" from the mother as a model? Is the mother providing a sort of "maternal prototype"? Recent suggestions that later in the first year the babies of depressed mothers may in fact be *more* active—in terms of gaze and movements—than the babies of "normal" mothers suggests that the situation may be more complex, at least in the second half of the first year.[31] A responsive—or compensatory—model of the engagement of affects seems more appropriate than a modelling one. This implies something like a dialogic process.

The idea that the 2-month-old detects only temporal contingencies and not the emotional relations or relevance of interpersonal acts therefore cannot be upheld. In attempting to reject the overly nativist heritage of infant communication research, Gergely's rejection of the 2-month-old as communicator seems to adopt the trappings of the very Cartesian model it is opposed to. It clings to a mind-behaviour dualism by distinguishing the physical features that infants can supposedly detect from the psychological features they supposedly cannot and by disallowing the infant from meaningful perception of emotion. Gergely argues that the infant gains dispositional meanings of emotion simply from observation of the action consequences of the emotion displays produced by others.[32] This is a fundamentally third-person theory—the observer deduces all, even the feeling of emotions. There is no room here for emotional responses in the infant to constitute either the dispositional meanings of the observed displays or indeed even to influence the emotional displays themselves. Ed Tronick uses a notion called dyadic expansion to capture the way in which the infant's experiences can expand in complexity within a dyadic base: dyadic engagement stretches the infant a step beyond her capacities, drawing her into skills and embedding her in patterns of feeling and doing that she would not otherwise have had access to.[33] These patterns afford a coherence to infant—or indeed adult—experience, not only reflecting current knowledge but also influencing what we can learn and know. They serve to invite infants into our culture. They can, however, just as easily be disadvantageous to the infant as advantageous. Armed with such coherent "affective centres of gravity," the infant is repeatedly pulled towards them.[34] In new interactions the infant acts—as do adults—in ways which reproduce such exchanges and feelings that at least have the advantage of being familiar and coherent. This induces a corresponding affective ethos even in new partners who sense and respond to whatever "dis-connecting" messages the infant is offering and inviting.

In sum, infant communication at 2 months seems to be much more than the detection of contingencies, involving a degree of sensitivity to particular emotional expressions in others and to the emotional tone of interactions—what Daniel Stern calls "vitality contours." These are the rhythms and tempos of ordinary actions, present in everything we do and say, and generally far harder to conceal and disguise than what we normally call emotional expressions. The meaningful perception of emotion in others may, according to Trevarthen, be the key to the evolution of affect. According to him and according to some communicative rather than "read-out" theories of the evolution of affective expression, emotions evolved *because* they were meaningfully perceived by others.[35] There is no point in being able to smile unless there is someone out there to feel its impact. There is no point in being able to express sadness unless someone can perceive and respond to it. Whether or not this was the case in evolution, the affective communication of the 2-month-old shows not only a sensitivity to the relevance and appropriateness of others' emotional expressions and rhythms, but also a remarkable ability to learn about their meanings from the responses of others to the infant's *own* emotions. The expression of emotion seems truly reciprocal in the sense that we are constantly expressing emotion in relation to the ongoing responses of others—their meanings changing for us, perhaps throughout life.

Functional Features of Dialogue and Communication: Openness and Recognition

Is using structural criteria the only way to ask whether something really is communication and dialogue? Using such criteria to identify a process of affective engagement can be very unsatisfying. There have been innumerable attempts across a variety of disciplines to capture something that, like "quality," is better experienced than reduced. Two aspects of such attempts at identifying what might be called functional features of dialogues are "openness" and "mutual recognition." These vague concepts may be better studied as properties of the relation rather than of the individuals involved in it. But it may be that we need to take them on board, at least as future challenges, if we are to understand dialogue and communication at all.

Dialogue cannot be scripted and predetermined. It must possess within it the possibility of going down a road which none of those engaged in it could have known about. When Martin Buber spoke about dialogue, he was capturing something of this quality of openness as well as the potential for dramatic change that openness to the unknown allows: "for what I call dialogue, there is essentially necessary the moment of surprise. . . . The whole charm . . . is that I do not know and cannot know what my partner will do. I am surprised by what he does and on this surprise the whole play is based."[36] And genuine dialogue—where each is really open to the other—involves what many have called a "confirmation" or "recognition" by the other. In every engagement, according to Hegel, there is the risk of not being "recognised" by the other in the way one has acted; it is only when we are recognised by another person that we receive confirmation about ourselves. If the engagements in early infancy show features of this openness to and being recognised by the other, then we may be shown how second-person relations really do work in the lives of infants and adults.

We take the unscripted quality of our conversations for granted, but it is precisely this that keeps us alive in our engagement, whether with the physical world or the social world. When things are open, the unexpected and the novel can happen, and whether rewarding or conflictual, they demand resolution and explanation—making a "lived story" as Stern puts it. And when such moments are shared, something bigger than either of the participants is released. "The moment when someone can participate in another's lived story, or can create a mutually lived story with them, a different kind of human contact is created."[37] I discovered something like this when I took on a management position at work. I started out with a plan to talk to everyone about their thoughts and feelings with a Kennedy-like what-can-you-do-for-the-department and what-can-the-department-do-for-you spiel. I discovered that my plan was largely irrelevant. The conversations I became engaged in, with the energy of the naïve and enthusiastic beginner, were themselves powerful vehicles for change. But this was the case only because what was needed was to be psychologically present—"authentic" in the dialogue. The rest emerged. Someone described it as the magic that happens when someone who isn't expecting to be heard is heard. What happens in such conversations? Why are they so powerful? And why do they strike me as *dialogues* in the full sense of the term? My hunch was that it took two things on both sides: honesty and courage—honesty in listening and responding to the other, and courage to be open to unexpected outcomes. In the therapeutic trade this is known as "trust in the process." It refers to the therapist putting his or her faith in the "now" of the therapeutic engagement and letting go of prior agendas, theories, and plans. It is similar to what we might call interpersonal harmony, particularly in dyadic interaction, at times when everything goes perfectly smoothly and beautifully right, such as between people who have newly admitted their love for each other or between people discovering the inviolability of childhood friendships. In relations between parents and children, this "openness" and "faith in the now" gives rise to a sense of wonder in each other, which defies rational justification but may be vital for development.

Does mother-infant interaction show these features? Infants certainly can be surprised by others' acts, as is evident in all of the perturbation studies which show that infants have at least by 2 months already built up expectations of what the other person will do and what the engagement will be like. It is also evident that infants are pretty sensitive to subtle fluctuations in others' moods and expressions, once again revealing their expectations from the relation. Their own acts in the engagement are influenced by the acts they experience from others: in terms of the openness of the infant-adult engagement, there is no doubt that we are dealing here with an open system. To use Ed Tronick's theory of dyadic states of consciousness, it seems that even at 2 months we are dealing with engagement in which both partners are open to and influenced by the other. Dan Stern's notion of "now" moments—where this openness results in startling moments of change and shifts of gear in the relationship—may be useful to identify just how infant engagements with other people actually develop through emotional sensitivity to the unpredictable.[38]

Infants also seem to *need* the unpredictable and the surprising; the totally predictable is boring. And when they start to disengage from adult engagements, even if briefly, adults often introduce intentional perturbations and violations of expectation—creating variations of intensity and action in games and songs and speech—primarily to keep the infants' interest continually engaged. Such intentional violations, however, aren't done *by* infants until a few months later, as we will see when we discuss teasing by infants. But once they start, they take the lead and do it to an extent that adults wouldn't do to them! Openness and unpredictability are central to teasing (and more generally, to playfulness). Infants, as we shall see in Chapter 8, are beginning to engage in acts which seem deliberately aimed at surprising other people; they tease and show off and clown with intense enjoyment.

Confirmation or recognition of the other can happen—or not happen—in many ordinary ways. In all the perturbation experiments, the adult (whether the parent under instruction to hold a still face or the experimenter manipulating the video replay) is explicitly *not* confirming the infant—not acknowledging or recognising the infant's previous acts or the infant herself. Mothers and other adults asked to engage in still-face experiments sometimes report finding them emotionally difficult. And this is why: they are being asked to act as if the infant isn't there—to not acknowledge the infant. Blank unresponsiveness may be a harsher "disconfirmation" of the partner in interaction than explicit challenge or rejection of the other. We do this in everyday life all the time, sometimes accidentally, sometimes deliberately; we often leave minor damage in our wake whether we know it or not. The perturbation studies show us (and in this they have succeeded in a moral victory) that it matters enormously to infants, even in these early months. What does this recognition and confirmation consist of? What does it feel like? Barbara Smuts uses the term *presence* to refer to something like such recognition: "the 'presence' we recognise in another when we meet in mutuality is something we feel more than something we know, someone we taste rather than someone we use. In mutuality, we sense that inside this other body, there is 'someone home,' someone so like ourselves in their essence that we can co-create a shared reality as equals."[39]

Perhaps this description will be largely dismissed as not valuable to science, for how do we reduce presence after all in our category schemes? But the question is important. If being recognised by another as a person is important for dialogue as well as for development as a person, then we need at least to acknowledge that we don't know how to study it. The discussion in the last chapter, of using imitation to reach the other person by proffering such recognition, may be the most productive way forward in exploring this issue.

Communicative Intentions: Towards Mutuality

Nonetheless, 2-month-olds' behaviour is still (at least implicitly) relegated to the category of pseudo-communication. According to a modern "cognitivist" argument most clearly expressed by Michael Tomasello, infants neither have communicative intentions themselves nor understand communicative intentions in others until they are about 9 months old.

The theory goes like this. To engage in genuine communication (rather than just interaction), the organism (infant, animal, or alien) needs both to have communicative intentions and to understand that the other organism has them. Communicative intentions are not ordinary intentions, for example, those which are directed towards things in the world. They are different in that they are directed towards minds and mental (or intentional) states. To be directed towards minds, communicative intentions must involve an "intentional object"—a thing which is represented in the mind; they must be "about" something. Shared "topics" of communication are not evident until the end of the first year, either in terms of the infant referring to them or in terms of the infant understanding the adult's reference to them. Therefore, it is concluded, the 2-month-old neither has communicative intentions nor understands them in others.

Communicative intentions, in this view, are seen as plans for action that exist in one mind and are directed towards another mind. The body is seen as a tool for conveying the communicative intention, and is not in itself intentional or expressive. The successful communication, then, is the idea that exists in one mind about the idea that exists in the other mind. It follows from this that until hidden entities can be conceptualised (late in infancy) communicative intentions cannot exist (the infant has no idea of a mind to direct them to) and cannot be understood (the infant has no idea of a mind from which something might be coming). This assumption of the mind-to-mind nature of intentional communication seems fairly firmly founded on a dualism between mind and bodily movements.

From that perspective, the 2-month-old's expressions of emotion towards another person, her reciprocal responses to the expressions of others, her seeking of engagement in face-to-face contact with other persons, and her adjustment to patterns of engagement become irrelevant to communication. They are bodily reactions to the bodily movements of others; they are not mental actions directed to others or reactions to the mental actions of others. They can be dismissed as bodily and biological because they are not representationally mediated.

Referring to the 2-month-old's reported inability to perceive others' perceptions of the outside world, Tomasello argues: "When the infant did not understand that others perceive and relate to an outside world there could be no question of how they perceived and related to *me.*" The grasp of a mental object is seen as a necessary prerequisite for understanding that others want to communicate, "for understanding that someone else wants me to attend to X, that is, for understanding a communicative intention."[40] Tomasello is reflecting a generally held belief that there must be a separate object in mind which is shared by both partners for the sharing to be called genuinely communicative (if we are talking about communication) or for it to be called genuinely joint attentional (if we are talking about attention) or genuinely joint intentional (if we are talking about intention). In other words, the crucial assumption is that acts between people must be mediated by representations of something else if they are to be genuinely mental. This implies that for me to genuinely communicate with you I need an intermediary—an idea, an object, an instruction, some other entity which you and I can share. There is, in this view, no direct relation possible in Buber's terms of an *I-Thou* relation. Or at least, any direct relation does not constitute mental relation, only bodily. The insistence on an "object" for communication, then, is also the result of a continuing, if unintended, commitment to a mind-body dualism.

Such an approach to communication adopts a traditional "telegraph" metaphor, in which you need a sender, a receiver, a common code, and a message. Just as in telegraphy, everything is believed to happen in a nice tidy sequence with each act of communication involving a clear sender and a clear receiver and a clear prior intention and message. But neither in infants nor in adults is there such a sequentiality and individuality to communicative intentions, nor are communicative intentions preformed and in existence prior to the communication itself. Although we can and sometimes do talk to each other in this way—planning to say something, conveying the message, and waiting for a response—communication is often far more chaotic and synchronous. Many writers, John Shotter and Alan Fogel to name two, argue persuasively that meanings, intentions, and communicative intentions change and unfold within the process of interaction and that therefore it makes no sense to look for communicative intentions and meanings as things independent of interaction.[41] In what he calls a "continuous process model," Alan Fogel argues that communication can imply "a negotiated and dynamic process in which whatever is shared is created through the process of co-regulation: not known by one person in advance and communicated as a message to the other."[42]

The Paradox of Communication

There is a strange paradox about communication. Language is often seen as the tool which opens the door to private mental experience. The use of language in dialogue can make private experience public. We speak of dumb animals and speechless infants and say that if only they could talk, we would know what they think and feel. Communication is seen as *leading to* the sharing of minds. This makes a lot of sense, at least in our highly verbal culture.

However, how does the infant acquire the means to use language to share mental experience? In order to use language, we must already know what is meant by it, and indeed *that* something is meant. Before a word can be shared, its meaning must already be shared in order to know what the word stands for, and people have to be understood as having minds with meanings. In other words, in order to communicate, we must already understand *that* others understand and *what* they understand.

Put this way we have a paradox. Communication is necessary to know about minds, but communication implies that we already know about minds. How do we resolve this issue? Paradoxes are frustrating things. But this one may be more apparent than real. It emerges from assuming that the communication of meanings is a representational act. That is, that the content of a communication (represented in the mind) has to precede communication itself.

Ludwig Wittgenstein showed that if you assume that representation precedes communication, you cannot explain communication at all. You have no way of explaining how the shared meanings originated in the first place. A meaning must be public—or shared—in order for it to be used in conversation or communication. The apparent paradox we have been considering then is simply a function of putting the metaphysical cart before the horse, by assuming that mind and the contents of mind (meanings) are private before they become public. If we accept Wittgenstein's solution, the question becomes: what meanings does the infant share with adults? When and how do these meanings emerge? If communication is taken as primary (i.e., if we accept the "hermeneutic circle" in this question), the paradox disappears. Words and gestures can achieve their meaning only if they are already grounded in shared agreement about what they mean or refer to. They have to be grounded in shared meaning before they ever emerge as separable and representable meanings. But they cannot do this in the absence of engagement. Thus, communication both sets the ground for and reflects mind knowledge.

"Nothing will come of nothing: speak again" said King Lear to his favourite daughter.[43] Communicative intentions cannot emerge out of their total absence. They develop, but from a ground which is simpler the further back you go in developmental time. Intentional communication is evident from early infancy. Its development is primarily in its referents, its informational content, and its scope. The processes of intentional communication become more complex over time, but they do not emerge, belatedly, as a result of inferences about others' mentality after many months of pseudo-communication. They must already be present in the early communicative engagements of the 2-month-old.

Summary

So, is the communication of the 2-month-old intersubjective? Does it show the infant's awareness of the other as a person, a psychological being? All depends, of course, on what we mean by a person and a psychological being. In this chapter we have described some structural and functional features of dialogue and communication and how these throw light on questions concerning the infant's awareness of the other. Attempts to dismiss the conversations and complex interactional sensitivities of the 2-month-old as pseudo-communication or mere contingency detection are clearly based on dualist assumptions about the (im)possibility of interpersonal understanding without representation. The 2-month-old seems to both invite and reveal a recognition of the psychological qualities of people. But what aspects of the other's person-ness or psychological-ness can the 2-month-old infant pick up? Two aspects are primary in any attempt to carve up psychological qualities into discrete kinds: attention and intention. In the next chapter I will explore the notion of attention as it has been developed in modern psychology and, using an embodied (non-dualist) definition of attention, ask what infants actually *do* with others' attention over the course of the first year of life.

CHAPTER 6

Experiencing Attention

I discover vision, not as a "thinking about seeing," to use Descartes' expression, but as a gaze at grips with a visible world, and that is why for me there can be another's gaze.

Maurice Merleau-Ponty, *The Phenomenology of Perception*[1]

You can't ignore attention, either in psychology or in everyday life. To have someone attend to us can soothe, exhilarate, frighten, inspire, embarrass, enrage, irritate, and in so many ways touch us at our core. William James was probably right: how could we survive being surrounded by people but not being noticed by even one other person?[2] The attention of others is probably the first, simplest, and most powerful experience that we have of mentality. Something about the attention of other people seems crucial for our emotional existence and our development. Why? And how—and when—does attention become meaningful to infants?

In this chapter I am going to show that an engaged second-person approach gives us a more complete answer to these questions than does either a detached third-person approach or a self-based first-person approach. Such an approach places the infant's own emotional responses to others' attention at the centre of their understanding of it. It is the other's gaze at grips with the infant, I am going to argue adapting Merleau-Ponty's image, that makes gaze meaningful to the infant. In this view, others' attention is first *felt* by the infant, neither as an intellectual deduction, nor as an empathic recognition of what it is like to see, but as a *response* to receiving it from others in engagement. In order to do this, we will need to have a look at how we (could) think about attention: about its perceivability, and about what counts as an object of attention. Because most of the data we have in this field is about visual attention, I will focus on visual attention to answer questions about infant awareness of attention, although the awareness of other modalities of attention is likely to involve a different and richer story. But first, let's start with a puzzle.

When Do Infants Become Aware of Other People's Attention? A Conflict

There is a bit of a puzzle in theorising about this question. The general conclusion is that human infants start to become aware of other people's attention in the last quarter of the first year (although infants are themselves attentive to people and things from birth). This conclusion began with a pioneering naturalistic and longitudinal study of pre-verbal communication and cognition in the 1970s, which was led by the late Elizabeth Bates together with, unusually for the time, an international all-woman team of psychologists. Around the end of the first year infants—sometimes quite dramatically—begin to point to things in the world communicatively (that is, checking to make sure an adult is looking). Interestingly, infants seemed to be doing this to serve two separate interpersonal functions: pointing to things in order to get adults to fetch the objects for them (customarily called proto-imperative pointing) and pointing to things in order simply to show the objects to the adults (proto-declarative pointing). This was powerfully suggestive that here was the moment in development when infants discovered attention in people: a simultaneous discovery that allowed them to use people's attention to obtain things and things to obtain people's attention. The simultaneous emergence of this single act with multiple functions seemed to point to the infant's underlying discovery of attention itself. Despite many more recent amendments and debates, the theoretical picture today remains largely the same.

But this makes infants' earlier engagements with others' attention a bit of a mystery. We have already seen infants engage in complex face-to-face exchanges with other people, sensitive to direct gaze to themselves even at birth, and engage in complex proto-conversational exchanges with adults from 2 months where they seem to respond to others' acts towards them with recognisable emotional responses, noticing when others look at them, and even initiating actions themselves to call others. If not involving an awareness that the other person is attending to them, what, then, is going on in the intricate dialogic exchanges of the 2-month-old that we saw in the last chapter? These exchanges are not usually considered by psychologists as relevant to the infant's awareness of attention; they are often compartmentalised into other domains labelled biological or social or affective attunement. But then what does the 2-month-old actually know about others' attention? Nothing at all?

I am going to suggest that the 2-month-old's interactions with other people do indeed reflect an awareness of other people's attention as attention and that this awareness is based upon the capacity to respond emotionally to it. I suggest that in the first instance, infants are aware of others' attention when it is directed to themselves. Gradually, as the infant's engagement with others' attention develops in complexity, the infant becomes aware of others' attention when it is directed to other things in the world. I suggest that infants do not discover attention towards the end of the first year. Rather, they are already aware of attention in others, and it is only through this awareness that they gradually become cognizant of further "objects" or "targets" or "topics" that others' attention can be directed to. Why do I make this argument, and what evidence do I have to support it? Let's look first at the why, and to answer it, ask what *is* attention anyway?

Attending Must Involve Engagement with Objects

Although there are many compelling theories about the nature of attention, a "space-based" or "spotlight" theory of attention has been most commonly used in studies of the infant's awareness of others' attention.[3] Attention, in this theory, is conceived of as a sort of psychological spotlight turned on to the world, free-moving and not bound to the things it alights upon, thus independent (or dis-embedded) from the world it roves in. And it has also been thought of as somehow separate from the body in which it operates, dis-embodied, not intrinsically concordant with the body's movements. From such a dis-connected definition, the only way in which we, as observers, could grasp or recognise attention would be to conceptualise it, to grasp it as an "idea." Any early evidence about pre-conceptual infants' apparent engagements with other people would not be relevant to the question of how or when they grasp attention. However, there is reason to doubt the spotlight view and adopt an alternative.

A spotlight can move about the visual field, picking up whatever falls into the specific region of space it shines on, whether a flock of birds, a puddle of water, the leg of a chair, someone's nose, or, indeed, empty space. The "organism" (whether person or animal) can be seen as the controlling agent, managing the spotlight and zooming in on particular areas. But the trouble is spotlights don't do anything with what they shine on. And they select *space* to light up, not *things*. But organisms don't work like that. They don't just wander about the world looking at this and that patch of space or this and that object but doing nothing with it. The objects of their attention are picked up, played with, given to someone else, eaten, smiled at, and so on. This fact, that unlike spotlights attending organisms have active and motivated bodies, must make a huge difference to what attention is like.

Neither do organisms relate particularly to space. In fact, they can focus so completely on the objects rather than the space they're in that they often don't even notice other objects in exactly the same space. An experiment conducted many years ago by Ulrich Neisser illustrated this point beautifully. He superimposed two images on the same piece of film: a hand-clapping game (two pairs of hands and wrists) and a ballgame (three men playing with a basketball). He asked adults to count events in one of the games, for example, the number of hand claps. While this was going on, the other activity was substantially changed, including a replacement of all the male basketball players with women. Quite incredibly, people did not even notice this change. More recently, this study has been replicated using a man in a gorilla suit who, walking across the "irrelevant" scene, turns to the camera, beats his chest, and walks on: people tend not to notice him![4] Attention, therefore, seems to focus on things, not areas of space. People are also better at absorbing many bits of information about one object than a similar number of bits of information about different objects—something that is known as a "same object advantage" in attending. When two overlapping objects are presented briefly, it is easier to detect two features of the same object than one feature of each of the objects. Or when two shapes are presented side by side and the task is to detect a target based on a prior cue, responses are faster when the cue appears in the same object rather than at equal distances but in different objects.[5] That we make sense of things almost in order to perceive them, we have known for a long time from the work of the Gestalt psychologists. For example, we don't even notice gaps in a line if the line makes sense to us, and we see lines completing a shape which isn't even there, if the shape appears meaningful. So if attention is a spotlight, it is a very odd kind of spotlight, engaging only with some things in its arc, omitting others even if in the foreground, changing the objects it shines on, selecting some, and obscuring others. We could think, instead, of attention more as an engagement with objects, not as something separable from them as the space-based theorists suggest.

Attending is an *engagement* that happens every time we feel the texture of a cloth or smell the air by the sea or see the bends in the road. In fact, whether attention exists at all may depend on whether objects exist to be attended to. Consider, for instance, the possibilities in a completely objectless or sensorily deprived environment. Could attention exist or develop in such a situation without anything to attend to? And the quality of attending too—that is, its intensity and fluctuation and duration and so on—must depend on the objects it engages with, a dependence that has powerful implications for the management of the perceptual environments children grow up in. The process of attending, according to the object-based view of attention, is fundamentally and intimately related to object-hood.[6] It may be more appropriate, therefore, to think of attention as an *activity* rather than as a "thing" inside our heads, and therefore to refer to it as attend*ing*—as a verb rather than a noun.[7] The implications of thinking of attention in this way are, of course, that someone else's act of attending is immediately public and transparent: if it's something that people do in the world, it's something that can be observed. And if it *can* be observed, then infants can, at least potentially, observe it. And we, as psychologists, can observe them observing it.

Of course, neither infants nor adults typically "observe" other people's attention as spectators; usually the perception of other people's attention involves the perceiver's interest, motivation, emotion, or responsive action. Let's look first at how attending can be perceived through its objects.

The Awareness of Attending Must Be Tied to the Awareness of Its Objects

If attending is the process of engaging with objects, then the awareness of attending in others must involve the awareness of this engagement between person and object. If attending is "intimately linked to object-hood," as Brian Scholl puts it, then in order to know about someone's attending, one needs to know about this relation between person and object. The awareness of attending must be intimately linked to the awareness of its objects. In other words, the *that* of attention, as Jerry Bruner had argued, cannot be separated from its *what:* it makes no sense to say that attention is understood if there is no understanding of what it is directed to, that it is in fact directed to *some*thing. If attention is conceived of as a spotlight, it doesn't matter, for an understanding of attention, what the spotlight shines on. Within an object-based view of attending, however, awareness of a (potential) object is crucial for an awareness of attending. What does this actually mean in practice? How do we perceive attending and its objects?

I am sitting here, as I type, watching two chickens walk by the window on the gravel drive, on their way to the compost heap behind the stable, and I am wondering, what can I see about the chickens' attending? Picture this. There is a big brown Buff Orpington chicken walking steadily and then looking down and pecking at bits that are invisible to me as it goes. A Black Rock chicken walks behind, pauses in front of the stable, and I cannot understand why it should pause. It cocks its head, looks at the stable wall, turns, looks at the ground, looks at another part of the wall, not pecking at anything; then walks forward a few feet and pauses in front of a fossil ammonite standing on a block of wood. It looks for a moment towards the ammonite, then turns its head sideways and pecks at something between the wood and the ammonite. It has a good struggle of a pull, not a brief peck, pauses again, looks sideways, leaves the ammonite, and walks around the side of the building, behind the Buff Orpington, which is still pecking steadily as it walks. I cannot see them anymore (but I can see that the horse is now turned with its back to me, looking out of the back window of the stable, in the direction that the chickens have gone).

The chickens' attending seemed to be a continuous process, constantly changing. I seemed to have no problem perceiving what the chickens were attending to, but I cannot describe their attention without talking about the objects they were attending to. The Black Rock's attention seemed much more obvious to me than the other one's—it was changing its "objects" more frequently. I was at one point uncertain about what she was doing and at another point much clearer about her focus of attention, precisely because of my access to the objects she was looking at. When I could see no object (perhaps she could not either?), I was puzzled and uncertain not about where she was looking (because I could see where her head was turned to) but about what she was attending to. Was it something small in the wall that she was seeing and considering? Was it that she was looking for something and not seeing it? Was she "gazing" into space not looking at anything at all? When I could see an object, I could see her attention. When I could not perceive an object, it was hard to think of her as attending. Perceiving attending is closely tied to perceiving the objects that are being attended to.

This seems to be the case for babies, too: some almost incidental evidence from experiments suggests that if they cannot see an object for someone else to be attending to, babies don't see or follow the attention at all. For instance, there is the intriguing finding from the late George Butterworth that babies cannot hold in their minds the space *behind* their own bodies until about the middle of the second year (when, interestingly, they also become capable of imagining absent and past realities). Not until this age—about 18 months—do infants turn around to follow an adult gaze or point to something behind them. To the infant it seems to be attending which does not make sense because no *object* exists for the infant. Furthermore, it seems that even if the adult turns to a spot in front of the infant, the likelihood of the infant following that gaze or head turn is much higher if there actually *is* an object in that region that the infant can identify as something which can be attended to! Several studies have shown that infants' gaze moves in roughly the right direction until it alights on a possible target.[8] And then it stops (even if inaccurately).

Amazingly, even by 3 to 4 months of age, the presence or absence of objects seems to determine whether or not an infant will follow someone else's head turn. Let's say you're talking face to face with a baby, and then you turn aside to look at something. A group of Japanese researchers found that the baby is likely to carry on looking at your averted profile for a while before turning in the direction your profile is turned in.[9] If the baby recognises something she is already familiar with or interested in, then she will look at the same object that you have turned to look at. If she cannot find any object near your head to attract her attention, her gaze will return to and remain on your profile. Perceiving you as attending to something in the world seems to hang on their perceiving that there is something out there to be attended to. Infants can even be taught to follow such head turns. Chris Moore and his colleagues showed that rewards could increase the accuracy of head-turning responses (that is, turning in the same direction as an adult model) in 8-month-olds. The study was aimed at demonstrating the possibly superficial nature of early gaze following. However, what was most interesting about their finding was that the training only worked if the rewards were consistent with the location of the target! In other words, while we can teach babies to be more sensitive to genuine attending behaviour (i.e., with objects which make sense), we cannot teach them to blindly respond to just any (head-turning) behaviour *as if* it were attending. Following or relating to another's attention does not seem to be possible (in the first year of infancy) unless the infant is aware of an *object* for that attention.

So, if it is so crucial to the awareness of others' attention that we should perceive the objects that others are attending to, then what do we know about babies' awareness of the objects of others' attention? To return to the puzzle that we started with, what do we make of the 2-month-old's engagements with people? In interactions with people, there doesn't even seem to *be* an object there for the 2-month-old to know about! But that's only if we take a simple view of *what* an object is. And this is the crucial issue. In the next section I will ask what we would—or should—count as a perceivable object of attention. The answer to this question will inform the answers to our empirical queries in the following sections about how the infant's perception of the objects of others' attention *develops*.

What "Counts" as a Perceivable Object of Attention?

The "External" Object

It is usual in this field of inquiry, when we talk about objects of attention, to think about objects which are external to both the attender and the observer of the attending. The concept of "joint attention" is often treated by developmental psychologists as synonymous with an awareness of attention, and anything that comes before joint attention is treated as something other than an awareness of attention. Joint attention requires that two people be knowingly attending to a common object in order to allow us to draw conclusions about infant awareness of attention. The triangulation is often conceived of as occurring in space (and here is where an unquestioning reliance on visual attention alone can mislead us), so the common object of attention is seen as something spatially separate from both infant and adult—the "third element," in fact, to use Elizabeth Bates' term.[10] There is very good reason for psychologists to focus on the external object: gaze following, as we have just seen, always involves an external object, and the infant's ability to follow gaze to objects develops with clear and identifiable patterns, depending on the geometry of their location in relation to the infant and adult.[11]

So, too, does pointing. Watching infants start to point could easily convince us that the externality of the object is somehow key to their understanding. Here is an example of its emergence in one child. Sitting on the floor of the living room, Shamini (who was 10 months and 4 days old) suddenly stretched out her right arm and with index finger extended pointed to something on the mantelpiece. With a conversational sequence of sounds she turned to her grandmother who was sitting nearby, and then dropped her arm. (I was so excited by this first communicative point I forgot to record what she was pointing at!) By the end of that evening, she had pointed at least ten or fifteen times. The third element had certainly entered the fray! A conclusion that this event signalled her discovery of our attention was problematic, however. After that evening it completely disappeared for twelve days, despite my attempts to elicit it by asking her leading "where is . . ." questions. Intriguingly, however, she seemed to point a lot to herself, noncommunicatively (that is, not within interactions with others and without looking at anyone) during these twelve days. One could argue here that the discovery, if there was one, may have been more the *act* of pointing itself than of attentionality in others.[12] Other people's attending, I am arguing, was already grasped well before this age, but to a different kind of object.

Beyond the "External" Object: Taking a Second-Person View

This general focus on the external object is problematic, not least because we all know as adults that we can attend to many different things other than just objects in space. What other objects of our attending could there be, which infants could perceive? They could be other *people* (whom we are attending to in the infant's presence perhaps), objects which are *close* to our bodies (like a mug that we are holding or the chair nearby), objects which are *part* of our bodies (like our clothes and jewellery), and even objects which *are* our bodies (like our hair or toes or belly). Thinking less concretely, they can be the *actions* that the infant (or someone else) does (like shaking their heads, waving their hands, wiggling their toes, smiling), or they can be *events* in time (such as the memory of a broken milk bottle or the anticipation of a party tomorrow) that we talk or are told about. They could also be *ideas* and concepts (such as the idea of this book or the concept of attention) but not of course for the very young infant.

Above all, the object of our attention can be the infant her*self*. As that beautiful line in the Song of Solomon goes: "Take away thine eyes from me, for they have overcome me."[13] Another's attention to oneself certainly can be observed and is probably the most powerful experience of attention that any of us ever will have had. Therefore, it would seem strange, on methodological grounds, to exclude the self as an object from this reckoning, even though this is customary in developmental psychology.[14]

The field needs to broaden the concept of the object of attention. In doing so, we could be opening up the area of study and obtaining richer data. If attending always involves objects, and the awareness of attention always involves awareness of this engagement with an object, then the nature of the objects (which others are attentionally engaging) must influence what they do in the engagement, and this must influence what infants perceive and understand about attention. For instance, when the "object" of the other's attention is a(nother) person, infants seem to show a different awareness of attentionality, behaving with different bids for and sharing of attention than if the object is an inanimate object. And speculatively, we could argue that if we had only holographic objects in our world, or if adults attended only to moving objects and never to static ones, the infant's understanding of attention would again be quite different. Or consider that if adults were all totally short-sighted and therefore never looked at anything but objects immediately to hand, the infant's grasp of attention would certainly have to be somewhat different!

If we broadened the concept of object, we could be doing even more than that; we could also be resolving one unnecessary theoretical conclusion in the field. This is the conclusion that while the connection between a reaching hand and its object is perceivable, the connection between a looking eye and its object is not, needing instead some intervening "idea" or representation to connect them. Amanda Woodward, for instance, suggests that this unobservability of the link between attention and its objects would explain the earlier emergence of infants' discrimination of intentional actions (more of this in the chapter on intentions, Chapter 8) compared to attentional actions. Discounting anything other than "external" objects of attending invites (and supports) the dualist view that the only link between "attending behaviour" and its objects must be a more or less inferential one. In this view, the psychological link between attender and object is presumed to be grasped as a deduction that there is an internal process such as "seeing" (from a third-person stance), or as a simulation (from a first-person approach) that the looking accompanies the same internal model of "seeing" as the self experiences. Of course, one could argue that it is through *intentional* action with the objects of *attention* that attention becomes meaningful. Michael Tomasello's argument that intentions are the first aspect of mentality that infants become aware of could make sense in this light. But I think this conclusion is not necessary: the meaningfulness of attention is experienced by the infant directly.

In effect, these theorists are arguing that the connection between a pair of looking eyes and their object is non-perceivable. But is this necessarily the case? Not if we accept the self as an object of other people's attention. When other people's attention is directed to the self, we not only perceive it as an action of looking, but we experience it in our responses to it. Assuming a sufficiently shared evolutionary history and a sufficient degree of "normality" so that a response *is* aroused, the connection between the looking eyes and their object is experienced as a perceptual/emotional/proprioceptive one. It would need to be *felt*. This is another reason for caution about solely visual metaphors; they could let us forget about other modes of experiencing mentality: not inferred or simulated but felt.

To summarise this section: expanding the concept of the perceivable object of attention allows us to explore more complex data about infants' awareness of others' attention than current models of attention allow. It brings in different kinds of objects, which might influence the nature of attentional engagements and changes the way in which the infant can perceive the connection between the attender and the object of attention. From a second-person perspective, the emotional responses to attention received to the self must be central to the *experiential* awareness of attention. This could then allow an expansion of the awareness of attention beyond the self to other objects. The key claim here is that—if this model can be supported by the data—others' attention may not in fact be discovered late in the day. Instead, I am arguing that it is the existing experience of attention directed to the self as an object which allows the discovery of newer objects of others' attention. The perceived objects of others' attention must expand.

Is the claim supported? Saying that attention can be felt and experienced emotionally/proprioceptively/perceptually to the self is no challenge; we all feel it as adults. And we know that in adults mutual gaze can lead to an increase in heart rate as well as to activation of specific brain areas.[15] But do infants really experience others' attention as directed to themselves? At 2 months? What is the evidence?

Self as an Object of Others' Attention: Responding and Directing Attention

Responding to, and Seeking, Attention at 2 Months (and Before)

We know that even newborns are "sensitive" to others' gaze directed to themselves, and that at least by 4 months, seeing someone look at them directly causes greater cortical arousal than an averted gaze. And 4-month-olds also show more arousal to still photographs of angry faces turned towards them than to those averted to the side (though intriguingly such a distinction is not shown to neutral or happy faces).[16] Even more excitingly, by 4 months, if an adult looks at them first and then turns away, infants are more likely to look at objects in the same direction that the adults are looking. Something about others' gaze to the self seems to be "cueing" the infant about the wider world.[17] But what does mutual gaze do in practice? One striking answer comes from a series of naturalistic interventions by the paediatrician Peter Wolff showing that 8-week-olds smile more when adults look at them rather than away. To any adult with an 8-week-old baby, this finding will seem an absurd statement of the obvious: of course, babies are going to smile more when there's someone looking at them! However, it isn't necessarily that absurd: babies, even foetuses, *do* smile on their own, and in newborns you can often see such smiles when they are asleep and especially after a good feed. Such solitary smiles don't entirely disappear (as any adult who has been caught smiling to themselves well knows) but from the end of the first month are outstripped by "social" or responsive smiles. Even solitary smiling is not unconnected to content-ment, albeit of a simple bodily kind. However, when smiling starts to be elicited by distal events, and especially "psychological" events (such as someone looking at you), the seemingly magical impact of mind on mind becomes strikingly evident. Perceiving that someone is attending to you can lead to emotional reactions which are "appropriate" (in the percep-tions of human adults) to *attention*. They need not only be straightforward smiles, but can have a varied mix of affect. Here's something from an early diary account which portrays this mix:

> Shamini: 7 weeks, 5 days: It feels . . . I can *make* her smile whenever I want—almost whatever mood she's in (not a frenzy or raging hunger though!). Today for example—she's (in the beginning stages of) crying— she's looking off to the side—while I'm changing her. I take my attention away from the nappy and talk to her and smile (i.e., I make one burst of . . . effort to catch her attention); she turns to me—mouth pulled down, crying stops for a few seconds, she smiles quiveringly, then grumbles/complains (rather than cries) with mouth down, still looking into my eyes.[18]

My shift of attention from nappy to infant's face led to a (brief) reduc-tion in crying, with an attempted smile and a complex communicative vocalisation.

Again as in adults, attention to self can also evoke negative reactions in infants. Persistent gaze at the wrong time can be distressing even for very young infants, especially if, as in the case of premature infants or those with central nervous system problems, they cannot disengage from it.[19] In healthy infants unwanted attention simply leads to attempts to turn away. Here are some observations from my husband on the first three days after Shamini was born:

> On the 3rd day, V lay close to her on the bed—about six inches away—and talked softly to her for the first time in this way. S looked at V's eyes (not hair or forehead) two or three times, each time for about 5 or 10 seconds, looking away in between. Then she looked down to V's chin or throat. V moved down to catch her eyes again. After a moment, S clearly avoided (V's gaze) by looking still further down. Such incidents of avoidance are common.[20]

When infants turn away in apparent indifference from adult attention, this can have a powerful effect on the adult. Especially when the baby is a few weeks old and has already been engaging in "chatting," impassive turning away can be distressing, as demonstrated in the following video clip from one of my studies.

> The mother says hello to her 7-week-old infant, trying to engage the infant for the camera. The infant seeming pre-occupied, looks away to his right. The mother says "Don't you want to talk to me, then?" and moves her head into the infant's line of gaze. The infant turns his head to the left. The mother is now amused but disbelieving "You are really not interested are you?" and playfully moves into the infant's new line of regard. The infant turns away again, unemotionally. This goes on for another couple of tries before the mother gives up, laughing awkwardly.

As shown in many studies, insistence on re-engaging when the infant keeps avoiding attentional contact can be distressing and counterproductive for the infant too. In cases of neurological problems where such turning away is not possible, the adult needs to be more than usually sensitive in detecting the infant's response and potential distress.[21]

Perhaps most interesting of all the emotional reactions to attention at this age are the complex smiling gaze aversions evoked by "greetings" from familiar people, even from the self in a mirror. Here is an example of Jennifer at 2½ months finding her own face in a mirror. Jennifer had recently discovered what her parents called "her little friend," getting excited and "chatty" whenever she looked into a mirror. On this occasion, her mother held Jennifer up to the mirror while her father was filming.

> Jennifer slowly turned from looking over her mother's shoulder and around the hallway. She turned towards the mirror with a pleasant, interested expression on her face. Her gaze slid down the mirror until it met her face. It paused, an asymmetrical smile started on her face, then she turned away for a couple of seconds as the smile intensified. She turned back to the mirror and the same thing happened again, although the smile was less intense this time. Her mother meanwhile, was smiling ear-to-ear watching this.[22]

Such reactions to other people and to the self in a mirror are not uncommon, especially at the onset of interactions. Infants of 2 and 3 months can smile in response to a greeting from a familiar adult and, as if overwhelmed by the closeness of the contact, turn away to the side with the smile still full, sometimes with the arms curving forwards in a single movement, and then turn back to meet the gaze of the person.[23] The significance of such reactions for self-consciousness (and their absence in autism) will be discussed in Chapter 7. The point here is that they are strong responses to the onset of attention to self.

The range and power of all of these different responses suggest that something in the attentional contact, and particularly in its onset, is perceived by the infant as significant enough to arouse strong emotional reactions. Both the presence and the absence of attention from other people have intense psychological effects on 2-month-old infants. But are these just passive responses? Is that all that infants at 2 months do with others' attention— react to it? If so, could it not be argued that the 2-month-old is merely hard-wired in some way to react to gaze or vocalisation with emotional arousal? (The richness and variability of the responses in each type of affect don't actually fit a "hard-wired" explanation, but never mind that for the moment.) But infants *don't* just react to other people's attention: they also direct it. It is in fact one of the arguments made in support of joint attention as a cognitive revolution—that only at the end of the first year can the infant actually *direct* other people's attention (rather than simply respond to it). But, as we shall see below, attempts to direct attention are prevalent a lot earlier than the end of the first year, and what is most exciting is that they vary appropriately with the infant's changing awareness of the objects of others' attention.

Do infants at 2 months *seek* to obtain attention when it is absent? Such initiative in seeking others' attention would seem a fair test of their ability to detect attention and, given the evidence of provocative "imitation" in newborns, would not be surprising in a 2-month-old. The data presently available in the literature are rather patchy, however. Infant responses to sudden inattention (as in the still-face and double video experiments in the last chapter) show that even 2-month-olds attempt to regain attentional contact through vocalisations and facial expressions. But those are both rather bizarre and "abnormal" situations in which the infant loses the other's attention to the self. The more typical situation is when parents are out of sight of the infant, having gone into another room, or are in sight but inattentive, almost always with the face turned right away rather than towards the infant, blankly, as in the still face.

Parents report that from about 3 or 4 months infants begin to call them when they are not present, or when they are present but inattentive. The calling is reported to be of a different vocal tone and intensity, sometimes involving shriller tones. A call even at the same distance sounds quite different from a vocalisation which is a "response" to already received attention. And the "calling" stops when the attention is regained; otherwise the parent would not perceive it as calling. The evidence for this is largely anecdotal at present, and what we don't yet know is how these "calling" vocalisations differ from more "responsive" ones, how frequently they occur, how they differ at different ages in these early months, or how individual infants differ from others. But the phenomenon of early calling should hardly surprise us. A trawl through the animal literature reveals a rich data set in terms of the calls of young "pups" (and recently also bats!) to their parents. The decision we have to make is how to interpret this "calling" for attention. It is not the kind of calling which could be translated as "Look at my painting," or as "Look at what I'm doing," nor even necessarily as "Look at me" but at the simplest level as "Come back to me." We don't know enough about the phenomenon as yet, but it is my guess that it involves more than just a regaining of physical contact or warmth or still-faced gaze. Rather, it involves a gaining of attention and attentiveness to the self.

This ability to seek attention to the self remains with us throughout life, but as we shall see, complexities emerge in the middle of the first year. Infants become able to use little tricks and funny movements to attract and retain the attention of other people well before they engage in proto-declarative pointing. Skills in directing attention seem to develop in parallel with skills in responding to attention.

Attention or Just Interaction?

So, very young infants respond subtly and appropriately to others' attention to them and seek it when it is absent. But the sceptic would (and does) ask: what is it exactly that the infant is responding to or seeking? Could it not be the interaction as a whole that the infant is seeking rather than the other person's attention per se? Of all the methodological reasons to exclude dyadic engagements and focus only on triadic engagements in studies of infant awareness of others' attention, this is the strongest: that in natural dyadic engagement we cannot tell whether it is the interaction as a whole that is being sought or attention alone.[24] In triangulated interactions, it is easier to distinguish the infant's attempt to seek, for example, the adult's head turn to a distal object from the adult's reaction to the infant herself, than would be the case in dyadic engagements where both the target of attention and the infant are the same. However, the presence of the methodological difficulty does not rule out the possibility that the responses and initiatives of the 2-month-old in dyadic engagement do involve a more specific awareness of attention. Focusing on different aspects of attention might help answer this question.

Take the example where I turned my attention from the nappy to Shamini's face and succeeded in getting her to turn to me and give a quivering smile in the midst of the tears. What was it about that shift in my attention that she detected? There is no reason to believe, for example, that it was just the gaze—the shift in my gaze was accompanied with a vocalisation and a smile—and it could be any or all of these aspects of attention that she was seeking, not just the gaze alone. What aspects of attention does the infant pick up—and seek out—in these early months, especially in mutual attentional engagements? Experimental studies provide some quite amazing answers to this question, even if these aren't the questions that the studies were necessarily seeking to address.

Attention in its simplest form involves orientation, whether of the body or the head or the eyes or the ears or the hands or even the tongue. Some scientists suggest that even at birth infants may have some kind of orientationally tuned detectors; we know that they certainly do by 6 weeks of age.[25] We also know very clearly that at least by 3 months of age infants are pretty good at detecting head orientation. Not only can they detect the difference between heads turned away and heads turned towards them, but (even in stark experimental conditions) they smile and gaze more at the latter. Infants in the first 3 months may be more sensitive to head orientation than to eye direction *per se*, or at least, they may not be very good at detecting eye movements if they are not accompanied by a head turn and they may be cued by movement—whether the movement of the head or even of the pupils.[26] However, certainly by 3 months there is evidence that they can differentiate between open eyes and shut eyes. In one interesting study, in fact, 3-month-old infants were presented with rather artificially posed adults in one of three conditions: turned away to the side, facing the infant with their eyes shut, or facing the infant with the eyes open. Infants smiled more to the "head-forward-eyes-open" condition even though, and this is crucial for our question, the adults were neither speaking nor smiling at the infant and were in fact in artificially static postures.[27] This suggests very strongly that neither smiling nor speaking is a necessary accompaniment to adult attention to arouse emotional responses in the infant. After three months of experience with the whole package of speaking, smiling, attending adults, gaze alone seems to be enough to elicit smiles! And it seems that even subtle shifts in gaze direction are sufficient for the 3-month-old to detect. Horizontal gaze deflections of as little as 5 degrees—that is, gaze directed to the ears rather than the eyes—are sufficient for 3-month-olds to respond differently. Interestingly, however, vertical gaze deflections of a similar size (i.e., directed to the forehead or chin) are not so easily detected.

But if this was the only evidence to suggest that attention is meaningfully perceived much earlier than—and in a different way from—that at the end of the first year, we could stop here. The argument would have begun, but not be much of a challenge to the idea of the expanding object of attention. But there is more.

Body Parts and Actions as "Objects"

You can direct others' attention to the external world, and you can direct their attention to your self. But somewhere in between you can also direct attention to things you *do*. We could have many debates about the interpretation of the following examples and phenomena. But one feature of their occurrence is striking. Infants don't call attention specifically to their actions at 2 months or 4 months, but they do sometime after 6 months. And this is a considerable time before they call others' attention to distal objects through pointing. The timing of its emergence is unlikely to be irrelevant to an awareness of attention. Before infants direct others' attention to distal objects, they direct others' attention to acts by the self.

Here is an example, which may well seem so trivial (if you have a baby around you) that you will wonder what the fuss is about. But is it so trivial after all?

> Rose sits in her car chair and shakes her head rapidly from side to side—apparently to herself, exploring the sensation of the movement. Her mother, watching her, comments on it with amusement and interest. Rose repeats the head shaking vigorously, now looking at her mother. For about two weeks after that, the head shaking is produced, expectantly, whenever the mother looks at her. (Mother of Rose, 7 months, interview)[28]

Infants at 7 months of age, and before they are capable of directing others' attention to distal objects through pointing and before they are capable of reliably following gaze to distal objects, are quite specifically directing others' attention to the actions of the self. In two different longitudinal studies of infants from around 7 months of age, we found that attempts to use actions (of body, face, hand, voice) to obtain the attention of adults was commonplace. Infants were zooming in with considerable sensitivity to those things that worked with adults. Sometimes they were attempting to get attention when it was absent, sometimes trying to retain it. At other times they were quite specifically focused on obtaining a particular reaction—such as laughter:[29]

> On one occasion before Christmas, my sister was sitting at the table . . . . And she (Vanessa) had a bit of a cough and she (my sister) said "Oh, bad cough, (cough cough)" and Vanessa went "cough cough" and they went on for about nine or ten different goes and each time she was laughing as she was going "cough cough" and looking at Jo with a big smile all over her face. (Mother of Vanessa, 8 months, interview)

And sometimes, with particularly obvious charm, infants attempted to bask in attention which was already on them or to gain attention for "clever" achievements. Here are two examples:

> She is also now starting to stand up a lot and seeking for you to tell her what a clever girl she is. She'll pull herself up and then look round to see who is looking at her. (Mother of Vanessa, 8 months, interview)

If any adult, or any new adult especially, comes into the room he tries to get their attention. . . . If it's other people, then he suddenly goes into this whole kind of clapping, waving hands (repertoire of things). . . . Well I went up to my Mum's the weekend before last and he had a massive audience there, 'cos they haven't seen him for 6 weeks, my family, and he was on cloud nine all weekend. So he was . . . he was just showing off the whole weekend. (Mother of Adam, 11 months, dictaphone and interview)

In their pioneering study, Elizabeth Bates and her colleagues described a similar example of 9-month-old Carlotta, who was always a star of the stage when she gave the comrades' salute on social occasions in communist circles in Italy. The phenomenon is well known to psychologists in the communication and language research tradition, and very familiar to parents. Piaget called this tertiary circular reactions—the ability of the infant to make a link between his or her own actions and the responses they obtain. However, the link between this phenomenon and the child's developing knowledge of attention has not really been explored. The reasons for this neglect may lie partly in our pre-conceptions of what the acceptable "object of attention" is and partly in our theoretical conviction that awareness of attention is not to be spoken about until a little later in development. The prevalence of these phenomena in infants is strong (in Britain anyway!). We found that well before they point to things, infants are skilled at repeating actions which have previously elicited attention in order to re-elicit it. In one study we found that 74 percent of 8-month-olds and 90 percent of 11-month-olds showed such repetitions for attention. As we will see in greater detail in the following chapters, there were different motives for re-eliciting attention—different forms of showing off, different kinds of clowning to make people laugh, and different types and levels of teasing to provoke reactions. The body and its actions were being used as objects with which and towards which the others' attention could be directed. The common object of attention had, by this age, expanded beyond the self to actions by the self.

The critic might argue, however, that when an 8-month-old shakes her head to re-elicit her father's laughter she may be using the head-shaking to get attention to herself rather than seeking attention to the act of head-shaking. In other words, as was the case several months earlier, the whole self (rather than the act itself) might still be the "object" towards which the other's attention is sought. However, crucial differences can be detected between the two aims. When the 4-month-old "calls," obtaining the other's attention to the self leads to *cessation* of the calling. In contrast, with the case of clowning and showing off, obtaining the other's attention usually leads to a *repetition* of the act, suggesting a clearer awareness of the link between the action and the attender's engagement with it. This does not, of course, mean that the self as a whole is not also a target. The other's attention may never be sought exclusively to the act even in adulthood: consider the case of the teenager repeatedly performing acrobatic manoeuvres for others' attention. The attention is clearly understood (by the performer at least!) to be linked to the act, although it may be sought for the self. Similarly, the 8-month-old appears to be more conscious of the link between act and attention than the 4-month-old, and more aware of attention to things other than the global self, rather than exclusively to one or the other. However far the infant has to go in terms of elaborating and differentiating her understanding of attention, this linkage is clearly an advance upon the previous linkage between attention and the global self. Furthermore, the motives for the directing of attention are, by 8 months or so, becoming so differentiated and so appropriately related to the actions that it seems unlikely that the infant is not aware of the other's attention to the action.

Does this expansion of the object of attention relate to previous emotional responses to attention to the self? We don't directly know. We can only speculate that they must, psychologically, be related. Does this expansion relate to subsequent developments in awareness of objects of attention? Here we do have an answer. Those infants who engaged more clearly in clowning or showing off at 8 months were more likely to have developed the ability to point by 11 months.[30] It seems very likely therefore, that these two ways of directing others' attention are linked. Further support for this link between later joint attention and clowning and showing off comes from our study of pre-school children with autism. We know already that children with autism have difficulty both in producing protodeclaratives and in understanding them when done by others. Joint attention in general, but a declarative sharing of attention in particular, is so problematic in autism that it has become incorporated into tests as one of the earliest indications of an autistic spectrum disorder.[31] In our study we also found a deficit in clowning and showing off, particularly clowning, in the children with autism, although it was present in developmental age-matched pre-school children with Down syndrome.[32] Moreover there was a strong relation in both groups between individual abilities at pointing on the one hand and clowning and showing off on the other. The typically developing infants who clowned or showed off at 8 months also pointed at 11 months, and none of them pointed before evidence of clowning or showing off. This was the same story for the pre-school children with autism and with Down syndrome. In both groups, the children were reported to engage either in both clowning/showing off and pointing or in neither. And there were no cases of children pointing but not clowning or showing off. The case for clowning/showing off as an intermediate stage in the development of awareness of attention seems strong. The actions of the body seem to form an intermediate object of others' attention, positioned between the early developing awareness of self as an object and the later developing awareness of external objects.

The critic could raise a further and seemingly more drastic challenge to my claims. Why could it not be that both directing attention to self and directing attention to the actions of the self have not got anything at all to do with attention? Why could not the infant have merely learned a series of cause-effect behavioural patterns and be experimenting on them, with no recognition that the other person's reactions are attentional? Only one answer is possible here: yes, this *could* be so. Indeed, this criticism has in fact been made about the pointing of toddlers: that they could just be experiments upon the physical reactions of others.[33] This logical possibility—that it could be mere attention behavior rather than attention as a whole that infants or even adults perceive in others—could always exist. But how plausible is this possibility in the case of typically developing infants? From what we know so far, it seems very implausible. The evidence seems to be mounting for a non-dualist alternative account in which infants seem to be aware of some objects of others' attention, that is of attention as attention in some cases, even early in infancy.

Other "Objects" of Attention: Other People, Things in the Hand, Events

This section will report on studies of three further types of "objects" of attentional engagement which provide some different pieces of the puzzle about how the awareness of others' attention develops during the first year of human infancy.

Let us take the simplest and least challenging case: the common object of attention can be another person rather than an inanimate object. Most approaches to the development of attention awareness would not put the "object" at the centre of the development: the process of discovering attention is largely independent of the objects of others' attention (except in a complicated sense of providing data). And so there is no reason why, if the "third element" were another person rather than an object, this should make a difference to awareness of attention.

However, two different research teams have found evidence suggesting that triadic attentional engagements are evident earlier in three-person triangles. Jacqueline Nadel and her colleagues in Paris showed that even in experimental situations a person-person-person triad works to establish joint attentional engagements in infants younger than 6 months old.[34] A second team with Elizabeth Fivaz-Depeursinge and her colleagues in Switzerland developed a clinical technique which they called the Primary Triangle for exploring triadic interactions with parents and infants. In these semi-naturalistic interactions, they found that even at 3 months infants showed prefigurations of the intersubjective triangular strategies not believed to happen until 9 to 12 months of age. At 3 months there was evidence of the co-ordination of attention—that is, a rapid and repeated alternation of gaze from one parent to the other—and a clear co-ordination of affect—transferring smiles, distress, and perplexity from a dyadic interaction to the other and on-looking parent. "For instance, an infant would warm up to mother, looking at her brightly, smiling and babbling; she would then turn to the father while maintaining her smile and vocal gesture. Or, in a difficult moment, her face would cloud, and she would turn with the very same expression to the other parent." By 5 months infants showed more co-ordination of attention with more rapid shifts, sometimes with three or more alternations, and more prefigurations of affect sharing, signaling, and even social referencing. By 9 months infants not only looked from one parent to the other when the one who was interacting with them stopped and turned to the other, but also made active attempts to reach forward and get the attention of first one and then the other parent. Infants, and indeed families, varied in how likely triangulated sharing was to occur: in problematic families these bids were much less likely to happen. Particularly interesting in this research is the central role of emotional events in prompting attentional sharing: "it is mostly at the height of pleasure, frustration or uncertainty . . . that triangular bids are likely to emerge" (p. 112).

But families differed in the extent to which the affect sharing bids with the on-looking parent were prompted by positive rather than negative events. Fivaz-Depeursinge challenges the assumption that triadic engagements emerge *from,* and therefore later than, dyadic engagements. It would seem they exist and develop in parallel, depending on the nature of the "third element."[35]

Another type of "object," according to a group of Japanese researchers, is the object in the hand. They find suggestive evidence of attentional engagements in the middle of the first year involving adults holding an object. They suggest that coming somewhere between a three-person triangle at three or four months in which the "object" is another person, and the more typical two-persons-and-an-object triangle at the end of the first year, is a triangle in which the object of attention is the hand-with-object. For them, the hand-with-object is the bridge between other person as "object" and thing as "object." They call this a P-P(O)-P (that is, Person-Person(Object)-Person) triangle. In other words, the infant's attention to the hand-object allows them later to attend to the object alone. If we add this to our collection of objects of attention so far, this intermediate step fits quite promisingly with the one about the self's actions. If we use this new terminology, we can call the self's actions a P-P(A)-P triangle, where the A stands for actions.

Now for the last additional type of "object" that I am going to introduce before we sum the story up: events (not controlled by the infant) as objects of attention. I mention these not because they are a structurally different kind of object, but because they allow us to introduce one new term: social or attentional referencing. We know a lot about social referencing, which usually refers to the infant's attempt to check the face of the adult when the infant experiences some ambiguity or uncertainty. The first and classic experiment on this was of course the one in which the infant was taken to the edge of the visual cliff and invited to cross over by a beckoning mother from the other side. But in the case of social referencing, given the largely "negative" events that it is paired with in experimental work, the infant is more likely to be checking the adult's face (for her reactions and non-verbal "advice") than her attention. However, it may well be that in positive situations, that is when confronted with some event that is positive, any look that the infant directs to an adult might also involve their attention to the event. "Affect sharing," as it has been described by Lauren Adamson, occurs earlier in infancy than does the classic "external object" type of joint attention and could be an attempt to seek others' attention to an object/event.[36] Take the following example of this 8-month-old:

> Janet is busy playing alone with toys on floor. (She has not looked up for at least 2 minutes to Mother (M) or Father (F) several feet away on one side of room or at researcher (R) behind camera. M and F and R occasionally talking to each other). The family cat makes a noise at other side of room (from M and F). Janet looks at it, then turns and looks at F, then turns back to the cat, squeaks herself in imitation of the noise and turns to look at camera/R. Everyone laughs. Janet turns back to her toys. Minutes later the cat makes a noise again, Janet looks up immediately at cat, then turns round with an imitation of the sound to M and F, then back to toys again. Twelve seconds later cat makes noise again and Janet looks at it for several seconds. R laughs behind camera. Janet looks at R, then turns to M and F with a smile and an imitation of the cat sound. (From video, Janet, 8 months)[37]

In other examples, the look to a nearby adult (or any person) can follow an accidental action (for example, a toy may have made an unexpected sound while the infant was playing with it) or an intentional action involving success or pleasure (for example, the infant may have succeeded after some difficulty in picking up a brick in each hand). In such behaviour, the infant is not making any attempt to call the parent's attention to the event; she seems to be assuming it. We do not know what would have happened if Janet's parents had not been responsive to her turning to look. Another name for such behaviour could be attentional referencing. In an experimental study by David Leavens and Brenda Todd, infants of 6 months of age (sitting in a fixed position in the middle of a room with their mothers to one side of them) were shown interesting things in other parts of the room. Infants at this age were too young to point these things out to their mothers, as they do in identical situations when they are over 12 months or so of age. However, their responses were in other respects identical: they showed signs of excitement and turned and looked at their mothers, then back again at the target.[38] Once again, the mother's attention is being checked up on, though not explicitly directed.

An Alternative Developmental Model: The Second-Person Story

I use the data presented so far about infants' dealings with others' attention to develop a model of the development of awareness of attention from a second-person perspective.[39] In Table 6.1 you'll notice the already familiar thesis so far that:

- The self is the first (and most vital) object of attention that the infant is aware of.
- Development in the awareness of attention involves an awareness of the expansion (from the dyad outwards) and differentiation of the objects of others' attention.
- Following the awareness of attention to self, the infant gradually becomes aware of other "objects," including, by the end of the first year, the distal object that is involved in pointing and gaze following.
- The age of the infant does not affect the variety and appropriateness of affective responses the infant shows on perceiving the adult's attention to different objects.
- For each object of attention, there is, at each age, both the ability to respond to and the ability to direct others' attention to it.

In trying to make sense of the data, I find a lot of gaps in the evidence that is currently available in the field. This is not surprising, given that the model I have been developing is not the dominant one in the field and psychologists haven't therefore been conducting studies that would help to fill in these gaps. For the most part, I have already mentioned these gaps in the chapter so far. Down the left-hand side of the table are some familiar categories: the self, other persons, frontal targets, objects in other's hand, acts by the self, and body parts and distal targets.

There are two categories that I haven't mentioned before: (others' attention to) objects-in-own-hand, and the very last category, (others' attention to) past events and non-visible targets. The category of objects-in-own hand is a speculation, based upon the knowledge we have so far, that somewhere after 8 months infants show/give objects to others (although the phenomenon of giving at around that age is not speculation). What we don't yet know, however, is how holding an object differs from showing it or from offering it to the other. It may well be that the two become functionally distinct only after many engagements. We have very little data about the infant's awareness and monitoring during the showing-giving of objects-in-hand or of the other's attention to the object. The last category, past events and non-visible targets, really refers to more verbal interactions (although not necessarily so) and usually comes under the heading of an awareness of others' knowledge and ignorance. Data concerning this are described in Chapter 10.

Table 6.1. The infant's expanding awareness of the objects of others' attention

Age	The objects of others' attention	Infants' engagements with the objects of others' attention
2–4 months	The self	*Responding:* Smiling, distress, indifferent and coy responses to attention to self. *Directing:* "Calling" and seeking attention to self.
3–5 months	Other persons	*Responding:* Responding to other's attention to a third person. *Directing:* Attention bids alternating between two other persons.
4–7 months	Nearby targets and objects-in-other's-hand	*Responding:* Following other's gaze to objects in front, nearby or in other's hand. *Directing:* No evidence yet of attention bids to these objects.
7–10 months	Acts by self	*Responding:* Joyful, avoidant, and ambivalent responses to attention to acts by self. *Directing:* Clowning and showing off to obtain attention to acts by self.
8–11 months	Objects-in-own-hand	*Responding:* Following other's gaze to objects in own hand? No evidence yet. *Directing:* Offering and giving objects to others.
12–14 months	Distal objects	*Responding:* More complex following of other's gaze to objects. *Directing:* Pointing, showing, fetching objects across a distance.
15–20 months	"Objects" over time and nonvisible objects	*Responding:* Varied affective responses to reported events; following gaze to targets behind the infant. *Directing:* Reporting past events and future plans; selective reporting of events and selective showing of objects.

For this account to be more than a mere empirical description, however, and for it to be credible as a theory of the development of awareness of attention, it must explain *why* change occurs. Why does the infant's awareness of the objects of others' attention expand? Why, in acting to manipulate others' attention, does the infant change from calling attention to the self as a whole to calling attention to particular actions and then to things across the room?

Let's take the findings from two sets of studies to answer this question. First, one of the studies exploring early gaze following to distal targets found something more interesting than the fact that gaze following occurred earlier than previously thought. They found that gaze following only occurred if mutual attention had previously been established. In other words, the infant seemed to bother to turn her head to look in the direction of the adult's gaze only if the adult had, immediately before, been looking at her.[40] Why would this be the case? Second, the Japanese study of objects in hand found that when infants were presented with an averted profile of an adult, they continued looking at the profile for a few seconds before turning to look at the adult's hand holding the object. They did not bother much with the hand-with-object if the adult's gaze remained on them, nor did they bother looking at the hand if it had no object or was doing nothing interesting. Why did the infant bother to shift attention to the hand?

The infant's attentional shifts in both these studies make the most sense if the infant is aware of the other's attention as a psychologically directed act. It is *because*, in mutual attention, this directedness is first, developmentally, experienced by the infant to herself as the object, that the shift to other targets *can* occur as development progresses. If the infant did not *feel* the other's attention to herself, she would have little more than academic curiosity as a motive to explore the other's attention to the world. It is this affective awareness of others' attention *to the self* that allows infants to develop a broader and eventually conceptual awareness of others' attention.

Adults play their own motivational part, unwittingly, in expanding the infant's awareness of their own objects of attention. Parents, we know, do things at the fringes of infants' abilities; they work in the zone of proximal development, to use a now popular explanation from Vygotsky. And we know that infants, like most juvenile mammals, seek and enjoy novelty and exploration. When adults at 4 months start to get subconsciously desperate at infants' waning obsession with them (looking around the room, for instance, is absolutely a marker of infants in the lab at 3 to 4 months in contrast to infants gazing exclusively at the mother's face at 2 months), they start performing more and more exaggerated actions—moving the infants' feet, singing songs, starting to invite the infant into rhythmic games, and so on to regain infant attention. This expanding horizon of adult actions, which is usually on the infant's own body, must have consequences. It must on the one hand *mark* the infant's body parts as separate entities—objects as it were—and it must make the process of engagement instantly more complex and essentially triadic. It would be surprising if the infant, faced with these new complexities and potential targets of attention, did not then herself bring them into interactions with adults. The motive for expanding objects of attention then becomes clear; the infants' horizons expand mutually—infants seek more and adults do more things. When the two combine, infants' awareness of attention expands a lot more.

If this explanation is valid, it must go beyond infancy. Even in adulthood it is engagement of this sort with the objects of each other's attention that continues to expand our awareness of what kinds of things can be attended to and what kind of thing attention could be. It is likely that in different relationships and different cultural contexts different aspects of objects and topics are confirmed, highlighted, or obscured as objects of attention.

What happens when things don't go right? There are some clear implications. The early experience of attention depends not only on the infant's biological predisposition to a particular perceptual/proprioceptive/emotional response to attention to the self, but on what then happens in the engagement. Infants engage in dyadic attentional interactions with adults from minutes after birth. What happens if the adult does not engage with the infant? Or if they only engage sporadically, not reliably? What happens if the infant is distressed or unable to engage? What happens if the infant finds the engagement disturbing and negative? What attention means to the infant must depend heavily on such histories. We can guess that an *absence* of emotional response to attention to self will divorce the infant's developing understanding of attention from any experiential reality of attention until it can be analogically inferred. We can guess that a largely *negative* (distressing) or neutral (disinterested) experience of emotional response to attention to self must inhibit further engagements with attention, leading to a spiralling negativeness of affect, and must influence the nature of later conceptual understanding of it. And we can guess that a largely *positive* experiencing of attention to self must enhance and encourage further initiations of attentional engagement as well as leading to a spiralling positiveness in experiencing and conceptualising it. In the case of autism, as we will see further, particularly in the chapter on self-consciousness (Chapter 7), there is reason to doubt the presence of attentional engagements (of the sort we see in typically developing infants) from about the equivalent of the middle of the first year. (This does not, of course, mean that these engagements did not occur in the first year for children with autism. Nor does it mean that children with autism cannot engage; it may just be that their engagement takes less obvious forms or that it only occurs under certain conditions.) Such absence of emotional involvement with others' attention—to its various objects—could be seen as directly influencing the absence of emotional responses to attention as we see in typically developing infants. The children with autism are developing an understanding of attention, but it seems to be a different sort of attention. The understanding that is developed outside of emotional engagement may be a more logical, deductive, protective understanding. However, we have no reason to believe that children with autism do not experience emotional responses to attention to the self as object. On the contrary, their responses, some would believe, may well be intensely arousing—so intense that they avoid contact with it in many situations.[41] Such questions have yet to be explored. But a second-person approach suggests that—whether for typically developing infants or children with disabilities or even adults—it is the emotional experience of others' attention that is crucial for constraining and constituting what others' attention means.

Summary

In this chapter I have argued that attention is better conceived of as engagement with objects in the world—as attending—rather than as an unobservable entity hidden behind behaviour. Attending is therefore fundamentally related to its objects. And the awareness of other people's attending is necessarily related to the awareness of its objects. The infant's awareness of others' attending begins with *being* the object of their attending in direct mutual engagement. The connection between the attender and the object of attention is thus first experienced emotionally. Emotional responses to this experience must not only inform the infant's developing grasp of attention, but must also provide the motivation for further engagements. During the first year, the infant shows similar emotional responses and similar attempts to direct or control, an expanding range of attentional objects. The awareness of attention develops not through a belated discovery of attention as attention towards the first year (which is what the literature primarily contends) but through an expanding awareness of the scope of others' attending. Links between early and late forms of directing attention can be seen not only in typically developing infants, but also in cases of problematic or atypical development, such as in autism. The clear prediction here is that without the direct affective experience of attention in mutual attention there can be no "appropriate" understanding of attention. In developmental psychopathologies involving disturbances in the experience of mutual attention, there is considerable evidence to suggest that what develops is a "bystander" rather than a participant understanding of attention. It would seem that the *I-Thou* relation (to hark back to Buber's term discussed in Chapter 3) is the only basis on which an appropriate conceptual awareness of attention can emerge.

CHAPTER 7

Feeling Self-Conscious

The *I* of the . . . *I-Thou* is a different *I* from that of the . . . *I-It*.

Martin Buber, *I and Thou*[1]

All thought of something is at the same time self-consciousness . . . .
At the root of all our experiences and all our reflections, we
find. . . . a being which immediately recognises itself, . . . and
which knows its own existence, not by observation and as a given
fact, nor by inference from any idea of itself, but through direct
contact with that existence. Self-consciousness is the very being of
mind in action.

Maurice Merleau-Ponty, *The Phenomenology of Perception*[2]

The Oracle at Delphi commands us as we enter its gates to
"Know Thyself." What is so important about the self that we need to discover
it in order to find truth? Why is it that the ultimate wisdom is seen to lie in
being true to the self? "This above all: to thine own self be true," as Polonius
urges in *Hamlet*. Self-consciousness has been seen as the most profound aspect that separates us from our fellow-creatures, the thing that allows us to
reflect on our place in the universe, and, more human than any of these, it
is the stuff of which romance is made. If it is such a profound and noble
thing, should we be talking about it in relation to infants? How do we become self-conscious?

When people talk about self-consciousness, they often refer to "thoughts
about the self." I am going to argue in this chapter that understanding what
self-consciousness is and how it develops takes quite a different slant if we
look at it instead as an emotional phenomenon. I will look at the development of two often neglected self-conscious emotional engagements—
shyness and showing off—which we can see even in the first year. The

awareness of the self as an object to others seems to emerge not from a concept of self but from an early feeling for the attention and attitudes of others directed to the self. In other words it comes from a second-person relation to people, experiencing, long before conceptualising, the self as an object to others. But first, let's take that familiar side-step and ask what it means to be self-conscious.

What, Who, and When Is the Self?

What Is the Self?

First, *what* exactly is this self that philosophers ask us to know and that poets are charmed by? It is strangely difficult to answer this question. And difficult also to say what we mean by a *consciousness* of it. Is the self that which we experience subjectively, from "inside" as it were, the "I," as William James put it, or is it that which we know as an object from the "outside," which we imagine is seen and experienced by others, the "me"? The distinction between subjective and objective self-consciousness is still commonly used today, with different ages predicted at which each develops. However, it is sometimes questioned, for example, in cases of "disintegration" of the self following bereavement or shock, when the "I" and the "me" become indistinguishable and both *being* an I and finding an image of me are disrupted.

The question of locating the self somewhere has an interesting history. If you are asked what the boundaries of your self are, your probable response will be your skin. Although this seems to be an obvious answer, it is clearly inadequate. Take, for example, your bodily self—a seemingly simple and clearly bounded entity. But even here the skin is not a clear-cut boundary. Imagine that you move your arm to pick up a heavy book: the tensing of the muscles is yours, but can only be understood in relation to the weight of the book. Similarly, your breathing is yours, but not only is it crossing the boundary of your skin, it is controlled by the nature of the air around you.

When we come to more psychological aspects of the self, the problem is more profound. Let's take a *feeling*—say pleasure. Someone smiles at you and you feel pleased. The feeling which infuses you is not separable from (and cannot be understood separately from) the smile of the other person; your feeling includes the other person's. Or take a *thought*—that Tony Blair was a disappointment as prime minister, for example. That thought, which we experience as individuals, is embedded in many conversations and news bulletins we have shared in. Our thought is not really ours alone; it is part of a bigger scene. Where does the action or feeling or thought or opinion of another person end and ours begin? The skin is hardly a boundary at all. We cannot identify that which is the self without including in it many other people. When we talk about the self, then, we are talking about this jointness, about something-in-relation rather than a single entity, something in the gaps, as it were, rather than an individual thing. And when we talk about self-awareness or self-consciousness, therefore, we must also be talking about an awareness of this *relation*, rather than solely about a separate entity.

Who Is the Self?

And *who* is this self? As Montaigne put it five hundred years ago, there is "as much difference found betweene us and our selves, as there is betweene our selves and other."[3] If the self is a relation rather than a thing in itself, then it stands to reason that each of us has as many selves as we have situations and relations to engage in. This multiplicity challenges the logic of the inside-outside distinction between the "I" and the "me" because as the self moves about engaging with people and things, it changes in the process—more like Heraclitus' famously changing river than his toe. The many "I"s and the many "me"s proliferate, changing, merging, the distinction between self as subject and self as object now seeming an artificial distinction, imposed for clarity but no longer clear or tenable. Like Foucault's face in the sand constantly erased by the sea, the self can only be described as a set of "arrested moments, artificially isolated from the flux."[4] So do we select a particular aspect of self in a particular situation at a particular time in our exploration of self-consciousness? Even if we restrict ourselves to what is now called the interpersonal self,[5] we still need to grasp the fact of this multiplicity and fluidity, and however hard it is to imagine this, perhaps talk as James did, of our many interpersonal selves.[6] So the question for us here is, *when* do we come to know our selves-in-relation?

When Does the Self Arise?

Adults might occasionally recognise having experienced a confusion between self and other in rare moments of intense emotional intimacy, or when looking in a mirror and seeing not oneself but the person one is speaking to in imagination, or even, simultaneously, that other person and oneself through the eyes of that person. In such moments, distinguishing who is the self and who is the other seems both irrelevant and impossible. However, the recognition of the "other" as different from the self is crucial for any communication and dialogue and for the awareness of the other as a person.

If one were to listen to some psychologists from the beginning of the last century, the infant at birth cannot even tell itself apart from the world around it. The beginnings of self-consciousness were supposed to be shrouded in a profound confusion between the self and the world. The human infant, according to Freud and Piaget, and many other famous theorists, actually begins life in a state of such serious confusion that she cannot tell in any way the difference between herself and the world of people or things around her. However, if it were in fact the case that the infant could not differentiate herself from the world, if adualism, as it is called, were the normal state of human neonates, action itself would be impossible. To act implies knowing that there is a world out there in relation to, and different from, my body and my actions. It also implies some degree of confidence in the coherence and continued existence of both. As Maxine Sheets-Johnstone puts it, "it is biologically axiomatic that to the degree an animal has to learn to move itself, it is self-aware" in a tactile-kinaesthetic sense.[7] And coherent neonatal action is not only characteristic of the lower animals, but also of humans: they can reach, they can cry, they can look, they can imitate, and they can move their bodies.

Even newly born babies are able to respond to events in the world with different reciprocal movements of their own. For example, if an object is dangled in front of an infant a few hours old, within about a foot of the infant's body in what is called "reach-space," the neonate may look intently at it, and then reach forward with one or both arms, attempting crudely (and sometimes successfully) to make contact with this object.[8] As we have seen in Chapter 4, human neonates respond to certain actions of others with imitative movements, not reflexively and in confusion between the other's act and their own, but often pausing with almost considered attention to these acts before imitating them. The phenomenon of newborns crying when they hear other babies crying (for example, the well-known chaos in neonatal nursery units in hospitals) was previously used as evidence of a confusion between the boundary of the self and the other (that is, that an infant hears another baby crying, and not knowing this is another baby, starts—or rather, "continues"—to cry). However, such crying is in fact less confused than it appears: newborns will cry more to the tape-recorded cry of another infant than to their own, showing an awareness of something different about their own voice that is hard enough even for adults to perceive.[9] Their crying in response to other infants' crying, then, seems to be some sort of sympathetic cry rather than one born in the confusion of not knowing that it was not one's own cry.

Intriguingly, it is not simply the case that neonates can distinguish themselves from others and can perceive similarities and differences sufficient to allow them to act coherently or to imitate others; they are also specifically *interested* in their own actions. Audrey van der Meer and her colleagues performed a series of remarkable experiments with 1-month-old infants in which they showed live video images of the movements of one of the infant's hands and even, in one of the experiments, hanging an extra weight on the filmed hand to make it more difficult to move. The infants were intently interested in watching their arm movements on film, and despite the extra difficulty, increased the movement of the hand whose movements they were watching. The co-ordination between the seen and felt movements was already sufficient to enable the infants to increase the felt movements in order to watch the seen. In another experiment, these researchers passed an invisible laser beam above either the chest or the stomach of the infant. When the infants accidentally discovered that the laser beam was activated and made visible by movement across it, they increased their movements at the place where the beam was, not anywhere else.[10] This may not even be the result of simple contingency detection and reinforcement. Another study with 2-month-olds showed that babies at that age not only suck more (on a wired-up dummy) to produce contingent sound effects, but recognise the matching in analog terms of the sound to their sucking and sucked just hard enough to play around the edges of the match. They seemed to be recognising not just *that* they had an effect on the world, but *what* sort of effect and were motivated to explore and modulate it.[11]

Even in extreme and odd cases, such as in conjoined twins where the twins often suck on each other's fingers, Daniel Stern showed that one pair of twins at 3 months of age could distinguish between their own fingers and those of the other twin. When the other twin's fingers were pulled out of their mouth, they strained the head after the hand as it was pulled out. They never did this to their own fingers when sucking was interrupted, trying instead to move their own hand back.[12] The self as a body, even in this odd case of conjoining, seems remarkably unified and distinct. The ability to distinguish between self-stimulation and external stimulation has been confirmed in an experimental study where neonates distinguished between their own touching of their cheeks and other people's touch, turning and rooting to the latter but not the former.[13] Even in utero the movements of the hands and feet of the foetus show basic intentionality and some action tendencies which persist in post-natal life.[14]

Confusion between self and non-self? I don't think so. Some kind of self-awareness is clearly present—not only an awareness of the body as distinct from the physical space and objects around them and of the actions of the self as distinct from the actions of things and people around them, but some awareness that it is *their* hand that they are watching or their actions leading to sounds and that *they* can act to increase visual movement or modulate sounds. Such abilities are now generally accepted as reflecting a subjective awareness of the body and its capacities. They are given different names: some call it "the machinery of the self," some call it tactile-kinaesthetic awareness of self, some subjective self-awareness, some the "core self," and some an awareness of the bodily or "ecological" self. What is important to note here is that few would claim complete dualism in self-other or self-world differentiation; instead, it is the self-in-relation-to-the-world which is known by the neonate. Nonetheless, some degree of adualism, at least in terms of relatedness, may in fact be a feature of all bodily actions, even in adulthood. How does this awareness of a distinction between self and the world and between self and other, and this awareness of the coherence and continuity of the self, develop further? Once again, a multiplicity of names is given to further developments in self-consciousness, in general distinguishing this early ability from later objective or conceptual self-awareness. Where the initial "machinery of the self" is believed to reflect subjective self-awareness from a first-person orientation to the self, the later developments are believed to reflect an awareness of self as an object in itself and to others from a third-person orientation to the self.

But there is a problematic omission here of a second-person awareness of self, a self first known as an object through experiencing oneself as an attentional and emotional object to another. Evidence of self-conscious affectivity from very early infancy suggests that "objective self-consciousness" develops far earlier than suggested within emotional engagements with people in which actions and reactions to others are experienced and used in play. The infant's awareness of others as attentive and intentional beings cannot be considered apart from her awareness of herself as the object of this attentional and intentional directedness. To experience your looking at me, for example, is also to be aware that there is a me to be looked at; to experience that you like me is to be aware that I am; to experience your liking for what I do is to be aware of what I do. This "me" that the infant is aware of in these simple engagements exists and *develops* within this relation to other people. It is contained within simple dialogues, existing as a relational entity in the perception of the other's psychological gaze. As the infant's perceptions of others' psychological existence become more complex, so also does the consciousness of the visibility of self to others become more complex.

Self-Conscious Affects: Emotions of the Visibility of the Self to Others

Self-conscious affectivity at its simplest can be thought of as those feelings and reactions in the engagement between people which arise from being *seen* or *known* by another person (or being thought to be seen or known); they arise from the visibility of one self to another. I will focus on two such reactions to "being seen" by another: shyness and showing off.

Blushing or bashful smiles or coy sideways looks, when they are spontaneous reactions to the heightened visibility of the self to another person, can be charming. This can be seen in the fact that romantic play and flirtatious displays often involve exaggerated or stereotypical versions of these reactions. Old-fashioned heroines, for example, may have formalised them in the traditionally recommended lowering of the eyelids on receiving the praise of an admirer, in sidelong (rather than direct) glances, or in the raising of a fan to cover part of the face, or of a kimono sleeve to hide the unstoppable, and too forward, smile. Even today, who amongst us hasn't been charmed by the shy smile of a child, by a tease with which we have succeeded in embarrassing a friend, or indeed by our embarrassment itself when someone we admire unexpectedly pays us a compliment? The charm of self-consciousness may lie precisely in this visibility of a previously hidden self—in seeing a self made ambivalent by the awareness of being laid bare by contact with another person. On the other side of the coin of heightened visibility is another emotional action/reaction: pleasure in display of the self, showing off.

One of my students was speaking one day about wanting to go on the television show *Pop Idol* in which aspiring members of the public are put to the test as performers. I asked, "Do you sing?" And she said, "Yeah . . . ?" cautiously, at which point one of her friends asked her to sing a particular song. The normally bold and teasing Sam turned shy in one second with her body curving away, smiling but half turned away, shaking her head "no." The demand on her was to reveal something about herself, a something she found too intimate or threatening in that moment for some reason. Her response was a sort of hiding of herself from those present, both body and face turning away a bit, although with some positive affect, still smiling, and refusing to reveal what was asked. No one would hesitate to call this a self-conscious emotional reaction; the self was attempting to conceal something about itself from the attention of others. Imagine in a similar situation that Sam had remained her ebullient self and had launched into a particularly loud and boisterous song—something slightly more than the situation called for. That, too, would have been a self-conscious reaction, although with the opposite intention and effect, the self would have been seeking particularly to show itself to others. In fact, Sam's reaction when I hesitantly showed her this text was of this sort—undisguised pleasure in being revealed, noticed, and written about! Reactions such as these are familiar everyday features of our interpersonal relations and certainly a regular aspect of interactions with children.

In these two kinds of acts the individual is seeking, in however simple a way, to protect/conceal/withdraw the self from psychological contact with the other, or to enhance/put forward/open the self to this psychological contact. In some sense, all psychological contact involves the mutual visibility of selves, as well as a continual play of selves within a frame of raising and lowering visibility. However, in both shyness and showing off, the focus of the play is more directly on visibility per se than it is, for example, in interchanges such as smiling in response to a greeting, giving in response to a request, complying in response to a command, gazing in response to a call, and so on. It is specifically the visibility of the self to others that is being managed here. There are also other kinds of interchanges in which the visibility of a self is the explicit focus—for example, in evaluating the self according to moral, educational or social standards. But this is an extension of shyness and showing off, of portraying the self positively or attempting to hide it, not just in terms of the positive attentional reactions of others, but in terms of criteria or standards that have been developed by society from such reactions. But let us leave these considerations for the moment and ask first, when and how such actions and reactions develop in infancy. When do infants either act to heighten their visibility themselves, or react by reducing their visibility, to an externally initiated heightening of visibility of their selves?

The Standard Developmental Sequence: A Concept of Self Leads to Self-Conscious Emotions

The standard story about the development of self-conscious emotional reactions comes from cognitive-developmental theorists who argue that these reactions emerge after the development of a concept of self. Darwin observed over a hundred years ago that infants don't blush, an observation since supported by others and used to argue that the child does not actually develop a concept of self until fairly late and certainly not in infancy. Different writers argue for different ages at which this conceptualisation of self occurs: some say that it is at 5 years of age following the development of a "social self," and others that it is at 1½ following the development of mirror self-recognition and a concept of self.[15] Based on the critical assumption that others as psychological beings can only be known through an imagined idea, it is argued that knowing about the self also requires an idea, an "idea of me" as Michael Lewis eloquently expresses it. This idea, it is argued, allows the infant to understand and use the pronoun "I" to describe and refer to the self, to recognise herself in mirrors by instantly matching the self seen in the mirror to the directly experienced self, and permits the rise of new kinds of emotions—secondary emotions as they are called—such as embarrassment, pride, empathy, and jealousy. These emotions reflect the awareness of the self as an object available to the view and attention of others. These dramatic developments are believed to emerge at around 18 months or so in human infants and not at all in most other animals, including most of the primates. Self-consciousness, according to the standard story, is primarily a late-developing conceptual idea, and self-conscious emotions are a response to this idea. Only much later, at around 3 years of age, do infants become able to mentally represent standards and goals, allowing the emergence of further emotions, such as embarrassment at doing something badly or guilt at wrong-doing, which involve the evaluation of the self according to these standards.[16]

The face validity of this argument is high: until there is a self in mind to be conscious about, the infant cannot *feel* self conscious because there is no self to feel conscious *about*. At first sight, the evidence seems to support this view. Michael Lewis and his colleagues found a strong relation between infants recognising themselves in mirrors and showing self-conscious emotional reactions to being over-praised or being asked to perform or to look at oneself in the mirror. Very few infants who failed the mirror self-recognition test showed any embarrassment at these things. If this story holds, then there is a problem with the claim for early other-awareness as well as for any claim of early awareness of self as an object to others!

But there's a problem with this story. If the self can be *experienced* as an object of others' attention (as I argued in the last chapter), there is a route to an awareness of self as object which does not rely on concepts. And the view that an awareness of others must also be mediated through concepts of some kind—third-person views—is problematic for all the reasons discussed so far. There is another reason for questioning the standard view—an empirical one. Self-conscious affectivity does not put in quite as late an appearance on the stage as it seems. Several recent findings have shown the development of jealousy in the middle of the first year.[17] Here I will focus on the emotional reactions of shyness, embarrassment, coyness, and bashfulness, which involve, in my terms, a response to, and a reduction of, the visibility of the self.[18] Using standard behavioural measures, we can see that such reactions arise in the first few months of life, developing in complexity through at least the first few years.

Reducing the Visibility of the Self: Shyness, Coyness, and Embarrassment

Simple shyness or apprehensive withdrawal from "stimuli" is not considered a self-conscious reaction. Rather, it is seen more as a primitive biological phenomenon resulting from the "primary" emotion of fear or wariness, although it has also been argued that embarrassment elicited by exposure is similar to shyness.[19] It is the ambivalent reactions of coyness, bashfulness, and embarrassment which are usually seen as self-conscious because they seem to indicate a much more complex tension between affiliation and avoidance with an implicit acknowledgement of the self that is exposed, and because, generally, they have been shown to occur much later than the simple avoidant reactions of shyness. So, what do we know of such behaviour in the first year of life? First, let's take a quick look at what embarrassment or coyness or positive shyness might look like.

Identifying Embarrassment and Coyness

Three decades ago Beulah Amsterdam published a number of sensitive observations on the self-conscious emotional reactions by toddlers shown to the self in a mirror.[20] She found that toddlers did a number of different kinds of things which could be called self-conscious emotional reactions. For instance, they engaged in preening and self-admiring (giving long, pleased looks at themselves or showing or emphasising to others particular aspects of themselves), and negative reactions (withdrawing from their own gaze and avoiding contact with the self in the mirror). They also sometimes became coy or embarrassed, smiling but averting gaze from themselves, cocking the head to the side, even holding the hands in front of the mouth or hiding the face. Lewis identifies smiling gaze aversion as the key component of embarrassment in toddlers, although additional features are tilting the head and looking up, with a sequence of return of gaze after aversion rather than a staying away of gaze.[21] For identifying embarrassed smiles in adults, two additional cues have been found: the *timing* of the averting of gaze, that is, turning away before the smile begins to fade; and the presence of facial attempts to *suppress* the smile like pressing or twisting of the lips and chewing of the inner cheeks, as well as turning of the face to the side and downwards.[22] For coyness and embarrassed smiles, then, the key expressions we are looking for are smiling with turning gaze and/or head away during the smile, movements of the hands towards the face, and possibly attempts to suppress the smile itself.

This expressive pattern can be seen to occur in embarrassed responses to teasing, in flirtation, in ritualised politeness such as hiding the smile while revealing the eyes by using the wide kimono sleeve, or hiding the teeth with the hand when smiling in the presence of a senior person or stranger, and in the explicit "act shy" behaviour required of brides in some traditional societies.

Coyness in the First Year of Infancy

When my daughter was about 2½ months old and had already been "chatting" to us for a few weeks, she started doing something when I or my mother greeted her. It only lasted about a week, but a typical incident went something like this:

> Her grandmother, sitting in a chair, is holding her face to face on her lap, and says a smiling hello to her; she smiles back but immediately curves her arms in a coy manner near her face, and turns her face away from her grandmother's for a moment, still smiling, then turns back. It seemed as if the greeting was rather too "nice" for her to bear without being briefly overcome.

I was puzzled about these reactions; I could not understand what they meant in terms of her engagement with us. They were not fearful or wary reactions. They reminded me of bashful heroines in Victorian movies (had there been movies at that time) or in Indian films from my childhood. It made no sense (given the theories of self-consciousness) for a 2-month-old to be doing that with adults she was so familiar with.

Some years later I studied this reaction in five other babies, videotaping them at home every week from 2 to 4 months of age in three different kinds of interaction: with their parents, with me as a stranger, and with themselves in front of a mirror. All the babies showed these reactions, though in varying frequencies. These reactions weren't just to me, the stranger, as could be expected if they were signs of simple wariness; they were as often to the mother or to the self in front of a mirror. Sometimes the reactions involved the curving of the arms in front of the face or the chest—and these were very noticeable to the parents. Our lab technician, Dave, who had been copying my videotapes from the study, came in one day with a story when his daughter was just over 8 weeks old. His wife had called him to come and have a look the previous evening, saying, "Here, what's she doing? What's she doing that for?" and showed him their daughter reacting with smiling gaze and head aversions with arms coming up and curving in front of the face. He, of course, knew exactly what she was doing! Similar stories can be found from parents of babies who are older (but still officially too young for these reactions) such as the following from the mother of 8-month-old Rebecca: "she's been doing that with Danny (infant's father) all the time, all day long, until he's beginning to get a complex about it, wondering, you know 'Is she shy of me or something?' "

Sometimes, however, and more so in some infants, they were just fleeting gaze or head aversions accompanying a smile, did not involve any arm movements and could only be seen on slowing down the videotape.[23]

There was no doubt about it—2-month-old infants were producing something very like the coy reactions of 1½-year-olds or even adults. Moreover, they were doing it in situations of "greeting," which made emotional sense to the adults involved as being positive shy or coy reactions to the attentions of others. So what do we make of these behaviours? Clearly, these 2-month-olds are far too young to have any conception of themselves as "objects" in the standard sense, and yet they were reacting to others' attention to themselves in roughly similar ways to older children. The significance of these reactions becomes clearer when we contrast them with other typical reactions at that age to positive greetings from others—fussing, distress, indifference, and, of course, undiluted positiveness. In the context of these different reactions to a "hello" involving mutual gaze and a vocalisation, it is difficult to argue that the "coy" reaction is not an emotional reaction to something that the other has done. But what do they mean in terms of self-consciousness? They cannot be self-conscious emotions in the sense of involving reflective awareness of the self. But if they do involve any emotionality (and it would be hard to argue that they are not emotional reactions at all), what sort of emotionality is it? If they are occurring as a result of some sort of awareness of the other's actions in relation to the self, could we class them as belonging to a simple level of that family of reactions called self-conscious emotions?

Functional and Structural Developments in the Expression of Coyness

One obvious place to look for the meaning of the reactions is the contexts in which they occur: what function are they serving? In adults and older children shy/coy/bashful/embarrassed reactions occur in two groups of contexts: one, in response to attention from others, either undesirable or unexpected or even desired; and two, in response to evaluation (positive or negative), or even the anticipation of evaluation, from others.[24] Adults show embarrassment, for example, on being seen by another person unexpectedly, on being seen by someone they like, on being praised, on being caught in some odd or anti-social act, and so on.[25] In Lewis's studies, toddlers showed embarrassment on being asked to "perform" (sing or dance) in the presence of a stranger, or when they were given positive (excessively positive, in fact) evaluations from strangers about their appearance or clothing. In the 2-month-old infants, in contrast, the embarrassment-like reactions were elicited only in situations of onset of attention (what Dacher Keltner might call failure at privacy regulation, or Michael Leary, unexpected attention) by mutual gaze and "greeting." The reactions were much more likely to occur in the first minute of renewed contact after a break than later on in continued interaction, and they were more likely to accompany the first smile after renewed contact than the second or later smiles. Clearly, the context is not one of evaluation (at least in the adult sense, though in another sense all gaze from another person contains some, and in this case, always positive, evaluation), but merely one of attention.[26] The 2-month-olds' reactions, then, fit appropriately into one of the two contexts for embarrassment displays but not both. They are simpler than the reactions of toddlers and adults, and only half the story, but are they structurally similar to even this half of the story?

A closer look at the structure of the 2-month-olds' coy reactions in comparison to those of toddlers and adults shows two areas of similarity and two of dissimilarity. As with those in older children, the reactions consisted of smiles accompanied by gaze or head aversion (the majority in fact had both gaze and head aversion, and the head movements were more marked, therefore, than in adults) and were also accompanied by arm movements (as in adults and older children). However, the arm movements that the infants showed were movements of the whole body, gross movements of the arms compulsively moving up towards the face, rather than the discrete body touching movements of the hands alone (as in toddlers and adults). They resemble more the impulsive face covering in situations of intimacy that Eibl-Eibesfeldt showed in his photographic records from many cultures.[27] They were not the nervous touching of body, hair, or clothing that reflects, according to Lewis, the person's active focus on the self as a social object. But neither were they reflective of the immobility characteristic of shyness, shame, or fear, nor of the automanipulation characteristic of shyness.[28] What, then, do these arm movements accompanying smiling gaze/head aversions show? In my study, their presence in 25 percent of the averted smiles (as opposed to only 6 percent of ordinary smiles) suggests a link between the two, which could well form the basis of the ritualisation of coyness, flirting, and positive shyness in many cultures using hands covering the face.

The second dissimilarity from embarrassed smiles in adults is the absence of facial attempts to suppress the smile. Smile suppression may well be a feature that develops in the second year, along with the discrete (rather than gross) hand movements. There is no clear literature addressing this issue, but two personal observations illustrate the difference.

I observed my son at 20 months with a mouth contorted in an attempt to suppress a smile, in which his lips were pressed together and puckered, with the smile still visible. In one incident, he called out looking for me from another part of the house; I answered from the verandah where I was sitting with a number of visitors. Hearing my response (and not knowing about the arrival of the visitors), he came into the room and headed towards me with a big smile, saw the visitors, was slightly taken aback, didn't stop smiling but puckered and pressed his lips together and moving more quickly towards me buried his face in my lap (with his back to the visitors); I could then see a broader, unsuppressed smile on his face when he lifted his head slightly. In a second incident a month later, a similar puckered smile (although less broad) was observed when he was asked to sing in front of a visitor. I never noticed such smile suppression again in him.

The embarrassed smile-controls in these two incidents could be explained as an attempt by the child to restore his dignity following an unexpected violation of intimacy (i.e., he was unexpectedly observed by strangers calling affectionately to his mother and smiling) or following a situation of conspicuousness. Smiles often signify a loss of dignity. Photographing traditional non-Westernised adults in India, for example, often leads to severe attempts to suppress smiles and look serious, with chastisement directed to the (Westernised) photographer who tricks them into smiling, and particularly into "showing the teeth." Smile controls may be initiated in order not to show one's feelings to an unfamiliar or unknown audience—either because it is potentially rude to be caught smiling in some situations (in which case unsuccessful smile controls could lead in a circular way to further embarrassment) or because it may be too intimate to smile as well as maintain mutual gaze in certain interpersonal situations.[29]

These infant coy smiles, then, are structurally similar to, but not identical to, the coy smiles described at the end of the first year or later in other studies.[30] As Harriet Oster notes, facial expressions change form with age, but nonetheless show continuities.[31] The differences appear to surround the extent to which the expression is a whole-body and less controlled reaction in early infancy. The change might come from the developing awareness, by at least around 9 months, allowing the control of expressions and their non-genuine use (see the discussion in Chapter 9 on artificial laughs and artificial crying). There is also evidence that the components of coy reactions are available for "use" to some extent even by about 5 months of age, as in the following observation using shyness as a game:

> Rohan, at the end of a successful day spent with a new childminder, is being carried by me while I chatted with the childminder. Chatting to me, the childminder finds herself suddenly distracted by Rohan looking at her and, as soon as he catches her eye, smiling and hiding in my shoulder. Oh hello, she says, then goes back to talking to me. She sees Rohan looking at her again, turns to look at him, he hides his face again. This goes on a few more times, while I am now fascinatedly observing what's going on. He is inviting interaction when the childminder is disengaged, then hiding when she obeys. Rohan's actions seem deliberately game-like, not uncontrolled reactions to intrusive gaze. I never saw this game again.

From about the middle of the first year, infants show considerable skill, and greater control and robustness than that shown at 4 and 5 months, in initiating playful games with others in which this visibility is being used and played with.

> Anyway, I'm usually carrying her when she does it. She starts it off entirely on her own, looks up at the person smiling cheekily, like that, and then dives into my shoulder. And then after a moment if nothing happens, looks up again slowly, same expression and then dives into my shoulder again. It's definitely an invitation to a game. But it's entirely her own invention. . . . And now we respond sometimes joining in and hiding ourselves, (we) sort of do what she's doing (the game dies out after about a month). (Mother of Rebecca, 8 months, interview)

Not only do coy reactions appear a lot earlier than expected, but they seem to follow a course of gradual differentiation and increasingly playful and conscious control.

One other type of response reported by parents—self-conscious refusal to perform on demand—also seems to occur around this time and is relevant here. The picture is incomplete and not entirely clear. We have stories of infants refusing to "wave" or do other new tricks to impress the visitor until the visitor has departed! We also have more subtle stories such as the inhibition of actions (starting to clap and then stopping) at the enthusiastic imitation of everyone around. Something like a self-conscious reaction seems to be occurring, linking others' reactions to specific actions, but clearer micro-genetic data is needed.

What is the dialogue that infants are engaged in with coy reactions? In adults, Keltner lists the following consequences of embarrassment: others' responses consist of laughter, affiliation, liking, trust, forgiveness. All of them are largely positive (although the more destructive aspects of embarrassment are easy to imagine).[32] Parents' perceptions of the infant coy responses are similar: they are perceived as charming and appealing. By 4 months, many parents reported that the infants were doing it particularly noticeably to strangers—at a swimming pool or while in the pushchair out somewhere. The parents' reports lend support to the observation that by 4 or 5 months infants are already *using* the reaction more deliberately as a means of engaging with others. If people perceive it as a positive and an inviting reaction, then they are likely to react to it as such. In the videotaped observations of the reactions when parents noticed it, they usually laughed if the infant was coy. Although their reactions in this study were likely to be confounded by their pleasure at the fact that the infants were performing as I wanted (they knew about the specific purpose of the study), their pleasure was intense. Infants, already sharply aware of the positive attention of others in the first few months of life, are more than likely to be drawn into engagements because of these reactions, and also, it appears, within a few months they are able to use them for initiating engagement. The dialogical meaning of coy reactions then is one of invitation even at 4 months of age. Little wonder then that this type of reaction becomes stereotyped in adults as one of flirtation.

Although they do involve invitations to engagement, these reactions are primarily aimed at reducing the visibility of the self to the other. What about the opposite side of the coin which we mentioned earlier—the deliberate heightening of the visibility of the self in showing off? Showing off the self is much more unambiguously a demonstration of the self and its actions as viewed by others. When does that develop?

Heightening the Visibility of the Self: Showing Off

When do infants attempt to seek to heighten the visibility of themselves to an audience? When do they start preening or self-admiring, as Amsterdam described it? To the self in a mirror, Amsterdam showed that these reactions began at around 14 months of age. But what about in interaction with others? If we look at others (as well as to the self in a mirror) as an audience for the self, are these reactions evident any earlier? We saw from the chapter on understanding attention that active showing off to an audience or doing something unusual, extreme, or clever with the self which actively directs attention to it does not begin until after the middle of the first year. Colwyn Trevarthen uses the French psychologist Wallon's term *prestance* to describe the infant's posturing and stance at around this age. The infant, according to Trevarthen, develops a presence, a self which can be presented to others. And this self is fond of displaying itself and posing and, in other words, showing off.[33]

In two studies we have supported these observations in larger groups of infants. Parents reported infants of 7 and 8 months to be very aware of others' attention to the things they did, to play up to unusual attention, particularly from strangers, by showing off from their repertoire of tricks, and to seek to repeat actions for signs of approval or appreciation. In order to count as deliberate showing off, we needed evidence that the infants were focusing not just on the pleasure of the action itself, but were repeating the action, at least partly, for their effect on others' appreciation. This evidence comes mainly from gaze to others' faces during the repetition and from reports of its decrease when others' attention wanes. The showing off at this age often involved extreme actions, shrill shrieks, squeals, or banging and splashing, as well as some newly learned skills, such as clapping, waving, crawling, and pulling oneself up to a standing position. Three different kinds of showing off are evident in the reports of infant behaviour from 7 months: trying to gain attention to the self by doing odd, extreme, or "silly" things; displaying a repertoire of tricks when already the centre of attention; and trying to perform clever or difficult actions for approval/appreciation.

The following excerpts from interviews with parents give a flavour of the kinds of things infants did *to gain and manipulate attention* and the simple everyday contexts in which these occurred.

Alec's just had lunch and he displayed some strange behaviour. I had been feeding him and he'll stop and take a spoonful of his dinner and then after the spoon has come out he'll start banging his head against the back of his highchair and sticking his tongue out, but still smiling at the same time and watching me. Again, when I bring a spoon up to his mouth he'll stop, take what's off the spoon and start head banging again. (Mother of Alec, 8 months, dictaphone)[34]

Although the mother's reaction to this behaviour is not reported, the infant's focus on the mother's attention to him in general, and his use of his unusual actions in order to manipulate that attention, seem clear.

Infants' *actions when already the centre of attention*, especially attention from strangers, were a rich source of data as the following examples show:

Well, in fact, when I went to the Poly last week. . . . She's really quite shy, and I thought she'd be getting worried about these four strangers coming into the room, but she just sat there beaming at them all, she just sat there holding the stage. I think she kind of knew it was her they were interested in, and far from making a beeline for me, she just sat there. She was a movie star. (Mother of Rebecca, 7 months, interview)[35]

She waves to the lollipop people when she's in the front of her pram, . . . she sits bolt upright and she waves to people as she goes by, and its like the royal wave you know, she does that to get attention and they say "oh aren't you clever" and . . . she claps as if to say "yes I'm a clever girl, I clap." . . . She does it quite a bit now, if you say "clever girl, she'll clap her hands at you or beam at you . . . she'll play with the bricks and you'll say "clever girl" and she'll do it again. . . . I'm trying to get her to build bricks up, but all she does is take them off and run off with them, but if you say "clever girl, clever girl" she'll do it. (Mother of Alice, 11 months, interview)[36]

In addition to the use of actions to get or retain general positive attention, from around 8 months infants also repeated *actions which were deemed "clever"* by those around them, and sought praise for them, looking around for attention when done. Some of these actions involved difficulty in achievement, some were repetitions of successful patterns recently mastered, some of them were idiosyncratic acts, while others were conventional forms of action.

He's rather pleased with himself now that he can crawl and pull himself up on the furniture and he'll crawl across the room and pull himself up on the toy box. . . . And then turn round and bang on the toy box and turn round and look at you and give you a big smile as if to say look at me. Look at what I've done. Very much so, cos its only in the last week he's been pulling himself up on the furniture and, you know, he definitely looks round to see, look at you and smile at you . . . ." The mother reports that she responds to such things by saying "clever boy. Look at you" etc. (Mother of James, 8 months, interview)[37]

What does such showing off tell us about self-conscious emotionality? First of all, do these actions reveal an emotion at all? There is little doubt about the emotionality of these behaviours. The infants are evidently acting intentionally in a conscious sense, selecting their actions for repetition with immense sensitivity to situations and to persons. They reveal many different signs of emotion in their faces, voices, and bodies; the expression itself is intensely positive and anticipatory of the response of the other. What sort of emotion we want to call it is another issue, but we will come to that.

But if infants are aware of the visibility of the self to others at 2 months, judging from their attempts to reduce that visibility in coy reactions, why don't they also, at least sometimes, attempt to heighten that visibility? One answer is simple: we haven't looked. Parents do describe infants of that age as sometimes "showing off," although in a different way from that of 7- and 8-month-olds. Here is an example at 13 weeks, transcribed from a videotape in which I had annotated in the inside of the sleeve the counter numbers of all noteworthy episodes, and this one, with no academic reason for it at the time, was marked as "showing off"!

> I sit beside Rohan and call to him for a chat. He is busy looking around at his sister and father and their actions. Turns to me on my initiation and responds with smiles and coos. I tickle him and talk playfully, he responds with near laughs and smiles. My energy seems to wear out and I quieten down, but still looking at him. I stop tickling him. After a brief pause, eyes still on me with a pleasant expression, Rohan initiates a long effortful vocalisation to me with protruding lips and pauses. I respond with a slightly querying tone "Noooo!? Don't you pretend!" then resume my tickling, saying "What're you trying to say? What're you trying to say?" with a rising intensity. He responds once again with cooing, and a smile, but with lower intensity, and then looks around.

He was in a very positive mood, not boisterous but pleasant and interested in everything around him, and was willing to engage. His long vocalisation could be described as a kind of performing, not a showing off in terms of repeating actions, but a simple heightening of visibility. That it occurred during a pause in the intensity of my efforts and was an initiation by the infant rather than a response to my immediate act is evident. The effortful, trilling vocalisation seems to have been done in order to regain my attention and engagement. He was not, however, keen to intensify the engagement, as was evident when I responded to his effort, but he smiled and then looked around elsewhere. More data are urgently needed, however, to explore this further.

What is the dialogue that infants are engaged in when showing off? The reactions of others to acts of showing off are generally positive and part of the showing off itself. The pleasure and appreciation of others, then, serves to define for the infant the actions that they are endeavouring to achieve and implement. In the instances reported here, the achievements of the self are simple ones, not judged against standards external to the dyad or triad. Much later, these achievements will become defined in terms of the standards of a larger group and will be spelt out in detachable terms. For the moment, however, the infant is basking in the immediate approval of specific simple achievements. The self is beginning to be an active elicitor of social appreciation for itself.

Reducing and Heightening Visibility of the Self in Autism

If it is the case that others' appreciation and attention are available to the infant very early in life, what happens in cases where children are known to have difficulty in perceiving such emotional qualities in others? What sort of awareness of self as an object of attention and appreciation do such children show? Autism provides a case in point. If the argument so far in this chapter about the awareness of the self as an object to others in simple emotional engagements is valid, then one would expect that children with autism would show deficits in terms of both displays of coyness and displays of showing off. Regardless of whether they can recognise themselves in mirrors (which previous research shows that they can, at the appropriate developmental age), they should nonetheless show different reactions to being attended to, such as not recognising or responding to the positiveness of the appreciation. In one study, we compared the performance of children with autism and children with Down syndrome (DS) matched in developmental age on the mirror test with reactions to themselves in a mirror.

What we found confirmed our expectation and raised some new questions. The children with autism passed the mirror test by the appropriate developmental age, as did the children with DS, but they showed very different reactions to themselves in mirrors, though they were all fascinated by mirrors. While the children with DS spent the majority of their time looking at themselves or at other people, the children with autism spent more of their time looking at things or the room reflected in the mirror. Even when they did look at themselves or at others in the mirror, what they did *to* the self or the other was very different. They tended to treat the person in the mirror as an interesting object, studying and playing with angles of reflection. The children with DS, on the other hand, tended to treat the person in the mirror as a partner for communication or as an audience for performance. These differences in reaction to the self in the mirror bore no relation to the children's passing or failing of the mirror test. For example,

> Maria approaches the mirror running, smiles into it, looking at herself, then at the observer, then says "Hello Mum," still looking in the mirror, then lies down on the carpet with her chin on her hands and her face about 4 inches from the mirror, smiling, and watching herself moving. Within a short time she says "hello" to herself, then starts to recite Humpty Dumpty, all the while looking and smiling at herself. Maria, 3 years, with DS, passed the mirror test.[38]

> Tommy looks at the mirror, smiling and excited, and leans close to his face and talking incessantly and happily, holds the mirror and tilts it side to side looking at some reflections in it. Still smiling and talking he then bangs his head lightly in the mirror several times, laughing, and ignoring his mother's protests. Tommy, 4 years, with autism, passed the mirror test.[39]

Furthermore, there were indeed no cases of self-conscious emotional reactions to the self or to others in the presence of the mirror by the autistic children, while some of the children with DS did show these reactions.

> Carl looks in the mirror, leans close and smiling broadly puts his face next to his face in the mirror; still smiling he turns his face and looks at his mother in the mirror; he then leans back and points to himself in the mirror. His mother says "Are you in there?." He looks at himself, smiling, and claps his hand over his mouth. Carl, 3 years, with DS, passed the mirror test.[40]

Indeed, in some intriguing experimental studies Peter Hobson and his student Gayathri Chidambi have tried to create a setup to elicit coy reactions. They tried it on me once (probably to give me a taste of my own medicine). An approaching teddy bear looked first at some objects and then at me, and I was asked questions about what he was doing in increasingly teasing and intimate tones as he approached me. Although I knew absolutely what reactions were expected, I could not help but respond with smiling embarrassment to the approaching teddy bear with that intimate voice. In their studies, they compared the reactions of children with autism and children with other learning difficulties. The latter reacted largely as I did; the children with autism, although showing some signs of smiling and gaze aversion, related to and re-engaged less with the experimenter.[41]

Parents' reports about emotional reactions to the visibility of the self in interactions with others (rather than in mirrors) in everyday lives showed a similar lack in the children with autism compared to the children with DS. Showing off was rare in autism, though not totally absent. And when it did occur, it was marked by a formulaic repetition of acts rather than flexibility and sensitivity to attention. What do these differences tell us about self-consciousness? Possibly that the children with autism saw and treated the mirror-self as an object, while the children with DS saw the self as an audience. Although they were quite capable of showing negative reactions to others' attention (as reported by parents) and sometimes even positive reactions to attention, the children with autism showed none of this in the mirror to the self. The mirror test didn't distinguish the children with autism and those with DS and does not seem to tell us as much about the presence and awareness of a sense of self as does the *way* in which children treat themselves in the mirror. The children with autism were clearly able, from the results of the mirror test, to recognise themselves as objects. The difference, however, seems to lie in *what sort of objects* they saw themselves as—objects as viewed by a psychological other versus objects as existing in a detached view. It would seem that while the children with autism didn't have such a problem with a third-person orientation to the self, they did indeed have problems with a second-person orientation. This finding supports the idea of a dissociation in autism between two aspects of self-consciousness—the emotional and the conceptual.[42]

Implications for Theories of Self-Conscious Emotions: An Alternative Story

Let's consider first whether coy reactions at 2 months can be called self-conscious affects. Both functionally and structurally, these reactions are simpler and narrower (i.e., they occur in more limited contexts and in less differentiated patterns) than those elicited in older children or adults. The absence of smile controls until—as far as we know, 18 months—suggests that the 2-month-olds' coy reactions are not deliberate attempts to hide the smile per se. They are impulsive global reactions to the positive attention of others. The nature of the gross arm movements also supports this interpretation; they reflect a global whole-body reaction rather than a specific focus on hiding a part of the self. Nonetheless, they are attempts to briefly hide from the gaze of the other. The similarity of reaction to that at older ages and the evident continuity in its development are striking and cannot be dismissed as irrelevant or trivial to self-conscious displays. So is it an emotional reaction? It is not a reflex or a fixed action pattern, nor is it a learned avoidance response. It *is* a reaction with distinct emotional tone. Perhaps the easiest solution is to describe it as belonging to the family of reactions of embarrassment/coyness/bashfulness rather than to call it an emotion in itself; this has the advantage of allowing it a vaguer boundary and content without denying its affectivity.

The evident continuity in self-conscious reactions cannot be explained—despite any amount of *decalage*—with the hypothesis that the "idea of me" is a prerequisite for self-conscious emotional reactions. One way of explaining these data and the changes in them with age is to reject the hypothesis that a conceptual "idea of me" is necessary for such emotional reactions. We could argue instead that these emotions are present from at least 2 months, reflecting not a concept of self but a different kind of awareness of self as an object of others' attention. The self as an object here is an experienced self, understood only in-relation-to-the-other. By 4–5 months, the non-impulsive use of the reactions in initiating interactions with strangers shows that the reactions are already differentiated to some degree, suggesting an awareness of a differentiated shy/coy self from an available-for-interaction-and-attention-other. Parallel developments at this age—a more controlled reaching for things, a clearer and more sustained interest in hand watching, and a greater flexibility in attentional acts—support this interpretation.[43] This awareness of self-as-experienced-object gradually differentiates to include a broader range of situations in which the self's visibility is perceived, as well as a more differentiated understanding of specific aspects of self which are available to others.

What about showing off? It, too, is affectively charged. However, is the emotion involved akin to pride in response to or anticipation of achievement or praise? Although these simple achievements which the infants are showing off with are not the same as the evaluations in terms of detached standards which Michael Lewis argues develop around 3 years of age, they are nonetheless achievements and known by the child as achievements in the eyes of others as well as of the self (in the case of the "difficult" actions). Standards in terms of objectively existing criteria for good and bad may indeed not become available to the child until 3 years of age. But markers for achievement *within engagement* seem available from at least the latter part of the first year in the form of appreciation from others for specific acts and in terms of success following difficulty. Use of these acts to re-elicit such appreciation cannot be ignored in the context of the development of a self which seeks to present itself in a certain way. From this perspective, it could be argued that showing off—or pride-like affect—is present within interpersonal engagements from the second half of the first year.

There appear to be strong continuities between these early affective reactions and later forms of self-conscious emotion such as shame and pride. Early positive shyness and showing off serve behavioural regulatory functions (serving to increase or decrease distance from the attentive agent, reducing or increasing "exposure"), social regulatory functions (communicating self as vulnerable and appealing or as competent and dominant), and internal regulatory functions (modulating arousal, aiding in acquisition of knowledge of self in relation to other). They reveal an awareness of the self as an object of others' attention and as an agent for eliciting others' attention and an appreciation of the other as attending to the self with positive regard. They show typical behavioural and possibly physiological reactions. The difference between the early and the later forms lies in the extent to which the self is reflexively thought about. However, the existence of these continuities suggests that, while conceptions about the self (and about the other) are yet to develop, the emotions themselves are in large measure already present in early infancy. They are rooted in perceptions of the others' attention and emotion towards the self rather than in thoughts about the self. By the end of the first year, infants seem to become aware of these perceptions not just as directed to the self globally, but as directed to things *done* by the self.

Since there is no evidence that conceptualisation of the self develops any earlier than about 18 months, the direction of effect proposed by cognitive-developmental theory must be challenged. The "secondary" emotions seem to be secondary neither in terms of developmental age nor in terms of derivativeness. The case for a reversal of the direction of effect—that is, that self-conscious affects *lead to* rather than *result from* a concept of self, which has been made by developmental psychologists such as Carroll Izard and Peter Hobson— seems strong.[44] This reversed direction of effect means that the occurrence and meaningfulness of these emotions must be crucial in shaping self-awareness. How might this work? The answer lies in a second-person engagement and experiencing of the other.

Commonplace in early (and later!) interpersonal interactions is a continual ebb and flow of increasing and decreasing visibility of one or other of the partners. Most of these changes in visibility involve some minimal level of affect. Some of them, however, involve clear forms of affect such as embarrassment at being praised, coyness at being greeted, pleasure in receiving appreciation, or pride in overcoming a difficulty. Consider the following sequences:

> She approaches and says hello, I look up with a smile, she compliments my appearance, I drop my gaze smilingly, she changes the subject.
>
> He comes up close and greets her, smiling, she is startled, looks up and smiles and turn away briefly, then steps back and talks about the weather.
>
> He smiles and turns away coyly when she speaks to him, she is charmed by the reaction and laughs lightly.
>
> She sees the appreciation in his face and confidently cracks a joke, he laughs, she cracks another one.
>
> He struggles and fixes the clasp on the suitcase and looks up at her, she raises her eyebrows in appreciation and he stands upright, pleased.

These affective interchanges make one point very clear: the individual's awareness of the self is inextricably embedded in the awareness of the other. The affects of positive shyness and showing off, therefore, must involve a consciousness of the self-in-relation-to-other and might be better labelled self-other-conscious affects. They perform both a regulatory and a constitutive role in interpersonal interactions. They are clearly helpful in achieving a comfortable balance of affective tension both within and between individuals, and they define and redefine the people who are thus engaged. They change within the engagement, from moment to moment, the nature of their engagement and the nature of the individuals themselves, thus changing the process of self and other awareness. First, in order to become aware of the self (or the other) the infant must also become aware of their affective aspects. In other words, the self (and the other) must be known to each other as affective creatures. Second, more importantly, it is *through* the medium of these affective states that the infant becomes aware of her self (or of the other). So the infant's perception of the other is "through the self's feeling for the other," and the perception of the self is "through the other's feeling for the self." This is true of any affective state that the infant is in, or perceives the other person to be in, during interaction. But it is particularly true of self-conscious affective states: to be joyfully aware of someone's appreciation or shyly aware of someone's attention directly influences the awareness we develop of the self or of the other in that interaction. In other words, the self (and the other) become known through the experience of the affects. The infant, then, is faced with the task of becoming aware of a self and of an other who often manifest affective reactions and who are affected by each other *while* experiencing these affects. The idea that self-conscious affects arise after and because of the development of a concept of self seems to be to put the cart before the horse. Neither in terms of chronology nor in terms of a plausible explanatory story do we need to adopt that position. A simpler and more fitting explanation would be to see self-conscious affects as leading to (both because of chronological sequence and because of their influence upon) the development of a concept of self.

However, what of the case of autism? Clearly, these children show evidence of a concept of self; they pass the mirror self-recognition test, they refer to themselves (albeit with some pronominal confusion in their language), but they do not show the kind of self-conscious affects described above. This could on the face of it be interpreted as evidence against the reversed direction of effects suggested above. Alternatively, the sense of self which children with autism are reported to develop could be seen as exemplifying the inadequacies of the developmental route suggested by cognitive-developmental theory. They do indeed develop a concept of self, but one which has certain deficits. If a sense of self is developed without experiencing or perceiving the kinds of self-conscious affects discussed here (involving a positive heightening or reducing of the visibility of the self), as must often be the case in autism, that sense of self cannot include those aspects of self or other and must have developed without the medium of experiencing those affects. The concept of self these children are developing must in respect of affects be a bystander concept; they are conceiving of the self and of the other without the advantage of feeling what the self and the other in typical development can feel towards each other. Literal heightening and reducing of the visibility of the self are unproblematic in autism—the attraction of peep-bo (peekaboo) with accompanying affect is well documented in children with autism. Similarly, the presence of what might be called negative self-consciousness, or distressed avoidance of the gaze or attention of others, has been documented in autism. This suggests that it is not a problem of literal perspectives on themselves that is impaired, or that there is no awareness of the self as an object of others' attention. It seems that the capacity to feel self-conscious affects in positive engagement is what is impaired. A concept of self can thus be developed with or without prior experience of self-conscious affects; however, quite different consequences ensue for each.

William James wrote that his search for consciousness left him only with the objects which entered into consciousness. The more he tried to catch consciousness, the less he could (despite a Cartesian confidence that the separate existence of the inner world cannot be doubted). "Whenever I try to become sensible of my thinking activity as such, what I catch is some bodily fact, an impression coming from my brow, or head, or throat, or nose."[45] Similarly, being self-conscious leaves us not with images of the self, but instead with images of the things and people that stirred the "self-conscious" feelings or thoughts and of their bodily or reflective attitudes towards the self. We might better, therefore, talk of self-other-conscious affects whether we refer to infants or to adults.

"We are 'seen' when our feelings are understood, or when something that is meaningful to us is empathically felt by the other person. . . . Touching another's felt experience," the relationship manuals suggest, can disarm us.[46] In shyness, the infant is revealing having been touched by being seen. And the recipient of the shyness is the toucher, the person who has seen but who then gets touched by the infant's affect. Within a sensitive relationship, positive shyness can work dramatically to deepen intimacy. Showing off, with its lower degree of vulnerability, is much less moving and deepening of intimacy, although it, too, can touch the adult with its evidence of caring for one's approval. In another sense, however, showing off genuinely is the other side of the coin of shyness: it reveals a confidence in taking the risk of rejection. Why is it significant that infants are capable of managing intimacy and attraction in relations with others from so early in life? Clearly, it matters for survival. The appeal of infants to adults is evidently not just in static displays of baby-facedness; they also have to do something to hold us. And this something could be the way in which they not only engage with us, but show that they themselves are engaged with us through demonstrations of positive shyness and show that they want to impress us—through demonstrations of showing off.

Summary and Conclusions

These data from the first year of infancy pose a challenge to the idea that what have been called self-conscious emotions are the result of the development of a concept of self. Embarrassment-like displays are evident from far too early in development in appropriate contexts, and develop in systematic differentiation of the display as well as the context, to be dismissed as mere biological phenomena. Displays akin to pride and preening are, similarly, evident from well before the end of the first year. It seems that the emotions typically called self-conscious are rooted in perceptions of the others' attention and emotion rather than in thoughts about the self. Since there is no evidence that conceptualisation of the self develops any earlier than 18 months, the direction of effect proposed by cognitive-developmental theory must be challenged. The case made by some developmental psychologists such as Carroll Izard and Peter Hobson that the so-called secondary emotions are in fact the primary movers in the development of conceptualisation of the self seems more plausible.[47] The occurrence and meaningfulness of these emotional expressions in interpersonal engagement are likely to be crucial in shaping the developing "idea of me" as well as in shaping the continuing development of these emotions.

Self-conscious emotions of these kinds can, therefore, be argued to exist in simple form from early in life. Such an argument not only makes better sense of the data of embarrassment-like displays and showing off presented here, but also of evidence for an early understanding of self as seen and matched with that which is kinaesthetically experienced.[48] A continuity in engagement rather than a concept-based disconnection in the development of self-conscious emotions seems evident.

Even if we accept that these "self-conscious" emotions are evident much earlier in life than cognitive-developmental theory allows, we still have not addressed their significance for consciousness of the self. The emotions expressed in early infancy could well be primary movers for the development of awareness of the self, but do they actually show objective self-awareness? The infants' actions and emotions seem more easily described as resulting from a consciousness of *other*, rather than of *self*. In all the cases discussed here, of coyness, of showing off, and even of evidence of early empathy and jealousy, it is manifestly not the *self* that is the object of the infant's attention but the other. The reactions may be better renamed "other-conscious emotions." The awareness of self as object could then be left where it is generally held to be, that is, that it emerges in the second year, except that the development of consciousness of self and of other are almost universally deemed inseparable.[49] What does this actually mean? It means that the self is an intangible and constantly moving point of flux; in the process of constant moving and engaging with the world of other people, it is constantly being re-shaped as an entity in relation and is gradually building up awareness of itself in these relations. The self is a dialogic entity, existing only in relation and therefore knowable only as a relation.[50] Other-consciousness, therefore, is inseparable from self-consciousness, and perhaps both should be called self-other-consciousness.

CHAPTER 8

Playing with Intentions

. . . to grasp the quality of a person's action is to have also the quality of his strivings and thoughts. . . . The paramount fact about social interaction is that the participants stand on common ground, that they turn toward one another, that their acts interpenetrate and therefore regulate each other.

Solomon Asch, *The Problem of Human Interaction*[1]

I had been looking for material to liven up a class on language development when I accidentally videotaped the following interaction. Shamini was almost 9 months old at the time, and about two weeks before she had started successfully offering and giving (actually releasing) things to others. She (and the family) really enjoyed the exchange of little objects; it was a great step forward and was always accompanied by that ubiquitous English word "ta." It was a very ordinary interaction for the family at that time, but it changed the way I saw things, not only in relation to my understanding of how we understand intentions, but also in relation to the role of playfulness in human engagement.

She stretches out her arm once again to her father holding out the little biscuit, her eyes on his face, watchful, a slight smile on her face. He obediently (but perhaps now wanting to get on with his dessert) stretches his arm out for it again. As his hand starts to approach she pulls hers back, smiling more and wrinkling her nose. He is surprised and laughs, saying "Give me, gimme, gimme!" and reaches further forward for it. She pulls it back further, smiling. He withdraws his arm, turns away. Her eyes have never left his face. She stretches her arm towards him again, offering the biscuit, watching his face with a half smile; as he reaches out in response she quickly whips it back.[2]

She seemed to be not only anticipating her father's intention—that he would seek to take the object if she proffered it—but herself *inviting* that intentional act and, with forethought, *setting him up* for failure by withdrawing her offer as soon as he reached for it. She seemed to be deliberately playing with his expectation that she would give him the object. She seemed to have no problem in predicting and manipulating her father's intentions; it was he who was fooled by *her* intention! How did she do it? It isn't always as easy as this to grasp what other people are intending to do and to coordinate your own actions with theirs so skillfully.

Temple Grandin, an exceptionally talented and creative engineer who is autistic, once described herself to Oliver Sacks as feeling like an anthropologist on Mars. Of her childhood she reported sensing that there was "something going on between the other kids, something swift, subtle, constantly changing—an exchange of meanings, a negotiation, a swiftness of understanding so remarkable that sometimes she wondered if they were all telepathic." As an adult she became aware of the existence of these social signals, but only inferred them, not being able to actually perceive them or to actually participate in this "magical communication."[3] For most of us, the mysteries of intentionality and communication that she experiences are themselves a mystery. How can she *not* be able to perceive others' meanings and signals and *not* be able to participate in communication with them? Perhaps the closest most of us will have ever come to such an experience is as children in a new school where all the rules are different, or on holiday in a very foreign culture when many of the gestures and actions of the people make no sense.

Even in the early months, it seems that the interpersonal world of typically developing infants is nothing like this: they not only seem *not* to find other people's actions puzzling or alien, but seem to be able to act in response to them pretty confidently and unthinkingly. Even newborns (assuming they are well and alert) seem to be able to find *some*thing in the other's actions that has meaning enough for them to be able to respond to. Neither the world of gravity, solidity, and energy nor the world of people's actions, emotions, and communication seems to be opaque or alien even to very young infants. How does this happen? How does the infant make sense of what people are doing, of their intentions? Why are intentions so easy for some to understand and so hard for others? And why has psychology found questions about intentions so troubling?

In this chapter I am going to explore these questions through looking at what infants actually *do* with other people's intentions, both in everyday life and in experimental situations. First, I will ask what are intentions: how should we think about them? It is customary in psychology to think about intentions as hidden behind movement, as mental plans about achieving goals. Such a definition is problematic, not only because it is unremittingly dualist, but also because it makes it difficult to explain how people actually engage with other people's intentions if they have to "attribute" and guess others' intentions all the time. I will argue that it is better to think about intentions as transparent within engaged perception. Adopting an "object-directed" definition of intention, I suggest that it is helpful to think of three features of intentional action: their perceivability in movement, their meaningfulness in context, and their engage-ability in action. Second, I will ask what infants actually *do* with other people's intentions and will describe the prevalence of five kinds of actions-with-others'-intentions that are commonly observable during the first year or two of infancy: imitating them, helping them, obeying them, detecting disruptions in them, and deliberately disrupting them. Third, I will ask how the awareness of other people's intentions develops. I am going to suggest that it can only be through engagement and play—a process of grasping intentions that does not stop in infancy and childhood but continues throughout our lives. Intentions as conceptual schemas—in the third-person—are useful to explain actions when we have problems understanding them, but that does not appear to be the way in which infants or adults typically and fluently grasp others' intentions.

How Should We Think about Intentions?

So, how should we think of intentions? Definitions abound. The dominant tendency in psychology, leaning on philosophers such as Brentano, is to define intentions in terms of goal-directedness. Intentions are seen as the intending individual's mental representations of desired (and therefore non-present) situations. While widely used, this rather individualistic definition is neither the only one around nor unproblematic. One obvious difficulty with it is that by, as it were, driving intentions underground, they become largely unobservable (and ultimately unknowable), leading to the danger of near theological debates about the timing of the entry of intention into the baby's body and the entry of awareness of intentions into the baby's mind. Another difficulty is that this focus on intentions as representations makes it difficult to explain how they *develop* and, even more so, how the *awareness* of other people's intentions develops.[4] Most psychologists share the intuition that having intentions and being aware of them in others is linked. Commenting on such a link made by James Mark Baldwin over a century ago, David Olson, in introducing a recent volume on developing theories of intentions, suggests that understanding intentions involves a dialectic between one's awareness of one's own intentions and one's awareness of others. However, the sociality of this process in this account appears to be an interpretive sociality: the outward aspects of other people's behaviour become meaningful through projection, through an attribution from the experiences of the self. As Olson puts it, "Third-person and first-person perspectives on behaviour are thereby synthesised."[5] Intentional actions defined in terms of mentally represented goals may only ever be grasped by others in this way.

A less dis-embodied and individualistic alternative developed within French phenomenology and favoured by more systems-based and ecological approaches focuses on *object*-directedness. This approach allows an explanation of how the developing "organism" can perceive intentional actions *as* intentional and therefore can engage with them without having to "attribute" or project intentions on to "outward aspects of behaviour." Taking sociality and the "other" seriously in the awareness of intentions is crucial. But the "other" as I have argued, is not a singular entity: the difference between second-person engagements and third-person observations is as necessary for explaining how the awareness of intentions develops, as it was for explaining the developing awareness of attention. Other people's intentions may be perceivable within direct engagement not merely through a synthesis of first-person experience and third-person perception, but through the emotional/perception/proprioception of their intentions in the second person.

Frequently, in developmental psychology, we tend to think of intentions as being something like "plans" inside people's heads which are going to be implemented in action and are aimed at meeting desires or achieving goals. It is clear why we think this way: there is something of a future-ness—a not-yet quality—to intentions, which the notion of plans seems to capture. But focusing on plans can mislead us. For a start, understanding plans can be really quite hard: even 3-year-olds fail at simple questions that ask them to differentiate "intending-to-do" from actually "doing" something.[6] For instance, shown simple cartoons of one child on a swing and another running towards an empty swing, or one child painting and another approaching an easel, 3-year-olds (but not 4-year-olds) failed to answer correctly questions such as "Which child is gonna/wants to swing (or paint)?" The idea of an intention for an action which hasn't yet happened seems (in these experiments) to be very difficult for the pre-school child to grasp. This is, of course, in complete contrast to young infants' performance in everyday interactions where, as we shall see, they seem easily able to anticipate, predict, and manipulate intentional actions that haven't yet happened. Something is seriously amiss in these apparent contradictions. Perhaps most problematically, thinking about intentions as plans gets us thinking about them as quite separate from their implementation—the intention as quite distinct from the action. But intentions often emerge *during* action (thus tying them inextricably together in terms of origins and causes) and are often negotiated *between* people (thus dislodging them from inside any one person's head). Nor are plans necessarily opaque: even something as obscure as a plan to propose marriage, for instance, is potentially perceivable by other people if they could only see the buying of the ring, the booking of a restaurant, the anxious pacing before the event, and so on (at least in old-fashioned proposals).

Given that we are interested in the early awareness of other people's intentions, I have deliberately opted for a definition in terms of object-directedness and look at intentional *action*. It makes intentions not only *perceivable* and fundamentally *contextual,* but also *engage-able* with by other people. First, let's have a look at *why* intentions ought to be perceivable and *how* they might be.

Perceivability

Intentions *ought* to be perceivable in their patterns of movement. Why? For two related reasons. One, however we think of them, whether as mental representations leading to action or as actions themselves, intentions must bear lawful relations to the constraints of the body, to the world around the body, and to the object to which they are directed. The intention to approach someone must involve a particular pattern of action that alters distance between them, as must the intention to kiss or turn away or even glance at. The intention to reach for something or to give something or to take something, unless one is deliberately being deceptive, has to have a systematic relation between the intending person, the object, and the recipient. Such lawful relations between the intentional action and its object can be perceived; they do not need to be inferred. Whether they are perceived accurately or meaningfully depends on their relevance to the perceiving in-dividual's body, capabilities, and experience. Two, if we are to explain the emergence of intentions in development or even in evolution, interpersonal intentions must be—and must have been—perceived by others in order to elicit a response. If other members of the species could not perceive them, it makes a mystery of why they evolved at all. And if we want to explain how infants make sense of, respond to, and play with other people's intentional actions from very early in life (as we shall see later on in this chapter), as-suming the perceivability of intentions makes sense.

But are they perceivable? And in what ways? What do we know about the forms and lawful relations of intentional actions and their perceiv-ability? How are they specified in patterns of movement and transparent to perception? The five perceivable features of intentional actions that I iden-tify as important overlap with some of the criteria that might emerge from a goal-directed definition of intentions (such as persistence, waiting for a re-sponse the use of rational or direct means to achieve an end, evidence of surprise, evidence of preference, the separation of means and ends in play as well as problem solving, and so on). The aim here is to focus on the per-ceivability of intentional actions and on features that often get omitted from studies assuming goal-directed definitions. They are neither exhaustive nor exclusive as descriptors of intentional action, but they will prove useful for thinking about infant experience of others' actions and for trying to draw distinctions between that which they (or we) may or may not perceive at different times.

These five features of intentional actions are *directedness, singularity, shape, deliberateness,* and *expectation of change.*

Directedness to Objects

Within philosophy, intentions are often defined as being "about" some-thing; they have an intentional (that is, mental) "object." The manifest ob-jects of intentional action (i.e., objects in the world rather than the philo-sophical "Intentional" objects) may be inanimate things, they may be other people, or they may be the self.[7] To understand an intentional action, as it seemed necessary for understanding attention in Chapter 6, it would be a good bet that we must recognise its object; otherwise, as in the case of at-tention, we risk ending up in the rather dodgy territory of separating the intention from its content, its *that* from its *what*. In fact, objects might be necessary not only to elicit intentional actions but to make intentional actions meaningful to others. A "reach" into space may be perceived as an odd and incomprehensible movement (how *can* it be meaningful as a *reach*) until we see that there is something there to reach for. Just as objects inform our awareness of others' attention, objects might inform our awareness of others' intentions.

Indeed, there is evidence, at least by 12 months of age, that infants show different affective responses when actions are performed without "objects." In an experiment using a fairly typical paradigm of presenting infants with direct or detouring actions towards an object, Henry Wellman and his colleagues found that those infants who looked surprised when someone reached for an object in a funny, roundabout way (as if around an imaginary barrier) *didn't* look surprised when the same action was performed but without an object present at all! Somehow, the recognition of relation between the reach and its object seemed to specify the (absurdity of the) intention of the reach, while, when there was no object at all, the action ceased to be either surprising or absurd. This makes perfect sense (in its roundabout way).

The perception of a psychological connectedness between an action and a "thing" actually seems to be present remarkably early in development. In a series of marvellous studies, Amanda Woodward showed that this connectedness is present well before the onset of language, by about 5 to 6 months. Presented with video clips of a (bodiless) hand reaching for an object, infants treated the hand reaching for a new object (even though it was in the same *place* as the previous object) as if it were a quite different action and looked longer at it, but they treated the hand reaching to the same object in a *different* place as if it were the same action and didn't react with longer looks. Indeed, even more interestingly, if the infants had already themselves *done* a reaching action (in one study they were helped to perform the action by putting mittens on their hands, which had velcro backing to stick to the objects), they could make this distinction in the object-directedness of other people's actions even at *3* months.[8]

If even 3-month-olds (and this is in a strictly controlled, non-social experimental situation where no faces are visible) can not only perceive hands moving in a specific direction but also as directed to a specific object, they must be able to perceive the directedness of others' intentional action to many different kinds of objects, including to themselves and to other people.

The subtle communicative responses of 2-month-olds which we saw in Chapter 5 begin to take on an even richer significance. And the fact that the vast majority of the intentional actions the infant is exposed to from birth must be directed *to* the infant herself becomes intriguingly promising.

Singularity

Intentional actions are *singular* because a reach, for instance, constitutes a single whole action rather than a series of small jerks. Being able to perceive this singularity is obviously useful; otherwise it would be difficult to tell when an intentional act was begun but then interrupted by a hesitation rather than by an external event. To be aware that someone is approaching you, it is imperative to see the approach as one act, not a series of disconnected steps.[9] Adults asked to "segment" a stream of behaviour on a videotape do this quite naturally, identifying the beginnings, ends, and lack of completion in everyday actions.[10] In a cleverly designed study using habituation Dare Baldwin has shown that even 10-month-old infants can "segment" actions on videotapes in this way, suggesting that this ability may well be a simple perceptual feature.[11] We don't yet know whether younger infants can perceive such segments too. Perhaps they might be able to do so differently for different intentions (as we saw in Amanda Woodward's success with 3-month-olds watching intentional actions they had already done themselves) or perhaps only for actions directed to the self. It would certainly make sense if, along with the perception of object-directedness, the chatty 2-month-old also could perceive the rhythms of intentions in communicative actions directed to her.

Shape

Another feature of intentional actions that makes them perceivable is that they are shaped in a coherent way. The *shape* of intentional actions does indeed appear to be non-arbitrary. (That is, not only do certain shapes of movement consistently lead to the same impressions in different perceivers, but also they seem to relate sensibly to the structure and kinematics of the body.) This is true of some very simple actions. If you move two rectangles along a line in a particular temporal relation to each other, you can create the powerful impression of simple actions such as swimming or crawling and even of complex actions of "pursuing," "joining and uniting with," "repelling," "distorting," "pushing repeatedly," "going to find and take away," and so on.[12] Impressions of actions such as attacking, defending, teasing, and chasing seemed to be unavoidable as reported by adult viewers in Fritz Heider's now famous experiments in which circles and triangles moved (in very animate ways) across a screen.[13]

There is now an enormous body of evidence that adults (at least) are good at making the subtlest of perceptual discriminations from filmed movements (often merely from watching a display of points of light placed strategically on body joints), and even from still photographs, about, for example, the weight of an object that someone is lifting, about whether they are trying to pretend that it is heavier than it is, and so on. Roboticists interested in re-creating these perceptual effects are asking fine questions about exactly what it is that specifies these intentions. We know little as yet about these features in relation to infants, although we do know that very young infants can detect biological motion (which is intentional), differentiating walking movements, for example, from mechanical motion. We don't know whether infants can identify a movement or even its emotional overtones from such "point-light displays"—something which we know that children with autism have great difficulty doing.[14]

Deliberateness

But what about the deliberateness that is such a central part of intention and volition? Can that be perceived? We can use an old definitional method—the method of contrasts—to define this aspect of intentions in terms of what it isn't. Three boundaries present themselves as *not* deliberate and therefore not intentional: actions which are *accidental,* such as tripping and spilling a drink all over someone else; actions which are *reflexive,* such as a hiccup; and actions which are *coerced,* such as being pushed by another person's force to perform a particular action. How can these be differentiated? This question is really about causality, about the dynamics of the action.

One suggestion has been that any movement which seems self-propelled (like that of a car) should be perceived by organisms as intentional. Certainly pre-school children respond with comments which would support this view.[15] But while self-propulsion may well be the key feature in the perception of deliberateness, it cannot be sufficient on its own. Amanda Woodward's studies showed that infants at 5 months distinguished between a casual, purposeless movement of the hand (moving the back of the hand towards an object) and an object-directed movement (with the palm turned towards the object, and perhaps containing more muscle tension). Both were obviously self-propelled but seemed to mean different things to the infants in terms of intention. And Michotte's experiments, referred to earlier in this chapter, showed very convincingly that the timing and speed of movement conveyed the impression of external pushing, pulling, knocking, and the like, characterising coerced actions. Distinguishing accidental actions may be slightly more complex. The source of external force when you trip and drop a glass of water may not even be visible. However, the disruption in the smoothness of the action (visible as a jerk interrupting a smooth flow) may indeed be visible.[16] Similarly, information about reflexive actions must be available in the manner of the action: its jerkiness, suddenness, speed of response to an external event, repeated and unvarying patterns of response over time, and so on. We don't know a lot, however, about *how* adults, let alone babies, make these perceptual discriminations, although we know that babies make some such discriminations and toddlers and chimpanzees make others.

Expectation of Change

The final feature of perceivability discussed here is the expectancy of change that characterises an action. Intentions are also about changing or doing something in the world, whether it is to pick up a toy or push someone off the sofa or move a cushion or tell someone to stop picking their nose. They seek to create change, however minor. If I can detect this aspect of your intentional actions, I can help you with achieving what you want—or indeed stop you from getting it. Even further, being able to grasp what others are trying to do allows me to understand when they are directed at my own intentions. That is, it allows me to grasp what you expect me to do or not do, to know your intentions for my intentional actions, as it were; and then to comply or indeed to tease or defy you by deliberately not complying. If I cannot detect this aspect of your intentions, then your behaviour might remain for me a well-shaped, coherent, directed spectacle, but it would not tell me that you are someone who wants things to happen in the world, someone who wants me to do things. Your culture (with its "shoulds" and "should nots," its intentions for my intentions) would be closed to me.

The expectation of change can be apparent in actions. Watching other people's intentional actions, we can observe satisfaction and cessation of the action when the object is reached, or persistence until it is, or surprise when the object disappears, or correction for direction if the object moves, and so on. For example, if I extend my arm with slight directional pressure on the computer screen, if the screen doesn't budge, or if it moves too far, or if I fail to make contact with it, my purpose is evident in my reactions (unless I am deliberately disguising them). I might look surprised, try again, try it differently, wait to see if it moves slowly, or I might eventually give up. If I tell my son to tidy his room, my expectation of the change in the world will similarly be evident in my pleasure (shock and incredulity, more likely) if he does it, my half-hearted repeat of the command if he doesn't, my looking and waiting to see what he will say if he doesn't respond immediately, and so on. The infant can potentially distinguish these different reactions, responding differently to the repetitions, to the waiting, perhaps anticipating and helping, perhaps complying with or perhaps deliberately obstructing the change that the other person seems to expect from her actions. In fact, if the infant really had her act together, she could tease the other person by anticipating what the person expected in the action and foiling it, or even more deviously, by inviting an intentional action with its expectation and then foiling it, as the observation with which I began this chapter appears to illustrate.

So, intentionality can be perceivable in action through its directedness, singularity, shape, deliberateness, and expectation of change. And we have seen that infants within the first year can already successfully grasp some aspects of intentional actions: by 3 or 5 months its directedness and by 10 months its singularity. Is this enough, however, to make intentions transparent to the perceiver in general and to the infant in particular? Not quite. The specific intentions need to be meaningful in some way. Two further aspects of intentional action—their contextuality and their engageability—allow the possibility of both adults and infants perceiving (rather than inferring) meaningfulness in intentional actions.

Intentions Need Context

The contexts of actions clarify their specific meanings. However, there is a tendency within psychology to see context as somehow separate from actions. So when theorists argue that the very same action can have different intentions and that therefore one needs to infer rather than perceive the differing intentions behind the "same" action, the theorist is often defining the "same" action in a very narrow way. Take, for instance, the opening paragraph of a recent paper by Mike Tomasello and his colleagues: "the exact same physical movement may be seen as giving an object, sharing it, loaning it, moving it, getting rid of it, returning it, trading it, selling it, and on and on—depending on the goals and intentions of the actor."[17] The implication here is that awareness of which of these intentions is involved in the same act of giving requires inference of some kind. You can't just perceive it.

But where should we draw the line around the intentional action of giving an object? Is the physical location in which the act takes place—shop counter or dining table or street corner—not a part of the act? Perhaps it is only the habit of thinking in terms of context as an "intervening variable" that would make us exclude the background from the act. Are the events preceding the giving of the object—outstretched palm, verbal request, physical offer of object—not a part of the act? What about the actual object that is handed over—chocolate bar, salt pot, white envelope? Or the manner in which the handing over is done—carefully, shiftily, casually, smilingly? Or the subsequent events—a smile, praise, refusal, acceptance, passing over of money? If we could see these things, we could hardly call the different kind of givings the "same act" anymore. A longer and deeper window into the act of giving—that is, its spatio-temporal context—makes transparent something more about the "meanings" of the specific intentions involved.

Cutting context out in order to find the pure physical action would be rather like doctoring a videotape of a "giving action," clipping the tape so that the preceding and subsequent events are omitted, blanking out the background, removing the object which is being passed over, ensuring that the passing over of the object is done in one uniform way, devoid of any expressive "manner." In fact, this kind of doctoring of actions is exactly what psychology teaches its students to do in designing experiments. In everyday life, however, we rarely see facial expressions or intentional acts without considerable contextual information.

Contexts are a part of, rather than additional to, the intentions that we grasp or don't grasp. And infants, when someone offers them a milk bottle at 3 months or a toy car at 5 months, do need to know the context to be aware of the specific intention in that act. What makes contexts informative? Infants would not need to be aware of shop counters or illicit transactions on street corners in order to be aware of some of the intentions of giving. The answer has to lie in engagement—contexts may be informative about intentions, provided that the perceiver has experience of engagement within it. The third and potentially most crucial aspect of intentions is that they draw us into engagement with them. Neither their perceivable features of directedness and shape and so on, nor their surrounding context are likely to be fully or typically meaningful unless the individual child or adult has engaged with them. The perception of intentions has to be an engaged perception and arguably an engagement in the second person—of experiencing someone else directing their intentional actions towards yourself.

Intentions Are Engageable-With

The third feature of intentional action that I think is essential to help us to understand infant awareness of intentions is its engage-ability. There is an openness—an incompleteness—in intentional action which invites participation from others. This can be the case even in simple actions upon physical objects (e.g., an attempt to push a fallen leaf away from your face) but is especially so for interpersonally directed intentional actions (e.g., an attempt to give a kiss or a toy to a baby). The action is open because it can change its course depending on the participation of the leaf (which may move again with the wind just as you reach for it) or of the baby (who may burst into tears as you approach) and because when it is directed to animate beings it is provoking participation. Sometimes it is simple muscle tension that conveys this openness or incompleteness and invitation to participate. There is a little clay sculpture on my kitchen window: a woman with her body twisted sideways, one hand gripping her own shoulder, her face rapt, listening, the sculptor told me, to an invisible flute player. Watching her, I can feel her striving in my own body. The key to the awareness of intentions may indeed be the experience of being moved by movement. This argument was made in the 1950s by Albert Michotte, who spoke about four levels of involvement of the perceiver and his body even in watching a film; by many of the phenomenologists; and more recently powerfully expressed by Peter Hobson. It is also, of course, a point that is central to all of the recent neuroscience research and its claims for the link between self and other.[18]

The participation which the incompleteness of intentional actions invites in an "observer" can be of two kinds. It can invite participation in the form of an empathic sharing, almost an adoption of the same intention. Or it can invite participation in the sense of a response from the other. Completion of the first kind, through *adopting* the intention of the other, can happen in the funniest ways. There is a probably apocryphal story that the philosopher Wittgenstein once went to the railway station with a friend who was leaving by train.[19] They were late and began to run. Wittgenstein got to the moving train first and jumped on to it as it pulled out. The friend who had intended to take the train was left astounded on the platform. The friend's intention in this case *became* Wittgenstein's own. Less dramatic examples of such absorption of others' intentions into one's own body can be seen everyday. Take Adam Smith's example of a crowd watching a tightrope walker. Every watcher's muscles tighten in sympathetic concern. Or the mother watching a child try to feed herself: the mother's head tips and her mouth opens in an attempt to accompany, strengthen, and correct the other's action. It is hard to imagine that unless one recognised the intention of the other, we would act in concert in this way, manifesting it in one's own body. It is tempting to conclude that this apparent adoption of the intention of the other involves a first-person empathic recognition of the similarity of the other to the self. But it could be more than this. The watchers on the ground or the mother opening her own mouth or even Wittgenstein jumping on the train may in fact be (unthinkingly) seeking to help the other, to complete their action for them, rather than see in their action the self's own, or in some way be confused about the difference.

Completion of the second kind is the more obvious sort of engagement we have been dealing with in earlier chapters in this book. A call seeks an answer; an outstretched arm with an object in the upturned palm invites at least a look, if not a "take." The infant's earliest experiences of other people's intentional actions (for reasons of visual perceptual immaturity at least) are likely to be primarily of those directed to the self. The infant's response to these actions must involve not only a perception of their form and a memory of their context but also a motivation and a feeling. The point here is this: intentional actions directed to oneself invite a response, and responding to them is crucial to development.

Intentions influence, and can be influenced by, others. The passive observer of intentions is rare. Someone reaches for the salt and you push it closer to them. Someone reaches out to hug you and instead you hold out your hand to shake theirs. Your sibling moves towards the comfy chair and you rush to get there first. It is hard to live with people and not be influenced by their intentional actions, especially when they are directed to us (that is, when we are the object of their intentions). And in being influenced, inevitably, we influence others' actions. Your action of helping to push the salt directly alters the other's reach. Your holding out your hand changes the other's intention to hug. Your dash for the comfy chair undoubtedly changes your sibling's intentions towards you and towards it. And it is precisely because they can influence *and* be influenced that intentions do lead to such complex engagements. Such involvement and reciprocal influence is unavoidably bound up with the question of awareness. It would seem that we cannot understand what infants understand without understanding what they *do* with others' intentions.

What Babies Do with Other People's Intentions

So what *can* be done with others' intentions? They can be copied, helped, obeyed, disrupted, directed or controlled, outwitted, given names, talked about, theorised about, and so on—as many different engagements as there are relationships (as Wittgenstein argued in his critique of Speech Act Theory). In the next sections I will take a few key infant actions in relation to others' intentions and summarise what we know about such actions. In particular I will focus on infants' attempts to disrupt others' intentional actions through playful teasing.

Imitating Intentional Action

Infants clearly imitate others' intentional actions, not only through the rather simple imitations of the neonate (already explored in some depth in Chapter 4), but also through more varied and "selective" imitations in later months. Imitation tells us not only about infants' motivations for engaging with people, but about the nature and extent of their awareness of others' intentionality. There is some reason to argue that you cannot imitate that which you don't in some sense "understand."

Is the neonate aware of the other's tongue protrusion or finger waving as an intentional action? When presented with objects, for example, a ping pong ball dangled in front of them, they don't usually "imitate" them by dangling or swaying! But instead they reach out or swipe or grasp or turn their heads to follow them. The neonates certainly seem to be recognising the directedness (towards them) of the adult's act, although we don't know whether it is the directedness to *them* that leads to the imitation (whether, for example, they would imitate a tongue protrusion when the model's face was turned to the side). Given the 2-month-old's sensitivity to small gaze deflections, however, it is quite likely that directedness is a fairly simple feature, serving to invite response. Given the conversational nature of the imitative exchanges, it is likely that neonatal imitation involves both a first-person and a second-person feeling (that is, I know what you are doing because I can do it myself, and I know what you are doing because I feel like responding to it). Neonates are not only perceiving intentional action, they are acting upon it: responding to it, inviting or provoking it if the model stops; they don't show the complex reciprocity of the 2-month-old, but they are doing something with it.

By 2 months, at least, human infants seem to differentiate between intentional and mechanical versions of the same action, imitating the actions of a human but not the movements of a mechanical toy.[20] Combined with the evidence that 2-month-olds direct more communicative actions (smiles, vocalisations) to people but react instead with attempts to *do* something with objects (such as reach, grasp, touch), this differential imitation becomes really interesting. However, the contrast of animate with mechanical agents is a double-edged sword (if used for demonstrating how different they are): they are only as different as you make them! Roboticists, seeking to specify precisely what information we use to identify intentionality, can turn the tables completely.

Take the remarkable study by Andy Meltzoff showing that 18-month-olds imitate the intention of people but not mechanical things. Eighteen-month-olds watching an adult's action (attempting but failing to pull apart a pair of dumbbells) will, when presented with the dumbbells themselves, imitate the intended action without a problem (without ever having seen it actually completed). They seem to have grasped the intention from the failed attempt. At 18 months this shouldn't surprise us. What was intriguing about this study, however, was that in the very same experimental setup, when the 18-month-olds were presented with a *mechanical* demonstration of the attempt, they did not imitate it. Why? Were the toddlers making an active assumption that only human (or organismic) actions of that nature could imply intention? Or did they simply not comprehend the "intention" of the mechanical demonstrator? Working with roboticists in Japan, Shoji Itakura and his colleagues explored this finding further. They presented children with both a complete demonstration and a failed attempt by a robot (a very robot-like robot, machine-like, with two arms, a faceless head, and two protruding eyes). For each of these conditions however, there was a further twist: the robot either turned and looked at the child (after succeeding or failing) or didn't look at the child. When the action was successful, the children imitated it whether or not the robot had turned and looked at them. However, when the action was a failed attempt, they only imitated it when the failure had been followed by gaze to them! This fine study suggests for a start that even non-human things, inanimate things, can (and in this instance quite accurately!) give us information about intentions. It suggests—although a huge amount of work is needed to explore this further—that many different aspects of action and the co-ordination of actions (e.g., failure with gaze) can constitute and be informative about intentions.

What *aspects* of intentional actions do infants imitate? It all depends of course, on what they see as intentional and on whether they are bothered about those aspects. Amazingly, 12-month-olds seem to select "rational" things to imitate. For example, babies who saw an adult turn off a switch with his forehead would "imitate" him exactly only if they could not see a reason for the peculiar action. If there was a rational explanation (for example, the adult was carrying something and therefore did not have his hands free), the babies simply turned the switch off with their hands. Children with autism, on the other hand, seem to ignore the odd "style" in which the actions were done (even when there was no reason for doing it that way). Peter Hobson and his colleagues in London found that, while children with language impairment do imitate the "style" of an action, children with autism don't, even when they do imitate the action itself.[21] Children with autism also don't shift their perspective to the other, so that when you stand before them and ask them to "do what I do," for example, waving your right hand, they wave their left hand! Identification with the other is Hobson's explanation for the significance of imitation—the inability to identify reflected in the imitation deficits in children with autism, whether of the style of actions or of posture or of gait (leading to the oft-reported oddity of gait) or of imitation itself.[22]

Helping Others' Intentions

There are many impressive anecdotes about young children's spontaneous helpfulness to others. For example, there is the toddler who notices that her grandfather has forgotten his walking stick and runs to fetch it without being asked to do so; the toddler must remember the grandfather's usual habits, recognise the deviation as a failure of memory, and anticipate his intention to correct the need. Setting up some ingenious studies to elicit such actions from infants, Michael Tomasello and Felix Warnekken showed that infants as young as 1½ years of age were helping not just family members, but total strangers in the laboratory, by opening cupboard doors for them to deposit heavy loads when their arms were full, or by fetching objects for them which had rolled out of their reach—all without being asked.[23] Anticipating what the other person was trying to do, and was either having—or going to have—problems in doing, seemed to these toddlers a piece of cake.

Where does this set of skills emerge from? What happens earlier in infancy, perhaps in simpler sets of actions and simpler situations? What about cooperation with simple actions by others—and actions which are directed to the self rather than only to other objects in the environment? There is some evidence that from around 3 to 4 months of age infants cooperate with, or accommodate to, other people's actions towards them before they have happened. The classic example is that of being picked up. You reach down to pick up a 4-month-old from a car seat, and you can often see their backs arching upwards as your hands approach. When you make contact, the body is already tensed and ready to be picked up. Parents report this as beginning after about 3 months of age, and it is a well enough known phenomenon to warrant taking seriously. What does it tell us? That in anticipating the action before it has been completed, the infant detects the *directedness* towards himself of the adult's action and recognises the particular *shape* the action is going to take.

Critics may point out that this bodily accommodation may be nothing more than a recognition of trajectory and that the infact could just be so eager to be picked up that she gets herself halfway there. It need have nothing to do with the adult's actions, but be merely, or largely, to do with her own desires. But two things argue against that claim, suggesting that such accommodation may be quite central to intention-awareness. First, children with autism don't make this simple bodily adjustment to being picked up, nor something else that typically developing 1-year-olds readily do—hold up their arms for being picked up.[24] This could mean that they are not interested in people and their actions and therefore don't bother to spend time and energy anticipating and adjusting to them, or that they cannot recognise the intentionality of others' actions and therefore cannot adjust to them, or that they cannot recognise the directedness of other people's intentional actions to themselves. Even such simple accommodation to others' actions may be a psychologically significant phenomenon. Second, Amanda Woodward's studies showed that infants of this age do in fact detect the connections between an action and its intended object (even over a distance), and even when it has nothing to do with personal desires for the action to be achieved. The idea that the 4-month-old is *helping* other people's intentions doesn't seem quite so bizarre a claim anymore.

Obeying Others' Intentions (or Not)

From about 8 or 9 months of age, infants seem to start becoming sensitive to others' intention to control: they start to comply with commands and prohibitions. Perhaps what is most impressive—and significant for the infant's cultural participation—is that others' intentions are now beginning to be perceived over a large physical distance with just words and tone of voice, outside of immediate engagement and serving to control the infant's own actions over time. What is evident is that these intentions are underspecified in terms of what the infant's act must be. Even when mothers demonstrate the action, as Colwyn Treverthen and Penny Hubley pointed out in their early study of secondary intersubjectivity in Edinburgh, they are usually only partially demonstrated—half-done and incomplete. The infant grasps the rest. Such anticipated completion of the end of the action suggests that the infant is aware of the shape of the other's incomplete or indicative act, its joint directedness to infant and to object, perhaps its deliberateness (that it is neither accidental nor reflexive), and above all its complex expectation of change (its intention for the infant's intention). Interestingly, this awareness is evident not only in compliance but also in clear non-compliance, whether it takes the form of defiant insistence or even a rather subtle stiffening of the back and pretending not to hear!

As yet, we know very little of just how these controlling intentions (or if we were being trendy we could call them meta-intentions) are negotiated between parents and infants. What does seem clear is that parents at somewhere around this age seem to detect the infant's interest in, and willingness to respond to, their "instructions," and start to attempt control at a distance. The clearest shift in parents' actions is that they start trying to control the baby's actions with their voices alone. Why do they shift? Although there are bound to be strong cultural differences present, the answer to this fairly widespread and unthinking shift on the part of parents must come from the

infants. Something in the infants' behaviour (whether it is the infants' increasing interest in the parents' intentions *for their own sake,* as Colwyn Trevarthen suggests, or whether it is something in the infant's responses to accidentally issued commands) must lead parents to seek to control the infant's
intentions at a distance, rather than just manipulate them physically.

From the little evidence that we have, compliance does not seem to be a
sudden acquisition, and it is not exactly an across-the-board acquisition.
Speak to the parents of 9-month-olds, and they may tell you that their baby
has become an angel, complying with prohibitions for the most tempting of
actions, such as pulling a sibling's hair! Speak to the same parents a month
later, and they may tell you that "Oh no—she doesn't understand 'No' really. She takes no notice at all of prohibitions." Compliance to different issues also seems to differ; parents may report clear compliance to issues such
as not touching the plug sockets or the fireplace, but deafness to prohibitions relating to not touching the video player. It would be difficult to argue
that compliance results from a generalised conceptual shift from not recognising to recognising the controlling intentions of parents. More local nego-
tiations seem to be at play.

How does compliance happen in other species? Again there are few data,
but what we do have suggests that in domestic animals compliance has to
be seriously trained for, even when, for example, as in sheepdogs, there is
intense desire to please humans. Compliance seems to be achieved through
reinforcement of responses rather than through a perception of intentions—
or, at least, more so than in human infants. Children with autism show yet
another pattern. With regard to autistic children, there appears to be little
interest in others' intentions (let alone others' intentions for the child's actions) and considerable difficulty with obtaining compliance. Regimes of
training for compliance are intensely based on reinforcement and on negotiation of rewards. Deliberate training and reinforcement will likely lead to
a very different—less flexible and less spontaneous—kind of responsiveness
and compliance than that which emerges from genuine engagement. Cathy
Lord, a psychologist who has worked with children with autism for many
years identifies an intriguing difference which is worth recapturing here:
she differentiates between social behaviours that, for non-autistic children,
are normally developed "out of routines" (that is, behaviours which emerge
in a "truly responsive" non-routinised way to the needs of others) and social
behaviours that are developed in autistic children "as part of routines" (and
remain routinised).[25] The latter process seems to need and involve little

awareness of intentions and feelings, the "behaviours" being maintained by reinforcements and routines.

Detecting Disruptions in Intentional Actions

So far, these data about smooth engagements are frustrating. They're telling us all sorts of things about intentional engagements and co-ordinations, but they're not enough: there is too much feeling around in the dark in using these smooth engagements to answer our questions. Their very smoothness could serve to conceal from us the infant's awareness of others' intentions during the course of these engagements. Philosophers often use the example of a blind man and his cane. When he is really using the cane to serve him, the cane itself tends to "disappear": "he is aware only of the curb (or whatever object the cane touches); or, if all is going well, he is not even aware of that, but of his freedom to walk, or perhaps only what he is talking about with his friend."[26] It is only when there is some sort of breakdown—let's say the cane breaks or cannot reach the ground or finds an unexpected texture—that the awareness shifts either to the cane or the objects it finds. One could argue similarly, that to become aware of others' intentions, or indeed our own, we also need interruptions or breaks or problems in what the German philosopher Heidegger calls the "tranquilised obviousness" of our everyday engagements.

Take the following example of an 11-month-old's response to an accidental movement within a repeated sequence of actions:

> Adam and his mother are playing on the floor. Adam has a breadstick in his hand and he takes a bite, holds it out to his mother and she takes a bite, he turns away, then turns back and offers it to her again, she takes another bite; he turns away slightly, then turns back and offers it again; smiling at him, she leans her face towards it but her bite misses and the breadstick jerks up slightly. Adam, looking at her, laughs at this. The mother laughs too, and so does everybody who watches this video clip.[27]

Although it is difficult to be completely certain from this video, it appears that Adam detected something about the accidental quality of his mother's action. We know very little about whether infants do laugh at accidents or even notice them. The only study to date on this topic suggests that this interpretation of Adam's laugh is not far-fetched. Mike Tomasello and his colleagues studied infants' reactions to an adult in a laboratory who had been playing with them by handing them toys. On some occasions the toys were not handed over, either because the adult deliberately teased the infant or just played with it herself or because the toy was accidentally dropped. While 6-month-olds didn't react differently to the two types of reasons, 9-, 12-, and 14-month-olds all did. Essentially, they showed more impatience when the adult was *unwilling* to give the toy rather than simply *unable*.[28] A similar question might be asked about mis-understandings in communication. Roberta Golinkoff's research showed that by 14 months infants are sufficiently aware of the other's "understanding" to correct communicative misunderstandings. Do 9-, 12-, and 14-month-olds also refrain from getting cross if an adult misunderstands their requests or desires, implying an awareness of the unintended nature of the other's mistake? We have few answers yet. We do know, however, that from around 8 or 9 months of age, when there is an unexplained *break* in the other's action (for example, if you are feeding the infant and suddenly stop, or while giving the infant a ball suddenly pull it back), infants look up at your *face* and not at the spoon or the ball or the hand which has stopped moving. Children with autism faced with a similar experimental task don't.[29] They continue to look expectantly at the hand. Why? It is intriguing to think that perhaps typically developing infants, unlike children with autism, are now locating information about the cause of actions in the face. This may be as much a result of a learning about the face and its expressions as it may be about "centralising" a notion of intention.

Disrupting Others' Intentions

Many years ago the ethnomethodologists—Harold Garfinkel, for instance—found that a powerful way of discovering people's expectations about other people's behaviour was to disrupt them (of course you had to first know *what* to disrupt). So for some years students of psychology took to strange practices, such as sitting too close to strangers on park benches, gazing too continuously at people's eyes, and watching for the reaction (practices which today's ethics committees would be unlikely to allow)! Known social patterns were being violated in order to confirm their existence. A similar strategy was adopted by developmental psychologists looking for infant awareness of physical laws: objects vanished in mid-air, disappeared form behind screens, changed shape incomprehensibly, and so on; surprised reactions in the watching infants indicated that they expected something different and therefore knew the laws that were being violated. Not only can we use this "method" of breakdowns to test infant awareness of others' intentions, but we can actually just sit back and wait for them to happen. Human infants, like other primates, seem to enjoy creating breakdowns in intentional engagements![30]

Teasing is fairly widespread in infants before the end of the first year, really taking off from around 9 or 10 months of age.[31] In our longitudinal studies we found that performance of provocative or disruptive actions with a playful or watchful look to the adult's face was *clear* in less than a quarter of 8-month-olds, but in three-quarters of 11-month-olds. Infants not only tease by offering and withdrawing objects (or in some cases themselves for a hug or a kiss), but also by provocative non-compliance and with deliberate disruptions of other people's actions. (I will take another look at the playfulness and humour in teasing in the next chapter, but focus here on its implications for the awareness of intentions). Probably the most common kind of teasing is "teasing with non-compliance," which most parents are all too painfully familiar with. Here is an example of a situation in which the infant doesn't particularly *want* to touch something, but knowing her mother doesn't want her to, "decides" to use it to tease the mother, repeatedly inviting the prohibition:

> Last week, I was round at my friend's and she's got a plant in the front room and she touched it, and I told her no, but she kept reaching out, like, not actually touching it, but like reaching out half an inch away from it, and then taking her hand away. Just so I'd say no. She was laughing, and she kept, she kept doing it, and she kept looking at me when she was doing it. (This was a one-off incident which did not recur.) (Mother of Melanie, 11 months, interview)[32]

Another common category of teasing is what one could call "teasing with disruption." What is interesting about this kind of teasing is that the initiative is on the child's side, happening even when there is no intrusive or constraining command for the infant to respond to or resist, nor a game to maintain. Arising from impishness and a fairly clear interest in others' actions even when not directly engaged with the infant, they offer convincing evidence of awareness of and interest in others' intentions:

> Her mother was playing the recorder, not specifically for Rebecca, with Rebecca close by. Rebecca reaches out and takes the recorder from her hand.

Her mother lets it go, not thinking any further. Rebecca then laughs and gives it back to M. M takes it, also laughs and resumes playing. Rebecca reaches out again and takes it, laughing. M allows her. Rebecca then gives it back with a "wicked grin." M laughs now because "it was so obvious that she was teasing." This was never repeated again, never became a game. (Mother of Rebecca, 11 months, interview)[33]

Teasing is relevant to the awareness of intentions only if the infant is capable of performing the serious versions of the actions (for example, of actually offering and releasing objects, or of complying with commands and prohibitions) and if it is clear that the act was not accidental, nor due to a change of mind, nor was itself a desired action, nor simply an imitation of someone else's act (although to reverse roles and imitate a tease would actually be more complex and demanding than teasing itself!). In general, though, infants seem to start to tease in a particular manner soon after they grasp some new interaction, whether it is being able to release objects or being able to comply with a command. This suggests that the teasing is directly related to something new that the infant is learning or exploring or discovering. The meaning of teasing actions is always a very fragile thing, even in adults: it rests heavily on the response it gets, and it cannot remain the same from one occasion to the next. In these young infants first attempts at teasing often—but not always—turned into games and became different routines, not quite teasing any more.

The first fragile attempts to tease are the most interesting in terms of the infant's awareness of the other's intentions. They often show a clear awareness of the directedness, shape, and purpose of the other's acts. In offer–withdrawal, for instance, the infant must know that the other's reach is directed to the object, that the reach can be elicited by an offer of the object, that the reach has a particular shape and form such that as soon as it begins the infant can start to withdraw the object, and that in some sense the other intends to influence the infant's act, that is by making her give the object. In provocative non-compliance, of course, the awareness of the other's intention to influence the infant's actions is most obvious. In the teasing disruption of the other's actions, there is clear evidence of the infant's awareness of the directedness of the other's acts towards something in the room or on their bodies, as there is of the shape and form of the other's act (in order to allow the infant to anticipate and disrupt it) and of the purpose of the other's act—this time in relation to something in the environment rather than to the infant's own intentions.

We could argue of course that teasing is "merely" an exploration of a mechanical reaction; that it need imply no awareness of intentions—only of contingencies and reactions; that such playing with the boundaries of things applies not just to people and people-related things but also to mechanisms—like, for example riding a bicycle. No sooner have children learned how to ride a bike than they may start to ride it with "Look, no hands!" or they test their own skills by steering in tight little patterns. There is certainly a similarity with infant teasing, which arises shortly after the mastery of a new skill (learning to give or being able to comply) and which also involves the spontaneous introduction of variations and difficulties into the interaction. And, even in the case of the play with the bicycle, the child is playing not with the machine, but with the boundaries of her own skill and desire/intention to stay upright. Teasing needs an intentional partner, and in the play with a bicycle the self provides such an intentional partner, though a poor substitute for another person. However, when we look at the emotional expressions accompanying infant teasing of others, the comparison to playing with a bicycle becomes daft. The infant in the first example in this chapter smiled at the other person, but not just in joy at success in eliciting an interesting reaction: the smile on two consecutive occasions, preceded both the withdrawal and the other's reaction, starting with the first offer as a watchful half-smile—which parents usually call a cheeky smile when combined with a brightness in the eyes,—and varying with the progress of the tease, increasing as the other reaches out. You wouldn't get such reactions from a bicycle!

Nonetheless, it clearly *is* possible to tease a person without recognising their intentionality. In cases of bullying, for instance, the victim's reactions may be treated precisely as mechanical reactions, and the interpersonal interest may lie in the reactions of the audience, or not at all. Little boys tying fireworks to dogs' tails, for instance, may be a million miles from thinking of the dog's emotions and desires. The evidence for the recognition of others' intentions lies in the manner in which the teasing is done, and the developmental history of the actions. There is some evidence that bullying seems to come from earlier experiences of parental insensitivity or non-contingency, possibly because such experiences influence children's awareness of the other people's intentions in relation to their own.

That teasing is indeed linked with awareness of intentionality is given further support by the fact that children with autism do not engage in it very well. They do in fact engage with simple games like peep-bo, showing some sort of awareness of intentions even there. However, they do not show the kind of teasing that typically developing infants start to engage in from around 8 or 9 months. Two different studies have now shown that children with autism do tease but less frequently and rather atypically.[34] Teasing with offer withdrawal is the rarest form of teasing in children with autism: in our study comparing pre-school children with autism and children with Down syndrome (DS), only 1 out of the 19 children with autism studied did anything like a tease with an offer withdrawal—and that too, only on request and only with objects in the mouth. On the other hand, amongst the developmental age-matched children with DS such teasing was common: three quarters of the children studied were reported to tease spontaneously with offer withdrawal, most of them in a variety of different contexts and with different kinds of objects rather than restricted to one situation. Teasing with non-compliance and disruption did occur in several of the children with autism, although it was not very common (less than half the parents reported their children ever doing such things) and not very frequent. But when it did happen, the incidents typically involved simple violations and were almost formulaic. I can list only five examples reported by parents of children with autism: increasing the speed of an act when told not to, grinning cheekily when told off for making a noise, banging or turning a chair over for reaction, taking clothes off, and calling for no reason, then laughing. In contrast, in the children with DS, in addition to its prevalence (85 percent of the parents reported their children doing such teasing), parents described a huge range of different kinds of provocation and disruption. I can list twenty quite distinct kinds of actions used to tease, varying from the very complex offering of a hug and then moving away laughing when the offer is taken up to the simpler putting a finger in the nose and waiting for a reaction!

These infant actions suggest that infants from very early in life perceive different features of intentional action as intentional and that these perceptions become more complex during the course of the first year. It is also clear that from birth infants are not "just perceiving" others' intentional actions, but are jumping right in to imitate, respond, anticipate and invite, adjust to and, before the end of the year, even deliberately disrupt them. Infant experience of others' intentions is solidly and primarily within a powerfully meaningful and "open" mutual involvement. What does this mean for explaining the development of the awareness of intentions in other people?

How Does an Awareness of Intentions Develop?

What is it about engagement (which must contain the answer somewhere in it) that leads to development and greater awareness? I think play and teasing, which are overlapping concepts in their broadest meanings, give us a paradigmatic answer to this question. In all genuine (i.e., open rather than scripted and routinised) intentional engagements, but in playing and teasing in particular, each partner is drawing the other *into* their intentions.

Let's take the case of a genuinely incomprehensible intention for an infant of 2 months, the meaning of which gradually becomes clear: playful "boo-ing." Mothers start playing peep-bo with babies from somewhere around 3 months of age, in a variety of ways—hiding their faces, covering the baby's face, hiding a puppet, simply looming with their whole bodies, and so on. Initially, the intention of these odd movements is unclear to the infant. Take the following example of Rohan when he was 2½ months old, revealing my ineptitude in gauging his response, which still embarrasses me:

> After a long sequence of intensely positive vocal exchanges with him (on camera) I was nearly laughing at his loudness and responsiveness. I sat back, and just for a change from the chatting I leaned forward and playfully—and fairly gently—"boo"ed him, looming in close to his face. I was expecting him to smile again, maybe even to give that breathy near laugh at my unexpected action. But he just continued to look at me— slightly surprised, but not at all alarmed—blank faced, serious, almost en- quiring. I suppose I was somewhat embarrassed—I had been caught making a social faux pas. I tried to recover the situation by doing it again— and again that sober stare. (My students seem to enjoy watching this more than any of my successful interactions!)

Clearly, he perceived the directedness of my action as well as its rather un- usual shape (the looming) and perhaps enough about me, my smiling and moderately pitched voice to trust rather than fear it. But he could not grasp its playful intent.

In a longitudinal study of peep-bo games, Nancy Ratner and Jerry Bruner showed that mothers had, albeit unconsciously, a very systematic way of drawing their infants into this understanding. In the early months, the different phases of the game (preparation, disappearance, and re- appearance) are pronounced, made salient, exaggerated, and drawn out.

Mothers seemed to be using something like a game-based "motherese" to emphasise and highlight these actions and phases. Dare Baldwin's notion of "motionese" captures this very well. She found that even outside of games, even in ordinary face-to-face interchanges, mothers exaggerate their actions when interacting with infants.[35] This may well be highlighting for infants, right from birth, the particular ways in which intentional actions begin, continue, and end, and the particular emotional contexts in which they occur. In the peep-bo game, this initial highlighting and exaggeration disappear over time; as the game becomes more familiar, the phases occur in almost brusque fashion. The "He's going, he's going . . . oh oh . . . oh he's gone!" (of a disappearing hand puppet, for instance) might become, for instance, simply "Oh!" The reappearance might be marked, not by a slow string of actions and words, but a simple and abrupt "boo!" without warning. This change in maternal "presentation" of the play intention is based entirely on the perception of the infant's emotional response at each point.[36]

Mothers are doing three things here: by starting with exaggeration and emphasis, they are highlighting the actions as salient events; by repeating them in sequence, they are making them and the sequence familiar, and in some sense transparent, to the infant. The third and most important aspect of mothers' actions involves their drawing of the infant *into* their intentions. A looming which is meaningless to the 2-month-old as a playful act of any kind becomes rapidly meaningful, not simply because it is repeated in predictable sequence and therefore its format has been learned, but because the mother is sensitively evoking and gradually managing the infant's emotional reactions to her own actions. It is through *these* that the intention of her actions is clarified. The mother's intention is *felt* by the infant because of the engagement, not in imitation, but through the infant's own *response*.

When infants explore or play with their parents' actions or more deliberately tease them, a similar process (though not with a remotely didactic function) is apparent. The infants are drawing the parent into *their* intentions. This can only happen, of course, if the parent is genuinely engaged with the infant. We can see this in even as simple a case as neonatal imitation (whatever judgement we might make about the significance of that for an awareness of others' intentions). In one video clip from Emese Nagy's study of neonatal provocations, the model finishes presenting her two-finger raising (she was clearly not British, as this is regarded as a rude gesture in the UK!) and moves slightly to adjust the wires above the infant's head. The camera on the infant's face shows a concentrated gaze still fixed on Emese's face. After a long wait, the neonate raises two fingers, eyes still on the busy model. Noticing this, startled, Emese looks down and curiously and responsively imitates the baby. The baby now does it again more quickly. And Emese imitates again. And both, one more time. Then the baby stops. This is a very simple exchange, but the equally simple point here is that if Emese had not been genuinely engaged with the infant's actions, she would not have imitated her in response, and the idea and future experiments with provocation could not have happened. The baby, quite simply, drew the adult *into* her intention. You could say the same with many other studies in psychology (my study of teasing, for instance): experiencing being teased by the infant was vital for me to become interested in it in relation to intentional engagements.

Teasing needs a partner. Our sheepdog, who generally is incredibly obedient and well-trained enough not to chase chickens, suddenly started teasing one particular chicken. This chicken was of a different breed from the others, bold and unafraid. Somehow the dog had discovered that this one wouldn't run away squawking in fear, but would turn round and be briefly aggressive if she teased it by pouncing too close. The teasing, which was delightful to watch, went on for a few weeks that summer but only with this one chicken! My point here is that the partner's response is crucial to maintaining a tease. In humans too, you wouldn't tease someone who didn't "understand" your intention. (Of course, where teasing is malicious, what may be desired by the teaser is precisely a not-understanding.) Parents, asked about whether they tease their babies, often say no, it would be too cruel (or at least this is true of British parents and mothers in particular), until, that is, their infants start teasing *them*. Similarly, parents of children with autism often report that they wouldn't tease their children even playfully; they simply wouldn't be understood. In contrast, of course, parents of children with other disabilities, like DS, who do get teased by their children, report enjoyable games of mutual teasing. The invitations for and disruptions of, the other's actions that we can see in teasing, seem to be possible only when genuine engagement and an appropriate response take place. If this can be established, at however simple a level, the route to developing awareness of others' intentions is open.

Engagement is at the heart of the *how* question of development. Intentions need something or someone to engage with in order to exist: they *only* emerge in engagement. The intention to give things to people is as dependent on other people's availability (and intention) to *take* things as the intention to walk is dependent on the existence of solid ground. This much we can take for granted. What is less obvious is that becoming *aware* of intentions, one's own or someone else's, must *also* be totally dependent on engagement; that is, it can only happen in engagement *with* the intention. We cannot discover intentions in other people's movements through voyeuristic peeping, nor by sitting in solitary reflection and inventing intentions as solutions to a problem of making sense of behaviour, nor from being given rules and formulae to understand them.[37]

In Conclusion

At the end of this chapter we have more questions than answers about how infants develop an awareness of intentions. There seem to be some patterns that we need to explore further and some ideas that we can reject, but we are still far from a convincing theory about its development in the first year. So what do we know so far?

Intentions in others are available to infants from birth, most vividly in actions directed towards themselves. It is clear that infants are deeply engaged with other people's actions from the start. Intentions are not only totally embodied in action, but they are also fundamentally *inter*-active phenomena, twice embodied you might say.

Others' intentions are potentially perceivable in actions-in-the-world, evident in their directedness, shape and singularity, deliberateness and purpose. They are also potentially experience-able, both through simple resonance in the infant's own body and through reciprocal reactions and affective response in real engagement. The fact that others' intentional actions *can* (and often *must*) be engaged with shows their openness to influence and completion by another person. This fact also gives the infant a power over them: they don't happen at a psychological distance but within the domain of the infant's own responses, almost seeking to be influenced and mucked about with.

Playing with others' intentions seems to be the most convincing answer to the "how" question in terms of developing awareness of intentions. Such play is strikingly evident in infants as well as in the actions of the adults they are involved with. It is apparent in the form of an exploration of the presence and absence of others' actions even in neonates. It is much more pronounced and clearly play*ful* in infant teasing towards the end of the first year. Playing as a powerful frame for intention awareness is also evident in *parents'* actions with infants in the middle of the first year during games and routines. In upping the ante during peep-bo, for instance, and through their sensitivity to the emotional reactions of the infant, parents seem to be drawing infants *into* their playful intentions. It is from this base of "play" that others' intentional actions towards other things in the world must gradually be understood: as resonant and contextually meaningful actions, largely affectively toned and inviting of response.

From this kind of perspective, the *how* question is easy to answer. The infant's understanding of others' intentions is experienced in the first person (through feeling the shape of the same action in her own body), in the second person (through having them directed at her and feeling them through her own direct response to them) and only gradually comes to be grasped in the third person (as abstract entities which have conceptual-linguistic labels). The direct experience of intentions (both in the first and second person) is essential to any further "normal" development of the awareness of intentions, determining the manifestation of intentional engagements throughout life and serving to constitute the abstractions and cultural concepts by which it is usually known.

The case of autism is a sad example of problems with this (first- and second-person) experiential base. What happens here is clearly a development of intention-awareness which is normatively inappropriate: children with autism don't engage with others' intentional actions in the same way as do developmental age-matched children with other learning disabilities, or developmental age-matched typically developing children. Nor do they talk about or think about intentions in the typical way. A concept of intentions can develop, as reports from autistic people themselves clearly show. Abstractions can be made and theories formed about what leads people to do one thing or another and what various actions and words mean. However, the experiential base for these inferences and theories remains problematic, as do their actions in response to others' intentions.

But what about the "what" question. What is it that develops? There are many possible answers. The majority of approaches see development in the first and second year as involving a generalisable grasp of intentionality. Sort of like getting the "idea" of intentionality. Some paint a developmental story in which the infant first perceives mere movement, then grasps that such movement involves animacy (others call it agency), next sees in the movement the pursuit of goals, and then finally grasps that this pursuit is based on a choice of plans.[38] In other words, development is seen to involve an increasing grasp of the intellectual components of intentional action with some observable components, some aspects of the observable which are detected only later, and some unobservable components, inferred after the first year. Others see the story more or less as a shift from a behaviourist to a mentalistic understanding of intentions—from a "teleological" to an intentional understanding.[39] Here, the *what* that is believed to be changing is not so much a detection of different components of the action as a re-understanding of the whole in a different way, a different stance. The observable components of intentional action are not considered to be about intentions; intentions are seen fundamentally as attributions. Yet others see the shift as being from a discernment of the properties of action—an action analysis as it were—to a deeper structural analysis of intentionality, very much in the way Chomsky argued that language emerged.[40] A very few voices, however, argue that intentions are understood in the plural, in a bottom up way from individual examples rather than as general ideas.[41] This explanation focuses more on local contextual understandings, explaining how the infant might be more aware of some intentions than others (for example, those that she might be able to engage in herself) and explaining how local engagements between people might leap ahead in some situations and not in others.

Most of these theories could cope with the data we have so far, explaining at least some parts of them. Few of them, however, take the infant's own affective experience of others' intentional actions as the central pivot around which awareness develops. And it would seem from all of these engagements that infants happily and actively immerse themselves in from birth, that affective experience—particularly the experience of intentions directed towards themselves—is central to our understanding not only of the *how* but also the *what*. The "components" of intentional actions cannot be solely intellectual. Allowing engagement and affect into the process of understanding shifts the psychologist's perspective: if infants can *experience* intentions in actions directed towards them, the need for analogy and inference as the primary routes to understanding intentions diminishes, and the distinction between deep and shallow awareness of intentions—at least in such intentions—becomes unnecessary. A second-person approach seems necessary to explain the developing awareness of intentions.

My goal at the end of this chapter has been to approach the "how" of the development of intention-awareness. And to do this we have inevitably had to tackle the "why"—the motive—why do infants even bother with others' intentions, why do they engage with them, why would they experience them in their own bodies, and so on. The answer is intimately bound up with why adults want to play with infants' actions, why they want to push the boundaries of their awareness, why they are interested in their actions at all. Neither intentional actions nor their understanding would exist without a world which engages with them/it. The mutuality is fundamental.

CHAPTER 9

Sharing Funniness

A jest's prosperity lies in the ear
Of him that hears it, never in the tongue
Of him that makes it.

Love's Labour's Lost, Act V, Scene 2

The tragic (and the dramatic) . . . are universal. The comic (is) . . .
bound to its time, society, cultural anthropology.

Umberto Eco, *Travels in Hyperreality*[1]

I remember Tom Shultz (a cognitive-developmental theorist of humour) giving me friendly advice years ago, not to build my career on humour research. But I will risk the threat to my serious academic image: humour is worth it. There is something about funniness (I prefer to use this less loaded term wherever possible) that is richer than everything we've been talking about so far, something wonderful and psychologically powerful, in which *dis*engagement is used to enhance engagement. It is fundamentally a relational thing, bound to its culture and time and place and relationships as Umberto Eco puts it. But it has a peculiar way of enlarging and deepening relation by violating it. To be able to find something funny reveals a pleasure in life visible in the poorest circumstances, and it *creates* as much joy as it reveals. The unexpected joke, the friendly tease, can lift the deepest gloom and lighten the angriest mood. The presence of funny colleagues can even make departmental meetings worth attending! We treasure funniness. We fall in love with people who make us laugh, we express the ultimate insult when we accuse someone of lacking a sense of humour, and we even pay money to buy laughter in joke books and comedy shows. Understanding what's going on in humour is potentially a rich source of mind knowledge (for psychologists *and* for infants): neither getting a joke, nor joining in laughter, nor making others laugh would be possible if we were unaware of or uninterested in others' thoughts and feelings. Humorists have skills at understanding people that psychologists probably don't!

Strangely, although laughter and funniness are a very frequent occurrence in the lives of most infants, and although, as I will show, such events are deeply social and very informative about infants' appreciation of others' interests, amusement, and expectations, infant humour is not often studied in developmental psychology. The literature on the development of humour adopts a largely analytical approach to "the joke" and "the comic" and offers a third-person conceptual route to explaining how children might understand what others find funny. In this chapter I will suggest that humorous "objects" emerge within social relations: funniness is very much a second-person phenomenon. The relation to the audience—the You—is crucial both to the defining of the humorous "object" and to the emergence of funny actions and their appreciation. I will show that evidence from what infants laugh *at* as well as from what infants *do* to make other people laugh suggests that funniness is based on an awareness of the psychological, which begins in interpersonal engagements in early infancy. First, before I look at infant engagements involving funniness, I will ask what sort of thing funniness is, consider two current cognitive-developmental views about when a sense of humour is believed to begin, and take a look at the nature and meaning of laughter.

What Sort of Thing Is Funniness?

One of the problems in trying to solve the mystery of the origins of humour is our inability to agree on what exactly the experience of funniness involves, even for adults. To try to provide a definitive formula for the experience of humour would be madness—it is too multifaceted and has puzzled too many people for too long to be constrained by definition. But different definitions and different emphases lead to very different answers to questions of when and how humour develops.

In general, the majority of writers have focused on it as a *thought* rather than as an emotion or an action. Certainly, as adults it would seem that we can *think* of something funny (and laugh at it to ourselves) without *doing* anything about it. The crucial element of humour identified by many philosophers and psychologists has been that of *incongruity*.[2] Incongruity is something like a contrast or contradiction—something done wrong, out of place, out of character, a juxtaposition of two things which don't really go together, bringing the abnormal or the odd into sharp contrast with the normal or expected. The classic examples of verbal jokes fit this pattern well: the Groucho Marx statement about clubs for young people being useful for beating them with, the song which goes, "If I tell you you have a beautiful body will you hold it against me?", the student who innocently asks when the "virus doctor" will next visit the department, and so on, all contain this juxtaposition of two "planes of reference" as Koestler called them, into unexpected and apparent congruence. Funniness, according to such thinking, lies in the individual's perception of an incongruity within the text of the joke, and the interpretation of this incongruity as funny rather than serious. Think, for example, of someone telling you a joke. You are listening, perhaps a little bored, with some anticipation of a punchline approaching. The punchline comes, and you are puzzling it out for a split second before you realise its sense, the joke bursts upon you and takes you by surprise, and you laugh, having worked out the logic (and incongruity) of the joke. The intellectual process here is obvious and convincing.

However, there is a question here: to what extent can one think of humour as an intellectual act rather than as an emotional response? Can you *think* funniness without *feeling* it? There is a physiological accompaniment to humour which consists of a rise and fall in tension, an "arousal jag" as it has been called. But is it the case, as the philosopher Henri Bergson argued, that emotional "indifference is the natural ground of humour," that the perception of the comic requires a "momentary anaesthesia of the heart"? When someone teases you, knowing that the opposite is true, for instance, "Okay, so you *don't* want to speak to me, then?" and you laugh at being caught out, or when someone mimics your too earnest tone and you laugh, or when you fish for a compliment and receive the deliberate opposite— your laughter in these cases is clearly a reaction to the unexpectedness of the thought of the tease, but the funniness is in the play of feelings between you and the other person, not in the thought alone. Emotional indifference would not allow the existence of humour in such cases. Consider also the fictitious case of robots (who cannot feel funniness) learning—and failing— to tell jokes: Marvin the paranoid android in *The Hitchhiker's Guide to the Galaxy* is comic but doesn't understand it; Crighton in *Red Dwarf* gets the formula right but fails to be funny; or Mike in Heinlein's *The Moon Is a Harsh*

Mistress deduces a code for humour, but plaintively keeps asking, "So that's *not* very funny?" In contrast to children who seem to find things funny without getting the joke at all right, robots seem to do the reverse: they know the rules, but can't participate in the emotional action. And when considering the question of origin and evidence from early development and from children and adults with disabilities, looking at humour primarily as a thought may be a particular problem.

But there is a more important question yet. If we had not experienced joking with other people, if we did not have a potential audience some- where in memory to tell jokes to or to laugh with, would we actually find things funny in this way? Humour, some people have argued, is first and foremost a *social act,* humour is what we *do* to or with other people; it can be neither a thought nor a feeling alone. What does this actually mean? As adults, in telling a joke, or in teasing, or in joining with the general laughter in a group, or in giggling with a friend at nothing much at all, we are fun- damentally engaged in social action. We do it to be friendly, to impress, to provoke, to hurt, to be polite, to ease tension, and so on. Humour, even when we laugh alone at a joke, is an act of communication towards at least a potential or remembered audience. As Bergson put it, "You would hardly appreciate the comic if you felt yourself isolated from others. . . . However spontaneous it seems, laughter always implies a kind of secret freemasonry, or even complicity, with other laughers, real or imaginary."[3]

To test this out, I try to think of the last five occasions on which I have laughed. There was that email last night with the list of jokes which were unusually funny and had me laughing aloud alone in my office. There was the rude comment from a colleague yesterday about my lack of fashion sense (obviously not serious). There was the moment when my son was lying beside me in bed and commented scientifically on the ripples that flowed through the fat in my belly when he lightly touched it. There was the laugh this morning when I deliberately mumbled an instruction to my husband so he could not hear it, and he, recognising the intent, playfully rocked me right off my rocking chair. Then there was that moment late eve- ning when my daughter's friend heard the phone ring and suddenly started to head for the gate in case it was his parents on the phone. In all of these cases the humour came from what people *did* (through words or other ac- tions) to each other, teasing, surprising, being cheeky, escaping punish- ment, taking revenge; they are all funny social *acts.* Even in the case of the email list of jokes, the jokes were funny because people *meant* them—they

were a list of problems routinely reported by Qantas pilots and the me-
chanics' (alleged) written responses of corrective action taken:

Pilot: *Aircraft handles funny.*
Response: *Aircraft warned to straighten up, fly right, and be serious*

Pilot: *Something loose in cockpit.*
Response: *Something tightened in cockpit.*

Pilot: *Left inside main tyre almost needs replacement.*
Response: *Almost replaced left inside main tyre.*

Pilot: *Evidence of leak on right main landing gear.*
Response: *Evidence removed.*

And so on! Perfect examples of funny incongruities though these are, what
I couldn't help laughing about was the image of some no-nonsense tough
mechanic expressing his contempt for pilots and actually risking putting
these responses on record. The wit in itself could be rendered totally unfunny without the social/emotional function it is serving. (Witness, for
instance, the very different responses we can have to black humour or to
sexist jokes, or the gruesome consequences of a political joke gone wrong
in Milan Kundera's *The Joke*.) And of course, the perception of the comic
seems to vary across cultures, as anyone will testify who has struggled—
and failed—to understand the funniness of Charlie Brown (well, I did!), or
of endless British punning or the daftness of the Goons or of Monty Python
or of cross dressing at student parties, or who has puzzled at the apparent
inability of some cultures to see the humour in that lowest form of wit—
sarcasm!

Further, our perception of the humorous changes in tune with the people
important to us; you can learn to find some things funny because they start
mattering in the interactions around you. At a more momentary level, a lot
of evidence shows that we laugh at funny things more—and louder—when
there are people around us. Laughter tends to be more like speech when we
are alone: muffled, indistinct, and weak rather than clear and strong.[4]
Laughter, arguably, is by its very sound a reverberation which seems to
need a partner, a returning voice to continue, needing an echo, to cite
Bergson once again. It is, however, fussy about who the partner is: we may
not find things funny at all if we don't know or like the people who are
laughing at a joke, while we may find things absolutely hilarious if the right

person starts us off. The phenomenon of "giggle incontinence" (familiar to adolescents at least!) illustrates this, where an external cause is very hard to find for the intense and sometimes unbearable funniness experienced. Laughter seems always to *contain in it* someone other than just the laugher. Not only is it the case, as the redoubtable Michael Crawford (and Shakespeare) put it, that in order for a joke to constitute a joke, it needs at least one person to laugh at it, but it may be that if there was no one (real or imagined) to share the joke with, we wouldn't experience funniness in the first place. Most approaches, however, see humour more as an (individual) analytic phenomenon, not as a *do*-ing thing. Looking for the origins of humour in what infants do must be a good way of answering these questions and illuminating these processes (as well as telling us what infants know of other people).

Two Cognitive-Developmental Views about the Emergence of Humour

Young children's tortuous attempts to construct alternative versions of "knock-knock" or "why-did-the-chicken-cross-the-road" jokes, in which the punchlines aren't remotely funny (even though the children are themselves in the throes of expectant laughter) might persuade us that a sense of humour doesn't really develop until late childhood. Indeed, the general story in cognitive-developmental theory has been much like this. One theory (Tom Shultz's, in fact) goes that, although humour begins at 18 months of age with the ability to symbolically represent the two different versions of reality needed to recognise incongruity, it isn't until much later—6 or 7 years of age—that children are seen as being able to "resolve incongruities" or to understand punchlines—that is, not just recognise the presence of an absurdity, but also see why it makes particular sense.[5] That is why, the theory suggests, younger children's punchlines are so amusingly unfunny!

Witty punchlines apart, what does it take to perceive humour in the first place? At the earliest stages, the standard cognitive representational account goes, it takes two things for the individual to perceive an incongruity and interpret it as funny: One, the ability to *perceive a contrast* between the expected and the "abnormal" (i.e., the incongruity itself), and two, the ability to *interpret it as funny* rather than as simply wrong. To perceive an incongruity you need, at a minimum, to hold in mind two different representations of reality at the same time. For instance, if you are to perceive John Cleese's strange walking in the Monty Python sketch "The Ministry of Silly Walks" as abnormal or wrong in some way, you must not only be able to see his movements, but be able to contrast them with a "normal" way of walking. This contrast must involve the recognition of his walking as "odd" or abnormal rather than just novel; in other words, the walking must be not only new or unexpected, but *mis*-expected. Exactly what it takes to perceive the latter is unclear—it is often assumed that some kind of concept, some range of normality and of the expected—must be present which an event can be judged against. Otherwise new events are simply *un*expected.

According to Paul McGhee, infants have what it takes to perceive incongruities by 4 months of age. They express surprise at "odd" events, for example when falling balls stop in mid-air, or moving objects disappear behind a screen and fail to reappear, indicating that something is being detected by very young infants which goes against their expectations of "normality." However, he argues, the infant doesn't perceive these events as funny; they are more likely perceived as something wrong or problematic. It isn't until the infant can understand pretence or make-believe that the odd is interpreted as funny.[6] John Cleese's gait, for example, may be seen by the infant either as a physical problem with his legs or as a problem with her idea of normal walking! McGhee argues that until 18 months, when pretending comes on stream, the infant cannot suspend reality and use a make-believe attitude to interpret the oddity as funny. Before 18 months infants *cannot* experience humour.

But do you really need a make-believe attitude to find things funny? Mary Rothbart thinks not. She believes that the suspension required is not of reality but of seriousness. What is needed to see incongruities or oddities or absurdities as funny is an attitude—of playfulness rather than seriousness. Funniness doesn't need the complex machinery of symbolic representation and make-believe, but very simply, the ability to adopt a playful attitude towards things. Things are funny, she argues, even within a reality frame, not just in a make-believe frame. Take, for example, finding it funny when someone wears a hat which is too large, or when someone slips on a banana skin. These don't require us to perceive the oddity as make-believe; they require us simply to see them playfully, as non-serious and non-threatening. And a playful attitude, everyone agrees, emerges around 4 months of age. So humour, according to Rothbart, can begin at 4 months.[7]

Here then is a theoretical deadlock within cognitive approaches: humour can begin at 4 months, or it cannot begin until 18 months. The solution must be to look for evidence in infancy. Surely that will answer the "when" question more definitively? But the empirical story so far is somewhat cloudy. Much research has looked at *verbal* humour and, moreover, has focused on pre-school children's *responses* to jokes rather than on their own creation of humour. With these limitations, little evidence has been produced to show that humour could begin as early as 4 months. The first clearly articulated claims to the *production* of humour in children come from early verbal distortions by toddlers. These allow the creation of spontaneous jokes, such as the 2-year-old laughingly inverting her name from Rosie to Sie-ro, or the 3-year-old inventing toilet humour by re-writing the words to Doctor Foster while sitting on the toilet and singing, "Doctor Foster went to Gloucester in a shower of wee wee"! The lack of any earlier evidence of humour may, however, owe more to a theoretical bias against its early existence and to the focus on verbal humour than to a true picture of infant capabilities. Is there any evidence at all of the *production* of pre-verbal humour in humans? Parents of much younger children—toddlers, even young infants—will tell you that their infants can definitely see the funny side of things, that the fun of their everyday lives often involves deliberate cheekiness and humour even before children can speak. What do we make of these views? They often hinge on evidence of laughter—that repeated and sometimes helpless shaking of the body that embodies funniness as nothing else does.

The Nature and Meanings of Laughter

> Take bread away from me, if you wish, take air away from me, but do not take from me your laughter.
> . . . when your laughter enters it rises to the sky seeking me and it opens for me all the doors of life.
>
> Pablo Neruda, *The Captain's Verses*[8]

Laughter does something special to us. It is good for our health (hence the recent eruption of "laughing clubs" in India!), enjoyable for the spirit, and certainly frequent in everyday engagements even with infants. Contrary to Nietzsche's pessimistic conclusion that we laugh to alleviate our pain ("Man alone suffers so excruciatingly in the world that he was compelled to invent laughter," he wrote), laughter seems to begin in infancy in palpable joy. But laughter itself, though associated with it, cannot be taken as evidence of humour. First of all, we can appreciate humour without laughing, even if "laughter is always in the offing."[9] And second, laughter doesn't necessarily indicate humour. The epithet of *homo ridens* (Aristotle's attempt to designate man as the laughing ape) doesn't seem to be well-founded: chimpanzees, and even rats, "laugh," although with different sounds from humans, during tickling and play—but not, as we usually understand it, from humour.[10] Even in human adults laughter is most often a conversational device, used for marking statements, exclamations, questions, and least often, only about 10 to 20 percent of the time in our everyday interactions, "caused" by preceding humorous utterances or events.[11] We laugh when we have succeeded in doing something difficult, from pleasure at success. We laugh from simple pleasure at experiencing something, from recognising a long lost friend, from joy, or from relief as when we are finally on the plane heading for a holiday after a nightmare trip to the airport. We laugh also from embarrassment, or embarrassingly, when we hear about tragedy (there have been reports, for instance, about laughing on hearing about the events of September 11), or in bitterness, or in anger. The laughter of the gods, according to Homer, was the "exuberance of their celestial joy after their daily banquet," and children too, in high spirits, often engage in "much meaningless laughter."[12] Such laughter, even if we wouldn't call it meaningless, is not necessarily prompted by funniness.

So laughter alone cannot be evidence of funniness, but it would be a mistake to dismiss it altogether. We don't usually have trouble in identifying the laughter of funniness from other laughs, even though humour is often mixed with other emotions. Laughter itself is not a single thing—acoustic qualities differentiate different kinds of laughs; the exclamatory chuckle, for instance, sounds quite different from a belly laugh or a giggle. These differences immediately indicate to us, when we hear them, what sort of feeling is being expressed. These features, and more particularly the suddenness of a laugh, often reveal its genuineness and allow us to distinguish laughs of amusement from those of joy, success, exuberance, anticipation, and so on.[13] Furthermore, our judgements are usually based on contextual information. A combination of these things, therefore, should allow us to use laughter as indicative of humour in the same way that it is used in everyday life. Parents, too, often use these features to distinguish between different kinds of laughter in their infants. Three things are interesting about infant laughter. One, babies laugh, like adults, with different types of laughs and for a variety of reasons. What they laugh at expands during the first year, and these prompts for laughter are interestingly similar to what adults find funny too. Two, parents don't find it hard to identify what their babies are laughing at. This is in sharp contrast to some developmental disorders such as autism, where although there is a considerable amount of everyday laughter, it is often incomprehensible and un-share-able with. Three, the prompts for early infant laughter seem to be totally embedded in engagement with other people. There seems to be something intrinsically social, even interpersonal, about our laughter. Let's have a look at some data about infant laughter and see what we can make of this sociality.

What Do Babies Laugh At? Different Kinds and Contexts of Infant Laughter

I will use data from three different studies (using a combination of video-taped interactions, dictaphone observations by parents, and interviews) on typically developing infants and pre-school children with autism and with Down syndrome (DS) to answer questions raised in this chapter about laughter and the perception and creation of the comic. Mothers of typically developing 8-month-olds report being able to distinguish different kinds of laughs in their babies. They differentiate, for instance, genuine laughs from fake or artificial laughs, with an intermediate category of the forced or polite laugh. They report that *artificial* laughs sound very different from genuine laughs, with a kind of unconvincing quality, and are often used to obtain attention or "join in" when others are laughing but not including the infant in their interaction. *Polite* laughs, on the other hand, are reported in contexts where the infant may have had enough of some game or joke, but continues to laugh in a mild and seemingly unfelt way to appease the parent's expectation and enthusiasm! This is somewhat similar to the "comment laughs" identified by Alan Fogel and Eva Nwokah in Utah.[14] Even when the infant does appear to be genuinely laughing, there are predictable differences between belly laughs, repeated giggles, brief chuckles, and the "screaming laugh"! There is the laugh of *success*, often just a snigger or a chuckle when the infant has achieved something with effort. There is *joy/exuberance*, usually expressed in a string of giggles and often during rough and tumble play. Then there is the very *physical* being tickled or having raspberries blown on the tummy or being chased. This can often lead to belly laughs or to screaming helpless laughter.

Although we might think of rough-and-tumble play as a simple, early, and not particularly funny kind of laughter, there are good reasons to take it seriously. Shultz argued that these are interesting examples of biologically primitive tendencies to deal with things that were once (and could well be again) dangerous for the infant, but are now occurring in a safe context. Peep-bo, for instance, is the story of the disappearing mother and produces in the infant that delicious torment of choosing between excitement and fear, provided that the disappearance happens within a familiar game and is neither entirely threatening nor entirely predictable and boring. Tickling is the story of the predator who can hurt you in the most delicate of places on your body— under your arms, on the soles of your feet, on your throat. Provided it is done by a trusted person who is responding to one's reactions, tickling, too, can maintain that balance between the predicted and the unknown, between desire and the fear of being overwhelmed. Chasing, of course, is the more direct threat of attack by a predator and again needs the right balance between fear and delight in order to work. For Shultz these are forms of proto-humour, involving an ambiguity and delicate balance between danger and safety, and in a simple way presaging the juxtaposition of ideas that constitutes incongruity. Darwin, too, thought that the tickling of the body is very close in spirit to the tickling of the mind by the ludicrous. And they are not, in fact, the first reasons for infants' laughter: even tickling seems to take developmental time to raise a laugh. More importantly, as we shall see in a minute, like other reasons for laughing, tickling and chasing and peep-bo are intrinsically social acts, wrapped up in an ongoing engagement, rather than "stimuli" on their own.

Laughs described as *amused* seem to vary in form from the chuckle to the snigger to what some describe as a "normal" laugh. They can happen in response to a variety of events such as exaggerated or abrupt acts or sounds, odd things the infant herself has done with an object, or mischievous acts on other people. In general, infants seem to start with visual and auditory slapstick (and some tactile contact like blowing raspberries) and then go on, towards the end of the first year, to laughing at socially inappropriate things and gradually more at doing the incongruities rather than just at observing them. Among the fifty or so acts that Alan Sroufe and Jane Wunsch asked mothers to perform in the laboratory to try to get their infants to laugh were many "odd" or incongruous actions, like making funny faces (although in everyday interactions these are almost always accompanied by a voice sound as well), vigorous shaking of the head, shaking of the hair, blowing a raspberry or making a lip-popping sound, making rising sounds with abrupt endings, and so on.[15] These are simple acts whose oddness lies sometimes in the contrast between them and the "normal" appearance of the body or voice, perceived incongruities in technical terms, and more simply at other times in the vigorousness or extremeness of the action or sound. What is interesting is that these acts elicit laughter from adults, too. We, too, laugh to see someone walking in a jerky manner, persons enlarging their eyes and sticking their tongues out, someone speaking in a squeaky voice, at sounds that speed up then stop abruptly, or at the fast forwarded videotape.

Our studies provided many examples of infants laughing at *visual and auditory slapstick:* funny noises, with rising pitch and abrupt end as Sroufe and Wunsch described, or people speaking in squeaky voices, and people making funny faces (although some infants at 8 months were reported to look puzzled, certainly if there was no sound accompanying the face—i.e., if a play context wasn't previously established or if there was no accompanying sound). All of the following examples are taken from the transcripts of one of our studies, with the names of the infants changed.[16] The sensory incongruity (if we want to use that term) could come from different sources: presented by the parent as in this example:

> Just . . . if you shake your head so your hair bobs all over the place and you go "brrr," he likes that, he'll giggle. (Mother of Adam, 8 months, interview)

Organised by the infant herself as in this one:

> She'll sit on my lap and . . . plays with my bra and pulls it towards her, even though she's not going for food, she just pulls it towards her and I'll make a noise going "aaaah" and she laughs at the noise as well and keeps on laughing . . . . at the response . . . she'll keep on pulling it to get a response. (Mother of Vanessa, 8 months, interview)

An accident as in this one:

> She was putting those tiny little pots into a long sort of box . . . when she put them in, the bottom opened and they fell out. . . . And the top and the bottom was open. . . she picked up (the box) and looked through it at us and cackled with laughter . . . she thought it was incredibly funny. (Mother of Fiona, 8 months, interview)

Or even, less frequently, to mechanical events:

> Oh it sounds daft . . . the other thing she really likes is er . . . the toilet flushing . . . so she . . . she tries to flush the toilet now . . . she'll hold onto

the handle, and she likes seeing that, and that makes her laugh and she wants to see it again. (Mother of Fiona, 11 months, interview)

In the case of popping up or chasing or tickling by the parents, what is involved is the infant's perception of suddenness, the experience of some ambiguity in anticipation, but not necessarily as yet an incompatibility (what might also be called incongruity) between an action and its expected pattern. Incongruity, however, could be interpreted as a matter of degree. Popping up in an odd place rather than the expected one is to some extent an incongruity, but not as much of one as would be just not popping up at all! The infant's experience of these events is clearly non-serious and is sometimes brief and sudden, consisting of sudden chuckles within an ongoing game, although it is more usually a prolonged experience of anticipatory enjoyment and laughter.

Adult Awareness of Reasons for Infant Laughter

It was interesting that when asked in our interview studies what their babies laughed at, none of the parents of the typically developing infants reported any doubt about the reasons for their infants' laughter. Only in one case did a parent report that she didn't on occasion know what it was her infant was laughing at:

> Sometimes she'll find something to laugh at just by herself, I don't know what it is, she'll suddenly have a little snigger to herself . . . and you go "what you laughing at" . . . sometimes it might just be a toy, or standing up or leaning against my mum's sofa you know with that pattern on that, she'll be playing with that and sometimes she'll laugh. I don't know whether it's the flowers or whether it's the fact that she's on her feet. (Mother of Vanessa, 8 months, interview)

None of the parents found the infant's laughter in itself incongruous or incomprehensible. This is important for the simple reason that if infant laughter is comprehensible to the adults around, it can be shared by them. If you cannot tune in to what someone else is laughing about, it is difficult to really engage with that person in their reaction. Of course there may be simple and uninteresting reasons for these certainties in the parents. If a researcher asks you what your infant laughs at, there is the underlying assumption that there *is* something to laugh at! (It would be rather like asking a toddler with a paint brush "what's that you're painting?" It invites an answer.) Parents must, like everyone else, be driven in any case to make sense of the acts of others close to them, and it could be that they seek comprehension even where none is warranted. However, parents often consciously report what their infant is attending to or doing just prior to the laugh, in the same way as they would the reasons for adults' laughter. Parents' answers about what their babies are laughing at are therefore not likely to be arbitrary.

Evidence for the importance of the confidence of parents of typically developing infants in identifying the reasons for babies' laughter comes from the very different answers from parents of children with autism. Parents don't *always* make sense of their children's laughter or offer explanations where none are warranted. When we asked the parents of pre-school children with autism the same question, we received very different spontaneous answers. One mother commented with sadness on the feeling in the laughter: "he laughs . . . but he doesn't have the emotion of laughter." Although the children laughed at many things which the parents could and did identify, there were also many occasions when all the parents felt that they could not understand what the child was laughing at. They reported finding the laughter incomprehensible, and sometimes not "real."[17]

> She'll do that quite a lot (just laugh without looking at anyone, as she was doing just now). She can be anywhere. I've been in shops before, walking round the supermarket and she'll be sitting in her buggy and all of a sudden she'll start laughing. And there doesn't seem to be anything about that she could be laughing at but she will be laughing. It doesn't matter what the situation is, she'll think of something and it'll make her laugh and you can't share it with her. We laugh sometimes because she does look happy but we don't know what she's laughing at. (Mother of Tara, girl with autism, 3 years, interview)

> When she was little we used to say she was strange, because upstairs in my bedroom I have got piles and piles of ironing . . . and Amanda used to stand in the corner, observe my pile of ironing and go into mass hysteria. . . . This was before she was diagnosed and we used to say gosh she is a strange child. (Mother of Amanda, girl with autism, 3 years, interview)

> But I also find sometimes he just giggles. You don't know what he's laughing at. . . . Sometimes you're lying in bed on a night and you hear him giggling. Its almost as though he had someone in the room with him,

you know, like he's having this little conversation. Certain times it's just a word that you've said. I mean one particular time we said the word "black," and it would have him so he was almost collapsing with giggling. (Mother of Tony, boy with autism, 5 years, interview)

In contrast, the same question put to parents of pre-school children with DS yielded very different responses. Only one of sixteen parents reported an incomprehension or lack of empathy with the cause of the child's laughter, reporting "laughing at horrible things like someone being smacked." But even here there was an identification of the "cause" of the laughter, not a puzzlement.

Infants Laugh at Things That Adults Find Funny Too

It is particularly interesting that the same things are found funny by infants and parents (even, to a large extent, by the children with autism and their parents). The lack of reports about incomprehensible laughter in typical infants and in DS suggests that parents are not simply focusing on what they recognize as funny. Moreover, there is often an identifiable pattern of incongruities in these laughter-producing events: involving violations of routines, accidental or intentional, and violations of normal facial, vocal, or bodily movements. A more plausible explanation of the similarity of "cause" of laughter would be to argue that infants and parents share the same world and the same ability to perceive *affordances for funniness* in events in the world. Affordances, a concept developed by James Gibson to provide an alternative to representational accounts of perception, are the potential for action that the environment offers the animal, the invitation it provides. Daniel Berlyne's specification of the perceptual features of "funny" stimuli—novelty, surprisingness, ambiguity—could be interpreted as the environmental affordances for humour (which may not always be perceived as such depending on other factors).[18] Parents and infants inhabit a similar (though given their different bodies, not an identical) physical world and possess similar (but again not identical) abilities to perceive some of these features. Children with autism, too, with their laughter at visual slapstick and their ability to respond to the surprises in peep-bo and tickling, hearteningly share part of the same perceptual world.

He loves being tickled . . . enjoys being swung around and he likes the bit about the okey kokey when you all go in together and . . . finds that really funny. If he's . . . he likes . . . he's watched Laurel and Hardy on telly and when they're falling over or done something he's laughed at that. . . . If we pretend to fall over he finds that hysterical. He thinks that's really funny . . . and (at the end of Telly Tubbies) well sometimes they sort of lay on their backs and wave their legs in the air and all the rest of it? He thinks that's hysterical . . . when we've done it. (Mother of Jake, boy with autism, 4 years, interview)

Say we're at the park and we see one duck chasing another duck. Or a dog chasing a squirrel. And he'll laugh his head off and think its really funny. (Mother of Alan, boy with autism, 4 years, interview)

This interpretation suggests that funniness need not be an inference or judgement about a perceived event, but may exist as an incongruous feature of the event itself, perceivable as such (given the playfulness of attitude identified by Mary Rothbart). Infants, before they develop complex representational machinery, may, therefore, perceive these features and, given a playful mood and context, laugh at them, as do adults. The data of infant laughter at these structurally incongruous events suggest that it makes little sense to continue to draw a line just beyond infancy for the onset of humour. A more appropriate developmental argument would be to see the development of funniness as a continuous process, beginning early in infancy and certainly developing, but developing in its *content*, broadening in its targets and its understanding, but not beginning as a late shift from non-humorous to humorous laughter.

But is the affordance for humour really in the "stimulus"? Is the joke really in the text of the event? Both representational and perceptual theories of humour can fall into this trap. An affordance, however, is a relational phenomenon, "something that refers to both the environment and the animal in a way that no existing term does. It implies the complementarity of the animal and the environment." This concept implies that the features of surprisingness, for example, are available to us because the world normally is regular and *not* surprising, and because we, while depending on these regularities, can detect and respond to surprise with laughter. We can imagine aliens from a chaotic world who would neither notice the breaks in regularity nor be able to respond to them with surprise. The funniness, then, is neither in us nor in the event but somewhere in the relation between the two. But even this account is incomplete. Where do other people fit in? How exactly does society wrap itself around the infant's developing sense of humour?

Incongruities-in-Engagement

The examples reported here show funniness to be much more complicated than a relation between the infant and features of the environment. The structural properties of the events the infants laughed at were in almost all cases perceived against a backdrop of the involvement and laughter of other people. This involvement is so widespread and seems so fundamental to infants' amusement that it becomes nonsense to say that a "boo" or a "squeaky voice" or even the bottom falling out of the cardboard box is funny solely because of the way infants perceive structure in the physical world. They become meaningful only within their use and response. All of these things are, from the start, *used* by people in order to elicit laughter, and they are also used by parents *because* they elicit laughter from infants. If you take the example of the infant laughing at the parent's action, both the infant and the parent are drawn into maintaining their respective actions by each other, the parent by the fact of the infant's response and the infant by the fact of the parent's act. The affordance for humour must exist somehow in a triple set of bi-directional relations between infant, parent, and event. The funniness of a "boo," then, is in the "boo" itself, in the individual *and* in the society. There is no real possibility of separating them. This is true for most simple funny things—making funny faces, odd sounds, and the like. If we take more complex funny things like teasing, it is even more impossible to separate the structural from the individual and from the social. They are based on expectations and norms, they presume surprise, and they cannot exist outside of social recognition. If you engage in a tease and no one ever laughs, it is simply not funny. One cannot, therefore, have either a purely social relations view or a purely structural view of funniness. Funniness is neither an arbitrary and ungrounded relativistic phenomenon nor a purely structural "objective" phenomenon.

Even the earliest laughter, developing from around 3 or 4 months of age, emerges within face-to-face social engagements. Darwin shows from careful descriptions of his children's early laughs that the first laughter develops out of smiles.[19] Both in terms of the contexts in which early laughs occur and in their actual form, they seem to be more intense versions of smiles, often leaving parents in the first few months of an infant's life wondering whether or not that slight hiccupping or almost-sobbing sound in the middle of a smile was really a laugh.[20] These first smile-laughs happen while "chatting" with other people, as extensions of the social smile, not in solitude.

"He never chuckles on his own at things, it is always when we're playing with him, trying to make him laugh," says the mother of 12-week-old Ben about the first three weeks of this early laugher. Four weeks or so after his first laugh, however, he was heard laughing on his own while playing with a mobile hanging over him. The following description from a video of Ben's early laughter (at 12 weeks) shows the intense face-to-face engagement, expectation, and dialogic motivation wrapped around every laugh of the infant and every laughter-eliciting act of the mother. It is long, and in some ways very ordinary, but conveys the complete embeddedness of laughter within a social exchange:

Ben lying on floor, Lucy leaning over him and asking (pretend grown-up questions) about his day

Ben looking intently at her and watching with a smile.

"That's a lovely smile" says Lucy.

Ben just continues smiling at Lucy.

Lucy repeats in a deeper voice "that's a lovely smile!"

Ben makes an almost laughing sound "Hmmmh, hmmmh!" still looking intently at Lucy.

Lucy imitates the laugh, saying "Ha ha! funny laugh!"

Ben makes the sound again, longer "Hmmh, hmmh, hmmh, ha!" and ending with a distinct chuckle.

"Funny laugh!" says Lucy again in a deep, hollow voice.

Ben almost chuckles once, reaction milder now, still watching intently.

Lucy puts on a fake chuckle in that same deep, hollow voice.

Ben just watches, smiling, but mildly.

Lucy says "What a funny laugh!" now her voice coming down to a less exaggerated, more conversational tone, matching his sobering up.

Ben looks at her, smiles once, then stops smiling.

Lucy says "Any more?" voice now normal level.

Ben smiles.

"Any more?" repeats Lucy quicker now.

Ben now seems conversational—mouthing something, arms moving and with whispering vocalisations, intently looking at Lucy, pleasant but not smiling.

Lucy watches, quiet for a bit. Then at another intent but not smiling conversational attempt by Ben, Lucy leans forward a bit saying "Bubububub!" as if in reply, mild tone.

Ben looks unsmiling for a second, then laughs suddenly twice.
Lucy repeats the "ubububububub!" now in a deeper, hollower voice.
Ben looks at her, smiling, then breaks into a higher pitched squeal,
Lucy laughs with him, saying "funny Mummy!"
Ben watches, now unsmiling again.
Lucy repeats the "Ubububububub" again, with reducing effort each time, as
Ben now watches but does not smile or laugh.

Lucy stops now, watches, and then just chats, voice now in normal register asking "Am I quite funny?" and so it goes on.

Every smile, every chuckle, and every attempt to elicit an action or a laugh from the other was completely embedded within the other's response.

Even something as apparently physical as tickling seems, according to parents, to require a build-up, a social wrapping to make it funny at least in the early months. It seems to be the *social interaction* of the tickle, not the tickle itself, which is funny at this age, the vocal and gestural build-up to it, the threat and anticipation of it rather than the physical sensation of it. The following examples are from our longitudinal study of typically developing infants:[21]

> . . . tickling his belly and you have sort of go "ticka, ticka, ticka, ticka" like that, and he thinks that's funny. I think it's probably the voice as well that makes him laugh. (Mother of Adam, 8 months, interview)

Even in chasing the fun seems to come from the social bartering, not the chase itself:

> She stomps along (away from her father) waving her arms, shrieking with laughter going da da da and he then chases after her, stomping his feet and making lots of noise and she shrieks with laughter and he scoops her up and swings her around and puts her down again. . . . And even when she's coming towards him she does exactly the same and then he just steps over her and she continues and she thinks this is incredibly funny, laughing hysterically as she sort of staggers off down the hall, laughing and sort of, she is laughing so much she can't always keep her balance. (Mother of Fiona, 11 months, interview)

And there were many instances of infant laughter which were prompted by social acts which were not incongruities at all, by, for instance, the other person imitating the infant or the infant imitating the other:

Stuart was making some strange growling noises in his pram, so I waited for him to stop and made the same noise back. He looked at me, laughed, and then repeated the noise. (Mother of Stuart, 8 months, interview)

We were all in bed, we had just had breakfast in bed and Adam was in a pretty good humour. He started pulling at his ear, so Graham started pulling at his own ear. Adam thought this was quite amusing so started pulling both his own ears . . . Graham did the same back and it just went from there. Adam started doing things, Graham would copy him, Adam would laugh and in the end he was in hysterics. (Mother of Adam, 11 months, dictaphone)

It is not incongruities per se—as abstract or acontextually representable events—but the incongruous-act-in-engagement that seems critical here. The roots of humorous laughter, it would seem, originate in interpersonal engagement. We don't know, of course, whether infants would ever laugh if there were no people to laugh with in the initial instance. (This is almost like that old question—Which language would infants begin to speak if there were no exposure to adult language?—which King James reportedly tried to test for by bringing up an infant with deaf-mute caregivers on an island in the Firth of Forth near Edinburgh). We do know that where children are brought up in troubled conditions, as in Rumania, with little joy in their lives, laughter is almost absent from their everyday lives. We don't know how soon after they begin to laugh in interpersonal contexts infants are able to laugh alone. It is likely, however, that such solitary laughter is rare, and rarer in the early months than later.[22] Reports of solitary laughter by infants come in the second half of the first year. The father of a 6-month-old girl reports that he was hanging the washing out in the garden one day, with the infant in her pushchair nearby. He heard her laughing and turned to see her looking at the sky and watching fast-moving clouds. By 8 months there are a few such reports of infants laughing outside social engagement at things like mechanical events. But these reports are still few and far between.

In our study of children with autism, we found that laughter when the child is alone is more frequent than in children with DS, as is "solitary" laughter when the child and parent are together (i.e., with the focus of the laugh unshared).[23] In adults, while we laugh alone on occasion (but always with an imagined or potential communicant?), we rarely let such solitary laughs remain unshared when we are with someone. The fact that laughter can remain unshared and uncomprehended in children with autism leaves the door open to the possibility that the comic can be perceived developmentally independent of relationships between people. However, the fact that this is the case in problematic development and is perceived as abnormal suggests that it is a strange and unusual process.

Sensitivity to Others' Laughter

Interest in and Desire to Join in Others' Laughter

Other people's laughter is itself interesting and may be the critical key to shared humour. As adults we know how contagious laughter can be in the right circumstances. Infants, too, from about 6 months of age can show not only an interest in it, but also a motivation to join in and share it, even when they cannot have a clue about its context. Such joining in laughter is not like contagious laughter; it is reported as being much more "fake," like a deliberate communicative (rather than uncontrollable emotional) act. The first time I ever heard such a laugh (and I would never have taken artificial laughter seriously enough to investigate it had this not happened) I had gone to visit Colwyn Trevarthen in his office in Edinburgh with Shamini when she was about 5 or 6 months old. She was in her car chair by the window in the big office some five yards from where we were talking. She could hear our conversation but was not in face-to-face contact with either of us. Suddenly we heard a forced "ha ha ha" from her. I realised that we ourselves had just laughed at something before she made that sound. It sounded like a (poor) attempt to join in with us. But such artificial laughter is frequently reported by parents in the second half of the first year.[24]

> She likes other people laughing . . . she actually has a laugh along with them . . . so if you, if you like pretend and you're laughing, she'll sit there and chuckle with you and even if there's nothing funny about, you haven't done anything, even if you just sit there and laugh, then she'll laugh with you. (Mother of Melanie, 11 months, interview)

Not all infants showed what parents called false laughter. Some did, and particularly for joining in with others' laughter. But others looked puzzled when they didn't understand why laughter was directed to them, and some grew out of it:

> He seems to have stopped that now actually (the artificial laugh) . . . he did have a sort of a . . . laugh that he would laugh almost because everyone

else was laughing. But he seems to have stopped that at the moment, to be honest. . . . I noticed it when the girls were laughing at something . . . and he would laugh . . . er . . . but now he's more mobile, he doesn't seem . . . so . . . I suppose because he doesn't have to sort of sit there and listen and watch them all the time, he can get off more on his own. (Mother of Stuart, 11 months, interview)

In children with autism, however, the interest in others' laughter is less evident. In an analysis of videotaped interactions with children and parents and the researcher present, we found that on over three-quarters of the occasions when other people laughed in their presence, the children did not even look up, in contrast to on average about half the time in the children with DS. Laughter in response to others' laughter was rare in the children with autism according to the parents. Although a few of the children did sometimes laugh when they heard others laughing (as opposed to three-quarters of the children with DS), the parents spoke about such laughter as "echoic" or imitative more than as attempts to join in or elicit attention.

Clowning: Doing Things to Make Others Laugh

The criteria for humour we've been discussing so far focus mainly on the individual's experience of humour on perceiving things that happen around them. There has been, as I said earlier, a relative neglect of humour created by the individual. Does the prankster, the joke teller, the teaser, or the clown experience the same thing too by creating humour? Freud observed that while one can laugh to oneself when one perceives the comic, one cannot make a joke and keep it to oneself; the processes involved in creating a joke and in receiving or perceiving it are slightly different things, though both involve funniness.

No one can be content with having made a joke for himself alone. An urge to tell the joke to someone is inextricably bound up with the joke-work; indeed, this urge is so strong that often enough it is carried through in disregard of serious misgivings. In the case of the comic as well, telling it to someone else produces enjoyment; but the demand is not peremptory. If one comes across something comic, one can enjoy it by oneself. A joke, on the contrary, must be told to someone else. The psychical process of constructing a joke seems not to be completed when the joke occurs to one: something remains over which seeks, by communicating the idea, to bring the unknown process of constructing the joke to a conclusion. . . . If I come across something comic, I myself can laugh heartily at it, though it is true that I am also pleased if I can make someone else laugh by telling it to him. But I myself cannot laugh at a joke that has occurred to me, that I have made, in spite of the unmistakable enjoyment that the joke gives me. It is possible that my need to communicate the joke to someone else is in some way connected with the laughter produced by it, which is denied to me but is manifest in the other person.[25]

In the creation of humour, the joking seems half an act, an act which can only be completed by the laughter of another person. But the distinction between the joke and the comic may not be so clear when we look at the creation (rather than the perception) of the comic. The creation of the comic seems even more inescapably social. What is it that drives us to become humorists? And how (and when) does it begin?

Infants, far from being constrained by their lack of speech and representational skills, not only laugh at other people's actions and sometimes at mechanical events, but they also deliberately *do* things themselves to make others laugh. Joking, which can be thought of as *play* with one's thoughts, feelings, or actions, can be non-verbal as well as verbal. And even by 8 months of age infants can be seen to be involved as agents in humorous engagements rather than just as observers and audience. Initially, however, the funniness of an infant's act in infant-parent humorous engagements is often in the parent's *response* to it (and on the sensitivity of the infant *to* this response). Most examples of clowning start off with the infant's interest in an action for the sake of its physical, sensational, and vigorous properties, becoming funny (rather than just interesting) by virtue of the fact that someone else laughs at it. The infant in the first year rarely seems to plan an act of clowning; she walks into it by accident. Once the accident has occurred, however, infants from this age pick up on the laughter of others and repeat the act deliberately, sometimes just a few more times on that occasion, but sometimes for days, until the laughter of others becomes strained to the point of impossibility! Here is one example of an 11-month-old infant clowning:

She imitated her great-grandmother's snoring face, looking around at the others. They laughed in embarrassment (because the video camera was on) and because her face was truly ludicrous. She looked at their faces, and now laughed (a social, almost complicit laugh, not a sudden chuckle) and then did it again, now deliberately, waiting for a reaction. They all laughed, unable to resist. She repeated the ridiculous expression, looking at them. She continued for several days to produce that face whenever something (like a yawn) reminded her and waited for the laughter. By the end of two weeks of this, the expression was hardly funny anymore![26]

Just as adult clowns pick up on things that amuse others and play on these things, so infants are sensitive to and interested in others' laughter and motivated enough to pick up on its causes and reproduce them. The descriptions of clowning episodes are clear in one respect: the infant at 8 months doesn't laugh initially, but does start laughing as well as doing the odd action once the other starts laughing. It would appear that things become humorous through the judgement of others.

Is the infant, then, really making a joke? There are two reasons to answer yes. First, this is often what adults and adult clowns do through their experiences. If we're trying to make people laugh, we use what works. And we all may, on occasion, start perceiving something as dull and then "see the funny side of it" when we hear someone (whom we like) laugh at it. Second, the things that infants do are strikingly similar (see Table 9.1) to the kinds of things adult clowns do to elicit audience laughter—hardly surprising, actually, since the audience in both cases is the same! The things that are done to make others laugh are in all cases incongruous in some way, violating either physical or social norms.[27] The infants have only a little of the understanding of how deeply these actions violate normality and of exactly why they are funny to others, but they certainly seem to pick up on the fact of the violation and their link to others' laughter.

What if rubbing the top of the head was found to be very funny in a culture where the head was considered a sacred part of the body? Undoubtedly, both adult clowns and infant clowns would develop rubbing the top of the head "tricks" to get people to laugh. The structure of the action itself cannot be completely separated from the social reactions. Clowning in infancy illustrates beautifully the way in which cultures of humour are created in engagement. Just as when we move to a different culture we start learning to appreciate humour which we didn't before, clowning in infancy shows how infants from the second half of the first year are learning what counts as funny in their world. Moreover, it shows that the roots of humour lie not just in the structure of the joke, but in the motivational/ emotional process of being interested in others' emotional reactions, in particular in this case, laughter.

Table 9.1. Typical actions repeated in order to (re-)elicit laughter from others: By adult clowns and by infants

Adult clowns	Infant clowns
Odd body movements: falling, slipping, funny walking, odd dancing	*Odd body movements:* squashes head into neck; shakes head; wobbles head; walks funny; throws self around
Odd facial expressions: odd eyes, painted smiles, dots on cheeks	*Odd facial expressions:* screws up face; sticks out lower lip; rolls eyes
Odd or loud sounds: bangs, squeals, gruff voices	*Odd or loud sounds:* squeaks, squawks, shrieks; fake coughing; fake laughing; saying "baa baa"
	Extreme actions: grits teeth on jumper and shakes self vigorously; effortful sound with tearing action; rattles headboard of bed; bangs, splashes
Acting absurd: hitting self, throwing pies at others' faces, splashing people with hose pipes, etc.	*Acting absurd:* pats mother on head; looks out from under arm; bites others' toes; puts dummy in mother's mouth; pulls M's tights; pulls M's skin; holds up smelly feet; kisses sibling's knee; puts thumb in mouth; touches toes; puts toy duck in mouth with funny facial expression; splashing others
Acting profane, abusive, acting hostile: Violation of taboos, uncouth behaviour	*Showing normally hidden body parts:* lifts dress and shows stomach pointing to navel
	Violating norms: teases with deliberate non-compliance; teases with offering and withdrawing objects
	Violating others' constructions: tips toys out, knocks others' bricks over; teases by disrupting others' ongoing or intended actions
Ridiculing the serious: Lampooning politicians, even religious figures and objects	
Mocking	*Imitating others' odd actions:* imitates great grandmother's snoring face; imitates grandmother's odd face; imitates mother's sound

(continued)

Table 9.1 (continued)

Adult clowns	Infant clowns
Adopting a grotesque appearance: false penises and vulvas (the Hopi), false breasts and male cross-dressing (Britain)	*Odd self-decoration:* puts on wedding head-dress; puts cup on head
Acting infantile, regressing: drinking/ eating urine, pouring over head (the Zunis), etc.	*Acting infantile, regressing:* blows raspberries with food or water in mouth; spits food out; makes spitting sound with water

Clearly, a structural analysis of acts or events alone is not sufficient for explaining humour, as a third-person perspective might assume. One needs to look at humour as a social process. The holy grail for the essence of humour may lie in a mapping of the paths of these processes of engagement rather than in the elements of the activity alone. That which is funny is an activity that develops within engagement, and in the case of clowning, develops simply by laughter from other people to accidentally discovered odd behaviour.

But not all children do pick up on the link between others' laughter and their own acts. See, for example, this report from a mother of a child with autism:

> There's nothing there that makes her think "If I do this it'll make Mum and Dad laugh and get our enjoyment." . . . It doesn't occur to her that she can do something to make us laugh. If she's done something accidentally like a few times you catch her hanging upside down doing something and you'll laugh and go "Tara, what are you doing?" and there's no recognition there that she's thought "oh, they're laughing 'cause I've done this" and doing it again. That's the big thing that you do notice, that stands out a mile from other children. . . . I can't think of a time when she's ever done something to make us laugh. (Mother of Tara, girl with autism, 3 years, interview)[28]

Clowning is not only revealing about an awareness of others' attention (as we saw from its correlations with proto-declarative pointing in the chapter on attention) but also tells us an awful lot about children's interest in and ability to influence others' emotional reactions. In comparison with the children with DS, the children with autism showed a marked lack of clowning. And the few children who were reported to repeat things for making people laugh usually used stock phrases and single acts. Clowning is difficult to do by formula. Teasing tells us even more, in this regard, about the awareness of others.

Distance and Disengagement in Humour

But there is another side to the sociality of humour—an almost paradoxical side. While humour seems to require tight engagement with audience reactions and sensitivity to social actions and patterns, it often involves a simultaneous detachment and disengagement from these very things. Humorists are "lateral" people: they show an ability to side-step from other people and other people's pressures and concerns, showing an almost willful refusal to participate in the expected, to engage on the same level as everyone else, to understand or accept what everyone else is moved by. It is as if, to extend an example from Bergson, they are stopping up their ears while watching people dancing. The dancers with their intense, self-absorbed or dramatic movements would seem absurd, funny, ridiculous. I remember one mortifying and tactless comment from a teacher when as an 8-year-old I was performing a dance on an open-air stage where the school sound system (unknown to me) simply didn't carry beyond the stage. "It was so funny watching you dance without the music," said the teacher! It is the perceiver's disengagement (in this case literally) from the music which moves another that makes that person's acts seem funny.

We often deliberately create such disengagement in many ways (some of us more than others), deflating a serious conversation, violating the routines we are caught in, creating wonderful absurdity by simply refusing to play the game or to accept the seriousness that others around us are absorbed in. We all know the feeling of being able to laugh at something which had earlier seemed a disaster, or those sudden realisations of absurdity that strike us in the middle of a meeting when the people around the table look like players in an elaborate pantomime. When this happens, we are breaking our connection with those others around us. It seems to be precisely a lack of empathy, a refusal to share the moods and thoughts and concerns of others that can both give rise to, and result from, humour. Mutual *mis*-understanding or *mis*-relation, it seems, is as much the natural birthplace of humour as relation and understanding. We need at the same time to join in and hold out as participants in a social group.

Can infants really be capable of such engaged disengagement? If simple compliance with the expected and simple attempts to elicit laugher through doing whatever "pleases" others were the only things infants were capable of, their humour would be impoverished indeed. But it isn't. Infants also show the ability to step aside from the mainstream and do the *mis*-expected. They tease.

Engaged Disengagement: Teasing in Infancy and in Autism

From about 9 months of age, infants show the ability to violate others' expectations. In two longitudinal studies of infants in the first year, parents reported three broad types of teasing acts by infants. The most common was provocative non-compliance, and we have already seen examples of this in the chapter on intentions. Provocations were not always done for the pleasure of achieving the action itself: the most striking examples were when the infant had no desire for the action—where the provocation itself was the goal, as in the following example from Rohan at 14 months:

> I was carrying him on my left hip while standing at the cooker and stirring a pot. On a previous occasion he had accidentally touched a hot pan (but very lightly) and almost burnt himself. He knew it was painful, often commented "hot" appropriately and was completely to be trusted not to touch hot things. Today, I was paying little attention to him, and he slowly reached out a hand towards the pan (looking at me with a slight smile on his face, which I didn't see immediately because I was looking down); I said "no, hot!" immediately, but he didn't withdraw. I looked up and found him looking at me with a slight, playful smile. (This tease had never happened before, nor did it happen again.)

Other types of teasing were the simple offer and withdrawal of an object, or more intriguingly, of the self:

> She's been crawling more now. And a new game . . . say, I'm holding her and my husband comes up to get her and she'll like pretend to go to him and then she'll back off. And that's with anyone, like even if my mum comes round and I say "go to nanny" and she'll put her hands out to go and then she'll like back off. . . . she'll laugh, she thinks that's really funny, because they go "oh, um" and she keeps doing it. (Mother of Dana, 11 months, interview)[29]

More general provocations involved disrupting others' activities:

> Holly's (sister, aged 3 years) in the sitting room at the moment playing with
> her duplo and Stuart seems to think it's really funny to keep breaking them
> down. Every time she puts the bricks together he basically breaks it up then
> sits there looking at you and laughs. Its almost as though he thinks he is
> going to get a good laugh out of it, even though you tell him no, he just
> thinks it's funny. (Mother of Stuart, 11 months, dictaphone)[30]

Beginning in single instances which are sometimes noticed by parents,
these acts often develop into games, but not always. Sometimes a single act
of teasing is never repeated beyond the immediate occasion. What is clear
in these acts is the mutualness of teasing. The tease works because the
teaser and at least one other person see it as important in the interaction.
(There is, of course, teasing which is not funny, where the teaser's expression is watchful and the reaction aimed for is negative. But these are less
common in the first year and are not humorous in their attitude). The tease
demands recognition as a tease and only survives if it gets it. It seems to be
not just a stopping up of the ears to the music the other is listening to, but
also the initiation of a *different* music for *both* to listen to.

Why Tease?

Why *do* infants tease? What is it that's funny in teasing? Why do we ever decide to stop our ears to the ongoing music (or start a different music)? Shigeru
Nakano from Japan argues that the motivation for teasing is an "incident-
affinity" (or "indecent affinity" as he once called it!). Studying the gentle
teasing of Japanese mothers of 9- and 10-month-old infants—through
jumping out sooner than expected or suddenly failing to clap hands in time,
and so on—Nakano argued that teasing creates an incident or perturbation in
communication. We are drawn towards such incidents because by perturbing
the ongoing flow, they demand a higher level of engagement to renew the
flow. In doing so, they deepen the communication.[31]

Two incidents of adults teasing older children stick vividly in my mind:

> One hot afternoon in India my sister was sitting on a large bed talking to
> her friend. The friend's 3-year-old son was standing by the bed playing
> with a toy train on his own. After a while my sister, bored, reached over
> and snatched the train away. The boy protested and demanded it back. She

gave it back, straight-faced. After a short while she took it away again, he protested, more strongly, and she gave it back. She repeated the disruption another few times. After a few occasions, the boy's grizzly protests turned to laughter, and she laughed too and the toy snatching stopped.

My invalid father was sitting on his bed while my 2-year-old son played on the floor with some toys. My father reached for his walking stick and prodded my son who was balancing on his haunches. He toppled aside a bit and frowned with a brief glance at my father, then got back on his haunches and continued playing. After a while my father repeated the prod. Within a few repetitions, my son gave up on his toys, and playfully attacked my father—both of them laughing, and now both started playing together.

The teasing in these incidents seemed to result from boredom (something that, interestingly, typifies some of the teasing by chimpanzees too) and makes sense even of a lot of adult teasing.[32] Teasing creates "incidents" or disturbances in engagement, which, when done and received playfully (even when, as in the instances reported above, the evidence of playfulness is concealed in the straight face and hidden from the recipient for rather a long time,) not only brighten the interaction for a while, but can create a new way of relating to each other. The playful tease could well be a way of making psychological contact, an attempt to touch the other at a higher level of intimacy and of successfully creating positiveness. There are, of course, many other reasons for teasing. It can be, as the anthropologists observed long ago, and as the majority of studies of teasing portray it, a form of bullying or social control disguised as humour. And certainly, its usage in groups of chimpanzees and school yards (where the status differences are very obvious between teaser and teased) show that this can be the case. However, teasing can be a powerful way of soliciting positive engagement and deepening intimacy. Teasing works because the teaser recognises the other's intentions and "touches" them unexpectedly. The teaser offers a reference to something hidden about the teased person. It works as play if the teased person recognises and is reassured about the teaser's intentions for the relationship. And if it works, playful teasing not only reflects, but creates intimacy, whatever age it happens at.[33]

In Conclusion

Participation is the alpha and the omega of humour. Umberto Eco argued that while the tragic is universal, the comic is particular to its time and social anthropology. What makes it particular is its origin and meaning within second-person relations. Like the dynamic process of culture, the process of creating and negotiating funniness reveals intense engagement as well as disengagement from other people. From the data about humorous engagements in infancy the cultural basis for humour seems evident. Shared affordances for perceiving funniness actually create further affordances for sharing it. Pure, genuine play, according to Johan Huizinga, is one of the main bases of civilisation, not leading *to* civilisation, but *being* it: "civilisation does not come *from* play like a babe detaching itself from the womb: it arises *in* and *as* play and never leaves it."[34] At its broadest, humour is play and playfulness (although unlike play, which can be serious, humour is the antithesis of seriousness). Nonetheless it is arguable that humour, with its incorrigible desecration of everything the self and the other holds dear, its side-ways thinking/feeling creation of the mis-expected, and of joy and close bonds in the midst of tragedy, is the spirit that creates and the glue that binds not only cultures (if not quite Huizinga's noble "civilisation") but also families together. Humour has *everything* to do with understanding other minds. We would not be able to join in with the feeling in another person's laughter nor be able to understand the sense of a joke unless we could understand something about others' feelings and thoughts. At the simplest level laughter epitomises successful and well-tuned engagement. Sharing a laugh with another person can open up moments of intimacy and mutual understanding which are hard to reach in other ways. Adopting a third-person or first-person approach to funniness would not allow this kind of mutuality.

In contrast to theories which argue that humour begins at around 18 months of age with the development of symbolic representational skills, the data from infancy suggests that from much earlier than that, typically developing infants laugh at the same sorts of things as adults do, and show an active interest in and ability to, make other people laugh. The commonalities in the things that infants and adults find funny reveal the existence of shared affordances for funniness, shared through our similar physiologies and our similar environments. The capacity to understand each other is already pre-figured in this sharedness. Infants' interest in others' laughter and their evident motivation to join in it even without understanding its cause show a motivation to share in others' emotionality. Funniness hinges on the infant's engagements with other people. Infants laugh at things that other people do because other people do them to the infant in direct face-to-face engagement. Conversely, other people do them to infants because infants laugh at them. Infants from the start are *participants* in humorous engagements, not just *perceivers*. And infants *create* humour, too. Their interest and motivation in re-eliciting others' laughter by repeating actions they have done shows an understanding of others as receptive audiences for humour. Clowning reveals an intriguing understanding of attentionality directed to specific aspects of the self (as discussed in Chapter 6) and shows the early processes through which cultures of humour are developed. Teasing, a much more paradoxical form of engagement, shows infants' sensitivity to the expectations and intentions of others (discussed in Chapter 8) and their interest in and ability to perturb engagements and build closer communicative contact. The experience of funniness, then, seems both a great tool for forging mutual understanding and, it would seem, a useful measure of existing understanding. The moments of mis-understanding and disharmony in humour seem possible only where there is also a basis of understanding.

The circularity involved in funniness is evident in all these interactions: infants would neither tease nor clown if others did not find it funny, nor would other people respond if the infant did not act in this way. The science of humour is probably better built through an explication of the structure of its processes than through trying to build processes out of its supposed structures. Fundamentally, then, it takes an engagement between two people (at least) for funniness to begin to exist. Painting humour as a textual phenomenon—focusing on it primarily as the structure of a joke—is destructive, not only for understanding when it begins, but also for understanding how it exists even in adults. Funniness exists only in relation.

CHAPTER 10

Faking in Communication

Semiotics is in principle the discipline studying everything that can be used to tell a lie. If something cannot be used to tell a lie, conversely it cannot be used "to tell" at all. I think that the definition of a "theory of the lie" should be taken as a pretty comprehensive program for a general semiotics.

Umberto Eco, *Theory of Semiotics*[1]

Psychologists have long remarked on deception as a paradoxical development: both a cognitive advance and a moral regression. Intellectual progress, it seems, accompanies a loss of moral innocence. Within evolutionary theories the ability to deceive others is often seen as the hallmark skill of social intelligence.[2] In evolution as well as in ontogenetic development, deceiving is taken as the closest we get to proof that the deceiver understands the other person's or animal's mind. Deliberate deception implies, at the very least, an ability to disengage dramatically from the immediate engagement. But *how* does deceiving begin? And, more importantly, *why* does it begin?

In this chapter I will explore the phenomena of early deception. I will show that contrary to the view that lying begins only later in childhood—around the age of 4 years—even toddlers can lie, flexibly, non-formulaically, and for interestingly "psychological" reasons. Such deceptions have their roots before speech, where, from before the end of the first year, infants are concealing and faking and distracting and pretending in their non-verbal interactions with other people. I will argue that deceptive communication is first and foremost communication, and like any other social and communicative phenomenon, it must emerge through a fundamentally dialogic process. Deceiving needs an intentional partner who will engage with the action and *be* deceived. I suggest that it is this experience of the other's "deceivedness" in engaging with the self—an experience in the second person—which explains why deceiving can develop. First, let us look briefly at why psychologists believe that lying is a late-appearing phenomenon, and why this belief sits uncomfortably with the findings about early truthful communication as well as with the evidence of early lying.

Deceptive Communication, Understanding Beliefs, and Truthful Communication

There is a theory in developmental psychology that only when children develop a "theory of mind"—which allows them to interpret people's behaviour in terms of hidden mental representations—do children become capable of genuine deception. The logic of the "theory-theory" as it has come to be called, is that in order to make other people think something different about reality than is really the case (i.e., to deceive them), children need first to be able to understand that people *can* think something different about reality than is really the case. They need to be able to understand that people have beliefs about reality rather than automatic knowledge of reality, and therefore work out that people's beliefs about reality can be false. Understanding false beliefs—as shown in many of the versions of the famous "false-belief task"—doesn't really happen until about 4 years of age.[3] Therefore, children cannot, on the logic of this theory, lie until that age. Startling support for the theory-theory came with the discovery that high-functioning children with autism, developmentally much more advanced than 4-year-olds, could not pass the false-belief task and were reported never to lie. The logic of the theory-theory was impeccable, and the findings impressive. But it adopts what could be described as the epitome of a third-person approach to communication, focusing on it as an internal juggling of propositions about mind and reality rather than as an interpersonal and emotional process.[4]

There are two empirical problems with this theory and its prediction. First, what about truthful communication? If it is the case that in order to deliberately mis-inform other people children need to understand that they can have beliefs (rather than automatic knowledge) about reality, what about communicating truthfully about reality? If children wouldn't bother to lie if they didn't know that beliefs about reality can be potentially different from reality itself, why would they bother to take the initiative in informing others about the truth? But they *do* appear to.

From about 12 to 18 months toddlers effortfully, selectively, and appropriately inform other people truthfully about reality, often telling people things they don't appear to know or may "need" to know. We know that at least by 12 months of age toddlers are spontaneously offering others information about reality, not only from a desire to share their own interests with others as seen in the proto-declarative pointing which we discussed in Chapter 6, but also with "proto-informative pointing" (a recently coined term) from a desire to tell adults what they seem to be unaware of, regardless of whether the topic itself is interesting for the child and motivated by need to know rather than desire for appreciation.[5] We know from Roberta Golinkoff's observations that by about 14 months toddlers are quite competent at correcting other people's misunderstandings of their utterances and intentions, both in contexts where the toddler wants something and in merely conversational contexts, and from Cintia Rodriguez we have the intriguing finding of proto-interrogatives in 12-month-olds (i.e., gestures seeking adult confirmation).[6] We know that by 18 months toddlers are able to understand other people's "referential intent"—that is, to infer what they are talking about even when they may be looking somewhere else.[7] At this age toddlers are also able to make denials—to contradict others' factual mistakes, for instance—by responding with a "No" when an adult points to a ball and says, "this is a car" or points to a picture of a cat and asks, "Is this a cow?"[8] And at this age, or possibly even earlier at 12 months, they selectively repeat information (about a new toy, for instance) for adults who have not heard or seen it, and identify which adults to tell what to.[9] For example, suppose there has just been a loud and exciting event outside the window which the toddler and mother witnessed together. Then the father walks into the room. The toddler may "tell" the father (but not the mother) about the event. Or even more selectively, if the mother leaves the room and comes back a little later with the father, the toddler is likely to tell the father (and not the mother) about the event even after time has elapsed. Explicit planning to tell others about events may be seen from around 2 years of age—for instance, a newly toilet-trained toddler refusing to let the nanny empty the potty in order to "Show Mummy!" when mother returns home in the evening. From around 2 years of age children even modulate the informational details in their requests for toys depending on the adult's knowledge of the toy's location.[10]

Given this wide variety of situations in which children far younger than 4 years are giving other people truthful information, it is strange that deceptive information should not appear until so much later. Is all this earlier communication about the world not really communication about the world at all? Or is lying not in fact as late to emerge as was thought? Two recent studies have shown that lying is in fact a commonplace much earlier than 4 years of age.

Paul Newton, a graduate student at Portsmouth, conducted two longitudinal studies to explore the last question.[11] He found a rich variety of lies in 3-year-olds and in one 2½-year-old, the lies serving a range of functions similar to that in older children. The prevalence of these lies was not influenced by whether or not the children passed or failed a battery of "false-belief" tasks. And individual children's lies did not seem to change during a six-month period from "before" to "after" they passed these tasks. What was particularly interesting about these lies was that not all were concerned with material gain or avoidance of punishment. Some of them were purely psychologically motivated, concerned with saving face in a variety of ways, and others were playful lies. Neither tricks nor lies, of course, should have been happening before the age of about 4 years.[12]

These findings have been supported by another study in Canada, this time analysing videotaped observations of family interactions of two siblings and at least one parent taken during research visits to their homes.[13] Anne Wilson and her colleagues at the University of Waterloo found that even on those brief visits, lying was observable. Lying increased with age: about 95 percent of the 6-year-olds and 85 percent of the 4-year-olds lied. However, so did 65 percent of the 2-year-olds—something the theory-theory did not predict. Lying was not frequent at any age (most children were observed to lie between two and four times during the study). Nonetheless, the finding that two-thirds of the youngest children, far too young to pass false belief tests, did lie, needs some explanation. The findings of these two studies potentially throws out of the water the theory-theory flagship claims. Children don't seem to need to understand false beliefs in order to lie about reality. But not quite. The response to data such as these is usually to reject them as pseudo-deception. What does this mean?

Early Lying as Pseudo-Deception?

The ringed plover deceives intruders by walking away from its rather vulnerable ground nest as if with a broken wing. The young child stubbornly repeats his "No!", denying a misdemeanour he is accused of. The 3-year-old dumps a spoonful of cereal on her baby brother's head and says quickly, "I didn't do it on purpose." The 2-year-old says, "I didn't do it, my dolly did it." A toddler says, "Hurt. Hurt" whenever he is asked to do something that he doesn't want to do. Something about these examples of lying is unconvincing: they don't look like they are connected with knowing about other people's thoughts. The solution by many writers is to dismiss them as merely *pseudo*-deception: something that looks like deception but isn't really—a deceptive deception in fact, worked on the psychologist by some evolutionary or conditioning process.[14] In general, three sorts of reasons are used for being sceptical about the intellectual significance of early lying: simple defensiveness and materialism of motive; implausibility and inappropriateness of content; and inflexibility and rigidity of form.[15]

Next I will describe some examples of bravado lies, probably the richest category of verbal lies found in Newton's research, which argues against these sceptical dismissals.

Bravado Lies

There were four kinds of bravado, which involved hiding or actually falsifying an emotional state, making a false statement about recent reality or making a false claim. These were: "Doesn't hurt" bravado, "Don't care" bravado, "I was right" bravado, and false boasts. A fascinating power play was evident in some of these instances where the child is either denying the experience of the pain being intentionally inflicted on him or her by a parent or denying the desire for something that he or she has no further hope of obtaining. There were some heart-rending reports of "Doesn't hurt" bravado in this study (all names reduced to initials).[16]

> You can smack her legs until they're red raw, and if she's in one of her willful moods she'll go: "Didn't hurt!" On a couple of occasions when she's been threatened with a good hiding for misbehaviour she's even dropped her trousers for you. The other day she did this and then said "It dun't hurt!" (Mother of L, 3 years, 6 months, interview)

Here's a subtle example of "Don't care" bravado from a child who hated a toy spider she had recently been bought, and wouldn't go near it. Once when she was being naughty her father threatened her saying, "If you don't behave I'll get that spider out." The child replied "I don't care, I've been playing with it all day" (she had not even been near it according to her mother). In Newton's study, a third of the children were reported to engage in each of these kinds of bravado over a six-month period in the fourth year and there was no change in prevalence with age. There was a similarity between these and the "I was right" type of bravado, as in the touchingly desperate example that follows from Newton's longitudinal study of R when he was 2½ years old:

> It was early morning, and S had been staying overnight at a friend's. I was still in bed when R came in and asked me "Shall we go and pick up S in a minute?" Contradicting him, I said "No, no. Not in a minute. Later." R exclaimed, "I said 'shall we go and pick up S later on,' that's what I said. I said 'shall we go and pick up S later on.'" This incident struck me and after a few minutes I asked him again "What did you say?" He answered, "I already said, 'shall we go and pick up S later,' I said." (Mother of R, 2 years, 8 months, dictaphone)

Or this one, which nearly caused a scandal!

> I returned home with the children as their uncle and aunt arrived for the weekend. After a brief chat the aunt asked "Where's your daddy?" R chattily volunteered "He's upstairs." A little later his father's voice was heard coming from the backdoor (rather than from upstairs). R said immediately "My *other* daddy's upstairs." His aunt (who had forgotten his previous statement) looked puzzled. I started laughing, realising the purpose of his statement (and there was indeed no one else upstairs!). (Mother of R, 2 years, 5 months, dictaphone)

There were also many tricks which didn't have any immediate gain for the child other than the pleasure of fooling the other person. That these tricks weren't just well-worn games—like peep-bo—whose meaning in terms of "lying" is unclear is evident from the way in which children tell them. Tricks were generally characterised by three stages: setting up a false expectation, for example, "It's the telephone!" or "I've finished (when on the loo)," then waiting for the other's reaction (running down the stairs to the telephone or up the stairs to the loo), and lastly, acknowledging the trick with laughter or an explicit "Tricked yer, tricked yer." The prevalence of tricks did indeed increase with age in Newton's study, but they were not unknown even in the 2½-year-old, as in the following example:

> On a visit to an aunt, R had had permission to keep the car keys in his pocket. When leaving, he was asked for the keys. R reached into his pocket, but then stopped (with his hand still inside) and said "They're not there.

I don't know where they are!" on being challenged, he then pointed to the grill of the car and said, smiling, "They're inside there." He did not then stop his mother from reaching into his pocket and taking the keys. (Mother of R, 2 years, 8 months, dictaphone)

Material Gain, Inappropriateness, and Inflexibility?

Material gain, inappropriateness, and inflexibility are the three common criticisms made of the claim that early lies are indeed lies. If early lies were limited to a few simple contexts and motives, or to situations of avoidance or intense desire, it would be easy to dismiss them. Both of these, the "theory-theorist" argues, put children on the spot in terms of finding some strategy to get out of trouble or get what they want.[17] One could of course, say the same thing for adults: that most of our lies happen on occasions when we are in hot water or want something badly. However, if early lies were only found in such situations, it would certainly warrant another look at how limited the deceptive words might be and just what sort of learning histories they might have. But in fact, although the majority of early lies were indeed aimed at avoidance of some punishment or accusation, the range of situations—and motives—that they covered was both varied and very similar to that in adults. In Newton's study, the only category of lie that these 2- and 3-year-old children did not seem to engage in was white lies, and it may be that these are different. In a study that we are currently conducting, it appears that, contrary to theory-theory expectations, children with autism may also lie, in all but, interestingly, the category of white lies. Otherwise the catalogue of lying went beyond simple defensiveness or seeking material benefits, ranging from the more banal false-blaming and feigning of ignorance to assertions of completion and of permission, and most interestingly, to the bravado, face-saving lies, and trickery illustrated above. The variety of motives, and their similarity across children who pass or fail false-belief tasks and indeed between children and adults, suggests that the psychological processes involved in these early lies are not fundamentally different from the later lies.

If early lies were largely inappropriate, then, too, it would be easy to dismiss them. But inappropriateness was rather rare. The classic example is that of an inappropriate lie that Josef Perner reports of his son: where Jacob tried to avoid going to bed by using the well-worn excuse "I'm so tired" but should have been claiming precisely the opposite if he wanted to stand a chance of avoiding going to bed. In both Wilson's and Newton's studies there were a few cases in which the children's lies were implausible but not inappropriate. In one of the examples above where Rohan tries to save face by saying—quite implausibly—that his other daddy was upstairs, he was clearly unaware that the lie *could* not have worked. But in relation to what he appeared to want to achieve—a saving of face—the lie was quite appropriate. Implausibility is evidence of ignorance about the constraints surrounding believing, but not evidence against an intention to deceive.

However, are early lies inflexible and rigid, suggesting that they are merely learned strategies? To say that something is "merely learned" is often to belittle its complexity, or to dismiss it as not "genuine" or "felt." This is an odd slant in relation to many things, but particularly in relation to lying. Learning from past success is hardly evidence that the lie is not "genuine." We would have to be foolish indeed not to learn that some lies work and some don't. Indeed, the situations in which children seek to lie *must* be learned. It is only the fact that society will, in principle, accept as adequate excuses such as "Daddy said I could," and that mothers might accept as sufficient "I promise I won't touch it again" that invites children to seek to use these excuses and make these promises. The knowledge that children or adults reveal in their lies is precisely a knowledge of the *legitimacy* of these excuses in their social context. We must in the deepest sense learn from experience of interacting with people what we can and cannot tell others, what we need to and don't need to tell them, what impact the information has at various times, and so on. Indeed, we would really have a problem understanding what a lie meant if the person did *not* learn from its effects.

However, the debate in relation to "learned strategies" is really about whether that's *all* there is to the lie. Is the strategy merely "blind"? As David Premack argues, inflexibility in lying can be robotic. The ringed plover is not only able to protect its un-defendable ground nest from intruders by walking around as if it had a broken wing, but also, as Carolyn Ristau has shown, to distinguish between pseudo-intruders who walk around the nest (by not bothering to deceive them) and serious intruders who head directly for the nest. Nonetheless, Premack argues, "The bird is analogous to a human who could tell lies only about pilfering fudge; he could not tell lies about dirtying the carpet, breaking the lamp, taking money from his mother's purse, or about lying itself."[18] We know already that the variety of early lies that 2- and 3-year-olds tell suggests that this is not what young children's lies are like. Nor are the early lies limited to one-word denials or simple formulaic utterances without the creative elaborations which older children and adults can display. In Newton's study none of the children were limited to one-word lies alone, and some were fairly elaborate. The false claim in the following example was unusually realistic: "Dad said yes, but (to) ask you as well" (when the father had actually said a clear No); and several lies extended over many conversational turns, resisting disbelieving challenges from others; for example, this apparently pointless lie in the face of an anxious father looking out for the postman. "The postman's already been," "No, he hasn't," "I saw him go past," "No, you didn't," "I did, I did, he came when you were upstairs." Just at the point when the parents were beginning to believe it, the child blew it at the last minute by adding, "He brought something for me." Lack of words was certainly not this child's problem! Although such elaborations do increase with age, Wilson's study showed that there was no difference between the younger and older children in their use of simple denials. In fact, denials increased with age as well! Another reason to doubt their rigidity is the extent to which lies were re-phrased and elaborated following challenges and doubts. Children certainly did not seem to be constrained to one response.

But the issue of learning really does need a closer look. Are these lies in fact "learned" through simple reinforcement? Of course, there is always the problem that we wouldn't know about the really successful (and therefore rewarded) lies because all observers would believe them! But if that were the case, any over-use of a single lie would reveal itself pretty soon. But apart from this caveat, it seems that parents don't usually believe the lies they are told, and they show their disbelief by factual challenges. Children are not usually rewarded by being believed or by getting what they wanted when they lied. Wilson's data showed that on average children either got away with or were rewarded for their lies less than 15 percent of the time. On these occasions parents believed the lie (the camera could actually record the truth in this study) and sometimes punished another child or on a few occasions redefined the lie or the transgression. A further 18 percent of the time the lie was simply ignored. The majority of the time, however, parents challenged the lie or addressed/punished the transgression in some way. Interestingly, however, children did seem to be influenced over time by watching parents tighten up on older siblings' lies, and in some contexts, reduce their own lies as a consequence.

Wilson's fascinating and unusual findings reveal two things about lying and learning. One, lying is not learned in the home from simple contingencies (since most of the time the lies are challenged or unrewarded and these contingencies don't exist). Two, children do not generally learn, especially from observation in the family, about parental tolerance for lying. The claim that these early lies are inflexible strategies—learned responses—is therefore untenable. If anything, children may learn a very general idea about whether lying is acceptable, perhaps even worth it. They do not seem to have to be reinforced to lie, nor do they seem to learn the content of lies in a blind way.

In general, the lies of these young children were neither simple and materially motivated, nor inflexible and implausible. Nor did they involve (as Piaget had suggested was the case in pseudo-deception) a blurring of the distinction between reality and fantasy, a "romancing." From the entire corpus of data in Newton's studies there were only five such stories. However, these early lies are still not as early as true information-giving: the earliest verbal lies reported here were from 2-year-olds while we saw that 1-year-olds are pretty skilled communicators of true information.

Concealing, Faking, Distracting, and Pretending: Earlier Non-verbal Deceptions

Deception is much broader than lying. We can deceive others by evasion, by omission, by distracting their attention from accusing evidence, by concealing the evidence before they get there, by faking emotional expressions, by falsely using conventionally meaningful gestures, and even by faking ignorance. The predictions from the theory-theory apply to all deception, non-verbal as well as verbal, and it could be that even before they are verbally skilled, children are capable of non-verbal deceptions. We have a large corpus of data about non-verbal deceptions in non-human primates. Frustrated by what many primatologists "knew" about deception in primates through isolated examples in the field, Andy Whiten and Dick Byrne complied a large collection of observations about primate "tactical deception" from different field primatologists and classified them structurally, functionally, and in terms of reliability of detail.[19] Some of Whiten and Byrne's most intriguing examples of deception—obviously non-verbal—involved concealment and distraction. Take the case of the baboon who carefully inches behind a rock to hide his illicit sexual intentions or the baboon who, being chased by a host of other baboons, suddenly stands up and looks intently into the distance; the others stop and stare into the distance too. Nothing is visible, everybody goes their own way and the chase is forgotten. We have only one such corpus of examples about human infants, using data collated from three studies.[20]

Infants seem to engage in many of the categories of tactical deception that other (adult) primates do. They conceal forbidden acts—either passively by waiting until they're alone, or actively, by hiding actions or objects from other people's line of sight. Passive hiding is common in the first year. Eight-month-old Philip, for example, had a passion for shutting the curtain in the living room. He usually waited for his mother to go into the kitchen before going to it: "if I just go into the kitchen to get something . . . (he) makes a beeline for the curtain . . . you can see him looking over his shoulder to see if I'm watching him, and if I tell him from the kitchen "no" he stops and looks at you and grins for a while . . . as soon as I've turned my back he makes another move for it."[21] Active hiding is reported in the second year: a toddler fiddling with a forbidden wrist watch may turn his back on other people in the room so that he can carry on unseen. Before the end of the first year, infants may also suppress their own responses: ignoring the clearly audible call of a mother by not reacting at all, but continuing with a stiffened back and still body, in a context where the infant is doing something she shouldn't is something that adult primates do as well—human as well as non-human.

Infants also distract other people's attention from the infant's forbidden activities in what appears to be a startlingly Machiavellian way as in the examples below of an 11- and a 13-month-old infant:[22]

If you give her toast and she doesn't want it . . . she . . . she's sneaky, she's very sneaky, she'll sit there looking at you and while she's got your eyes looking at her eyes, she picks it up and puts it under her arm like that and throws it behind her . . . and she thinks you can't see. (Mother of Anna, 11 months, interview)

. . . continuing to undo the tapes on his nappy. . . . Although now he is much more serious about it. He lies on his changing mat . . . and he wants to pull the tab off he almost sort of stares you out. . . . And really fixes his eye onto my eye and is exceedingly serious, as though he hopes that because he is looking at you and making you look straight at him, you won't notice him undoing . . . his nappy tab. It is really rather funny actually but he is so dead serious about it. Doesn't go on (at) every nappy change, but has certainly happened 7 or 8 times. (Mother of Jonathan, 13 months, dictaphone)

Within the first year of life, there is no evidence that infants can distract others' attention in the complex way that the baboon in Whiten and Byrne's corpus of examples did: that is, by distracting others' attention to a distal location. In the preceding examples, the infants are using what Whiten and Byrne called "close-range" behaviour—a distractor which is close to the body of deceiver and deceived. There is one example in the second year, observed by Sully a hundred years ago, of distal distraction. In that example, a 17-month-old infant who has been told off for repeatedly throwing gloves out of the pram, calls to the mother with the dog's name, reportedly in order to get the mother to turn away, enabling the throwing out of the gloves again.[23]

A similar finding is evident in relation to another of Whiten and Byrne's categories of tactical deception—false attraction—that is, falsely attracting the other's attention to a certain location in order to get something at that place. Within the first year of life, infants don't lead others deceptively to a desired location. However, they do use fake actions and expressions in order to lead others to *themselves*. Fake crying is a good example of this and is evident from about 8 or 9 months. It is easy enough to detect the difference in sound between genuine and fake crying, and the situations in which fake crying can occur are often a dead giveaway. One common situation is one in which the infant fakes upset at being told off:

> Victoria definitely knows when she is doing something she shouldn't. She headed over towards the video, looked round to see if anyone is going to tell her off and then actually . . . gone to touch it. When Paul told her off, she actually sat there and tried to make herself cry, but the tears just wouldn't come. (Mother of Victoria, 8 months, dictaphone)[24]

And another is where the infant wants something and uses fake crying to get it. Surreptitiously watching 8-month-old Carla in the middle of the night, her mother saw her "shout, sort of as in crying, but no tears, for about thirty seconds and she'd stop and listen to see if she could hear me coming or moving . . . and she'd start again. . . . She just lay there and she'd shout and then she'd stop and listen and when she realised I wasn't there, she'd carry on screaming but no tears, not one single tear, and she carried on and on and on."[25] Faking laughter, too, as we saw in the chapter on humour, can occur in the middle of the first year in an attempt by infants to join in with others' laughter. Whatever the basis of these acts, the falsifying and manipulative use of a previously "natural" expression is evident. The interesting similarity to deception through "distraction" discussed above is that here, too, there is only "close-range" behaviour, and no involvement of a distal location.

These developments in deceptive actions seem interestingly similar to the developments in the awareness of attention that we discussed in Chapter 6: earlier examples of deception seem to involve dyadic engagement between infant and other person, with triadic deceptions emerging later. It does not appear to be the case that deception itself is a belated occurrence; rather, its content changes. Deceptive communication seems to be occurring even in the first year of life, but in a simple way, and primarily involving the infant's own body and actions rather than a distal object or target.

Pretending is the word that parents often use to describe such faking. In the psychological literature, pretending is usually reserved for imaginary actions upon objects. A standard definition of pretend play, for instance, identifies three different types: the pretended existence of a non-existent object or substance, the pretended identity of one object as another, and a pretended action. However, there is no good reason to limit pretending to the meanings of and actions upon objects. The meanings of gestures and expressions, for instance, and actions towards people, are just as commonly open to pretending. In fact, what is intriguing about these instances of interpersonal pretending is that they happen a good nine months earlier than does the well-documented object-related pretending.

Not only do 8- and 9-month-olds "pretend" to cry and laugh and be deaf, but they also "pretend" the meanings of gestures and words. As we saw with infant teasing in Chapters 8 and 9, offering something with the playful intention of withdrawing it, or requesting something only in order to refuse it, is well-established before the first birthday. In serious contexts, too, gestures can be misused to "pretend" a different intention: the 11-month-old who is apprehended heading for the forbidden soil in the rubber plant scoops his hand up in a funny manner, "as though he was waving" rather than going to touch the soil, and repeats this whenever his mother says a warning "No."[26] These newly learned conventional gestural forms are being played with—"pretended" to use ordinary language—in much the same way as a newly learned skill with an object, speaking on the telephone, for example, might be played with by the 18-month-old. Skill with words, too, can be mucked about with. The Russian poet Chukovsky reported (a now famous) example of his daughter, having recently learned the equivalent of "miaow" and "bowwow" and their association, respectively, with "cat" and "dog," comes up to him one day with a giggle, and says, "doggie miaow!" In a similar way we have 11-month-old Anna, who had just started pointing to her own body and naming her self as "Baby" (she had already been correctly naming her mother as Mummy and her father as Daddy), suddenly pointing to her mother and saying, "Daddy." The mother's puzzled correction led only to an insistence of the "error" until her "cheeky look" with "her head on her side" gave the game away.[27]

Pretending seems to begin with the meanings of expressions and gestures and words rather than with the meanings of objects. (Interestingly, in all cases, when the pretending is playful, it seems to be the newly learned meanings which are manipulated.) Even when the pretending concerns the existence and meaning of objects, however, it is in interpersonal contexts that the pretending seems to gain its earliest significance. A mother's funny little observation—of 12-month-old Jonathan at a mealtime—shows this really well.[28] In a good mood throughout the lunch, Jonathan kept pretending to pick up something from the table of his high chair and handing it to his mother. She went along with it and held her hand out for "it" and he gave it, looking at her with a smile. This was repeated three times but, apart from the first time, with a serious rather than smiling expression. Interestingly, at this stage, the pretending only seemed to work one way. The "game" continued for a few weeks after which the mother tried to initiate the game: "now, rather than just take it, I sometimes pretend to put nothing, which it is, on the table, then look at him, pick it up and give it back to him." But, according to the mother, when she tried to pretend back, Jonathan wouldn't have it: "[he] actually thinks that's a bit ridiculous and doesn't play along with that." The "pretending" for the infant is clearly rather fragile at this age, not based on or "caused by" an abstract "understanding" of the act of pretence, but tied to the specific context of the activity and the do-er of the act. Despite this fragility, the fact that the infant initiated this act of pretending to pick something up and offer it to the mother makes it difficult to call this anything but pretending. The question of interest for us in this chapter is how this relates to deception.

The simplicity and very early appearance of such non-verbal faking, concealing, and distracting suggests two things. One, that the verbal lies of 2½-year-olds are already founded on a long tradition of non-verbal manipulation and mis-representation of shared meanings. Like the verbal lies, these non-verbal deceptions too occur in more than just a single context and are motivated by more than a simple desire to escape punishment or seek rewards. The fact that they occur in play as well as seriousness suggests that the meaning they are mis-representing is not confused with its mis-representation. Two, these early occurring deceptive attempts do seem to happen more or less simultaneously with the earliest attempts to communicate anything at all. In other words, they occur at least as early as truthful information giving. But how and why does all this develop?

Why Does Deceiving Develop?

Why do infants begin to engage in deceptive communication? A groundbreaking finding by Kristine Onishi and Renee Baillargeon, since followed up by a number of other similar studies, showed that if they are given a non-verbal habituation task, even 15-month-olds seem to detect that other people can have false beliefs about reality.[29] So the findings of these early deceptions could simply be attributed to an early discovery by infants that other people can have beliefs about reality which may be different from reality. This would certainly resolve any contradiction between truth telling and lying—both could be based on the same theoretical and computational understanding of other people's representations of reality. Indeed, Alan Leslie who had been a lone voice arguing for many years that the crucial development in mind knowledge happens at 18 months with the development of pretending, suggests that infants have an innately developing "theory of mind mechanism" which can explain pretending as well as deceiving.

However, this explanation doesn't quite do a couple of things. It doesn't explain the continuous emergence and *development* of a number of these different communicative features, and it doesn't explain *why* deception should actually emerge.[30] Infant deceiving doesn't burst out at a single age, whether at 18 months or 15 or 12 or 10 or even 8 months. Rather, different kinds of deceptions seem to happen at each of these ages, although we know too little about whether the differences are really age-related or much more individually variable. At any rate, there are so many variations of deceiving that to attribute them to a discovery—however implicit—of false beliefs, would require a rather un-parsimonious attribution of several points of false belief discovery through the first 2 years. Nor does it quite seem sensible to use a concept (of other people's beliefs) developed for 4-year-olds and apply it unmodified to 1-year-olds. It would require an incredibly a-contextual logic for a concept to survive such a change. Can the idea of beliefs be anything like the same at such diverse ages? Can understanding the *that* of other people's beliefs be unrelated to changes in the *what* of other people's beliefs? If an intimate connection between the that and the what (i.e., between the aspect of mind and its objects) is true for a grasp of attention and intention as that we saw in Chapters 6 and 8, and for the developing awareness of self as we saw in Chapter 7, then it may be equally true for a grasp of believing.

And does this explanation really *explain* why infants engage in such deceiving? Like all cognitive representational explanations, it can only offer the following answer to a "why?" question: it happens because it can. I think it is possible to tackle this question further.

Deceiving, like any other form of communication, *is* first of all, communication. And like any communication, it needs an intentional partner: to occur at all and to *mean* something. If an act of deceiving isn't acknowledged or responded to at some level as a deception, what can it mean for the developing child? And second, like any other communicative action, deceiving happens within the unscripted openness of conversations. It is often drawn out in dialogue rather than typically planned as an individual and insightful act. The other person's reactions, invitations, encouragements, and tolerance *must* influence what sort of deceptive actions children can engage in. Deception cannot be a single head achievement.

The crucial feature explaining the emergence of deception may be the infant's perception of other people's *deceivedness* in the very early engagements involving subtle sensitivity to and manipulation of other people's reactions that we have seen in the examples from the first year. Beginning from a motivation to engage and a reciprocal emotional responsiveness (both evolutionary givens for humans at least), infants may get drawn into deceiving others within engagement. Engagement—or emotional dialogue—often involves acts which are unexpected by the other; dialogue which is totally predictable is hardly dialogue. That which is unpredictable can cause surprise. When someone the infant is engaging with responds with such surprise or alarm or discomfort to an action by the infant, these responses can be emotionally experienced by the infant in her own reactions to the response (for example, with delight at the other's surprise or discomfort). This experience is possible within second-person relations that link emotion with proprioception and perception, as argued in Chapter 3. The infant experiences the other's *deceivedness* in this way and gets drawn into emotional dialogue with it in specific contexts.

The infant's deceiving develops in complexity and scope with age—a development which is evident in the content of the deceptive acts (moving from close-range to distal distraction, for instance). The origins of deceiving, however, must lie in the infant's experience of others' *deceivedness*. A prediction can follow here too, as it did in the case of the awareness of attention: that the development of the ability to deceive another person depends upon the ability to *feel* in the self, the process of true and false "close-range" communication with the other. Perhaps if the infant cannot deceive in a dyadic situation, more distal deceptions become impaired and, in some formulaic or other way, "inappropriate." Dialogic emotional engagement may provide the fuel both for the emergence of deceiving and for the developing complexity of the objects or topics of deceiving over time.

CHAPTER 11

Other Minds and
Other Cultures

. . . one has only learnt to get the better of words
For the thing one no longer has to say, or the way in which
One is no longer disposed to say it.

    T. S. Eliot, *East Coker V*[1]

The story of this book has been that, in order to understand how infants develop an awareness of other minds, psychology needs to pay attention to what they do in engagement with other people. A disengaged observation of people can never, I have argued, lead to an awareness of what other minds are like. To develop an understanding of this process, we need to centralise the second person—the You—in dialogic engagement. A first-person route to the awareness of other minds (emphasising simulation or modelling from the self) and a third-person route to others (prioritising detached observation of movements leading to inferences about mind) both give the perceiver different kinds of information about self and other. However in both routes, the infant is essentially a perceiver of others, a spectator. On their own, these routes cannot explain how infants understand other people as *others* and as *people*. I have sought to illustrate my argument by looking at a range of domains of infant engagement with mentality—imitating, communicating, engaging with attention, playing with intentions, hiding, and exposing the self to the other in self-conscious affects, sharing amusement, and deceiving.

Being a participant within an engagement with another living being allows the infant to perceive that someone is acknowledging and responding to her being and to experience a response to this other person. Many philosophers have remarked on the crucial role of this experience: William James called it "being noticed," Bakhtin, the recognition of an "answering consciousness," Hegel, the awareness of recognition, and Buber, the experience of the *I-Thou* relation. These concepts refer to more than just "interpersonal interaction," more than just a recognition of the similarity of an other person to the self, and more than just an inference from observation of movements.

The second-person approach that I have been developing in this book argues that both developmentally and experientially recognising and being recognised by a *You* is primary for understanding other people. The view adopted within much of developmental psychology is that an understanding of people and their mentality can be obtained either by simulation or by deduction or by some mix of the two. In contrast, a second-person approach suggests that unless the baby can feel and emotionally respond to aspects of mentality directed to her, her engagement with them, and therefore her understanding of them, will be "different" from and less "appropriate" than the understanding of other people that we typically take for granted in our everyday lives. The absence of a participative involvement with others' mentality seems to lead to the more theoretical, detached, and rule-based understanding of people that is evident in disorders such as autism. Typically, developing human infants seem to start life with dialogue, however simple its form, in exchanges of neonatal imitation and an easy emotional connectedness to other minds. A second-person approach seems not only to explain infant behaviour better than either a first- or third-person approach, but also to change the problem of other minds as it is still, very often, posed within the literature—that is, as a "spectatorial" process of observation of "mere behaviour" across a gap. The important difference between this approach and a first-person approach is that the emphasis here is not on recognition of the similarity to self of other people's acts, but, crucially, of the *experience* of a reciprocal response to the other's acts. The gap between minds becomes hard to find in this re-embodiment and this re-embedding.

Infants seem to be capable of entering into dialogue with other people remarkably early in life. From birth they prefer to look at faces which engage them in direct mutual gaze, and they are capable of engaging in imitative exchanges with adults that reveal not just an ability to recognise similarity between self and other but a motivation to invite engagement. Within two months of birth, infants become more robust at dialogic exchanges with people, showing not only prolonged turn-taking and sensitive detection of the contingency and relevance of others' responses, but a sensitivity to many emotional nuances. Before there is any "topic" for conversations to be "about," dialogue functions in early infancy as an open medium within which self and other develop. That these engagements play a constitutive role can be seen in engagements where the openness of the engagement is perturbed, especially for prolonged periods.

The significance of second-person engagement—the idea that one must experience a response to an other in order to "know" them "appropriately"—can be captured most clearly in the awareness of attention. Others' attention is meaningful to the infant because she experiences herself as the first among the objects that others can attend to. The meaning of other people's attention for the infant expands in scope with the objects that others attend to which the infant can engage with. A similar argument—that the meaningfulness of an aspect of mind is first experienced through the self's response to it—can be made not just about attention, but also about the awareness of intentions, the awareness of amusement, and, intriguingly, the awareness of other people's beliefs. Play within (and always just beyond) the boundaries of others' intentions serves to draw infants out into more and more complex intentions and awareness of intentions. The experience of other people's reactions to one's tricky, playful, and deceptive actions—the experience of their "deceivedness"—may explain why infants begin to deceive in simple ways. Self-conscious affects, perhaps better termed self-other-conscious affects, may similarly provide a better explanation of the pre-conceptual development of self-consciousness and of various types of humorous initiatives by infants in the first year. Experiencing aspects of other minds within one's own responses may be crucial not just to the beginning of awareness of mentality, but to its continued emergence and development. Such engagements must draw the infant into further entanglements, further complexities, and further awareness—of self as well as of others.

Engaging with other people in the second person therefore seems crucial to becoming aware of them: the information available is more meaningful and detailed, it is experienced rather than simulated or inferred, and it creates new aspects to *be* aware of. Two broader implications come from this conclusion. One I have already discussed in Chapter 3: it is the issue of how psychologists get to understand the people they work with—their "participants." If participative knowing is crucial for understanding newly met other minds, then it must be as true for adults and psychologists as it is for babies. This suggests a very different methodology from that which we normally value in psychology.

The second implication is for understanding people from other cultures and how we, as adults, deal with what can sometimes be a difficult process. The question of how you can "understand the natives without *being* one" might be a rather unfashionable way of putting it nowadays, but in many ways the question of the inaccessibility of other cultures is startlingly similar to that of other minds.[2] The very expression of the problem in terms of needing to get inside someone else's skin in order to understand their "culture" has Cartesian overtones. Cultures, like minds, are assumed to be inside bodies (in this case perhaps a group of bodies), not directly available to others, only to be speculated about from the outside, and never really understood except from the inside. In both cases there is a subtle implication of static-ness—that a culture or a mind is sort of sitting there, waiting to be known. This view portrays culture as a product rather than a process: something that you either possess or not once you "get" it, depending on the chance of birth.

The answers to both questions, about culture and about minds, are similar as well. For culture too, you could adopt a first-person approach (laborious in terms of using and extending analogy from personal experience, and always constrained by limitations), or you could adopt a third-person approach (reflective, theoretical, deductive, powerfully rational, but emotionally unconvincing), or you could adopt a second-person approach. Like minds, cultures only emerge and exist within engagement.[3] Culture needs dialogue and engagement in order to continue to *be* a certain way. And dialogue and engagement, necessarily being unscripted and open, must *change* some cultural practices and emphases as well as affirm and sustain others. If this is the case, then culture—as a fluid and potentially changing practice—is open to be known by those who engage in it. The development of shared meanings can take time, but it is not closed to strangers or newcomers, just as adult minds are not closed to infant newcomers either. If we think about meanings as existing in participation and dialogue, in shared and public practice rather than in privacy, they stop being occult and opaque. They are open precisely because they can only exist in practice, and are constantly reaffirmed by and changed within it. The meaning of a ritual or a gesture or a word or a look, a shriek, a smile, a greeting, an averted face—all exist only in their expression to, and response from, another person. No dictionary of minds and cultures can hold their meanings still.

In both cases, that of other minds and other cultures, participation with emotional openness to the "other" seems to be the key. And this, of course, can be absent: denied deliberately in conflict or withdrawal or unintention-ally in an inability to achieve a shared rhythm. In both cases, participation and emotional responsiveness need common ground to begin. And what is that common ground? It involves the body, the world, physiological needs, attraction and motivation for companionship, and activities to be done. This is true for infants new to an adult world—they already share a common body and world and needs and motives and, later on, activities. Without this common ground, the process would be much harder. And this is true for knowing other cultures as well. The common ground doesn't limit under-standing to that which is already in common: it provides the ground for di-alogue within which shared meanings can develop. But when some of this common ground isn't there, there are problems.

But the essence of a second-person approach is that the "knower" must *feel* a response towards the person or thing to be known. And why is this necessary for knowing other cultures? Why can't we live in other cultures and do what they do and observe what they are about? Why do we need to *feel* anything for them, let alone something positive? Because feelings for the other not only colour our perception of the other, but critically, they move us to action and engagement. And positive feelings open our eyes wider, making new things happen, allowing us to see them, and making better sense of them. They allow us to look beyond our noses, fears, and bi-ases when we are confronted with other cultures. Culture seems to be as little a closed system as mind is; both require engagement to exist and are therefore immediately open to being known, but only through engage-ment. Intriguingly, this similarity also raises the possibility that we can see mind itself as a cultural practice and infants as participants in this practice from the start of their lives.

NOTES

INDEX

Notes

1. A Puzzle

1. Macmurray, J. (1961). *Persons in relation* (p. 28). London: Faber and Faber.
2. Clark, A. (1999). Embodiment: From fish to fantasy. *Trends in Cognitive Sciences, 3*(9), 345–351. A good review of the attempt to develop a robotic blue fin tuna in a swimming tank can be found in Triantafyllou, M.S., & Triantafyllou, G.S. (1995). An efficient swimming machine. *Scientific American, 272*(3), 64–74.
3. Stern, D.N. (2004). *The present moment in psychotherapy and everyday life.* New York: W.W. Norton.

2. Minding the Gap

1. Ryder, A.W. (1914). *Kalidasa: Translations of Shakuntala, and other works* (p. 92). London: J.M. Dent & Sons.
2. Descartes may be somewhat unfairly blamed for this dualism. He writes, for example, that mind is not to the body like a pilot is to his ship, and he writes—very un-dualistically—of the "passions of the mind." The philosophical problem of other minds pre-dated Descartes but didn't become a real problem until the nineteenth century with John Stuart Mill's attempt to develop a solution to it.
3. For an explicit discussion in psychology of the idea of behaviour as factual and mind as inferential, see Hebb, D.O. (1966). *A textbook of psychology* (2nd ed.). Philadelphia: Saunders; see also the discussion in Costall, A., Leudar, I., & Reddy, V. (2006). Failing to see the irony in "mind-reading." *Theory and Psychology, 16*(2), 163–167.
4. Coulter, J. (1979). *The social construction of mind.* London: Macmillan. See also Penn, D.C., & Povinelli, D.J. (2007). On the lack of evidence that non-human animals possess anything remotely resembling a "theory of mind." *Philosophical Transactions of the Royal Society of London, 362*(1480), 731–744.
5. For an explicit suggestion of such stages in the child's understanding of other minds see Olson, D. (1988). On the origins of beliefs and other intentional states in children. In J.W. Astington, P.L. Harris, & D.R. Olson (Eds.), *Developing*

theories of mind (pp. 414–426). Cambridge: Cambridge University Press. See also Cheney, D.L., & Seyfarth, R.M. (1990). Attending to behaviour versus attending to knowledge: Examining monkeys' attribution of mental states. *Animal Behaviour, 40,* 742–753.

6. Costall, A. (2006). "Introspectionism" and the mythical origins of scientific psychology. *Consciousness and Cognition: An International Journal, 15*(4), 634–654.

7. See Leudar, I., & Costall, A. (2004). On the persistence of the "problem of other minds" in psychology: Chomsky, Grice and "Theory of Mind." *Theory and Psychology, 14,* 601–621.

8. LeGuin, U.K. (1974). *The lathe of heaven* (p. 153). London: Granada.

9. Merleau-Ponty, M. (1945/2003). *The phenomenology of perception* (p. 354). London: Routledge.

10. But see Hinde, R. (1985). Was "the expression of the emotions" a misleading phrase? *Animal Behaviour, 33*(3), 985–992 for the suggestion that by continuing to imply in his language—for example, in the title of his book *The Expression of the Emotions in Man and Animals*—that expression and emotion are two different things, Darwin perpetuated the dualism in psychology.

11. For a critique see Hobson, R.P. (1991). Against a theory of the "theory of mind." *British Journal of Developmental Psychology, 9,* 33–51.

12. Perner, J. (1991). *Understanding the representational mind.* Cambridge, MA: MIT Press. Astington, J. (1994). *The child's discovery of the mind.* Cambridge, MA: Harvard University Press.

13. Diaz, R.M., & Berk, L.E. (Eds.). (1992). *Private speech: From social interaction to self-regulation.* Hillsdale, NJ: Lawrence Erlbaum Associates. Delgado, B., Gomez, J.C., & Sarria, E. (in press). Private pointing and private speech: Developing parallelisms. In A. Winsler, C. Fernyhough, & I. Montero (Eds.), *Private speech, executive functioning and the development of verbal self-regulation.* Cambridge: Cambridge University Press.

14. Frijda, N., & Mesquita, B. (1994). The social rules and functions of emotions. In S. Kitayama & H.R. Markus (Eds.), *Emotion and culture: Empirical studies of mutual influence* (pp. 51–87). Washington, DC: American Psychological Association.

15. Donaldson, M. (1992). *Human minds: An exploration.* New York: Allen Lane. The notion of "care" from the phenomenological philosophers is relevant here, where "being" is never a matter of indifference, but always involves "care" and involvement in life.

16. See Astington, J.W., & Gopnik, A. (1991). Theoretical explanations of the child's understanding of the mind. *British Journal of Developmental Psychology, 9*(1), 7–31 for another significant alternative solution to the problem of the gap: the "story" alternative, which (being agnostic about the existence of minds and focusing entirely on "talk" about minds) is less appropriate for exploring the beginnings of awareness of other minds in early, non-verbal, infancy. If extended to non-verbal narrative, however, this solution comes closer to the second-person approach suggested in this book.

17. The origins of the use of the term *first person* in this context are unclear. I use the term not to refer to any theorist who emphasises the significance of experience

within the self, but rather to refer to those theories which argue that awareness of the self is the starting point for awareness of other and which see the similarity between self and other as the primary and principal bridge to other minds.

18. Meltzoff, A.N., & Moore, M.K. (1998). Infant intersubjectivity: broadening the dialogue to include imitation, identity and intention. In S. Braten (Ed.), *Intersubjective communication and emotion in early ontogeny* (pp. 47–62). New York: Cambridge University Press. Meltzoff, A.N. (2002). Elements of a developmental theory of imitation. In A.N. Meltzoff & W. Prinz (Eds.), *The imitative mind: Development, evolution, and brain bases* (pp. 19–41). New York: Cambridge University Press.

19. Tomasello, M. (1999). Social cognition before the revolution. In P. Rochat (Ed.), *Early social cognition: Understanding others in the first months of life* (pp. 301–314). Mahwah, NJ: Lawrence Erlbaum Associates. Tomasello, M., Carpenter, M., Call, J., Behne, T., & Moll, H. (2005). Understanding and sharing intentions: The origins of cultural cognition, *Behavioural and Brain Sciences, 28,* 675–735.

20. Gopnik, A., & Meltzoff, A.N. (1997). *Words, thoughts and theories.* Cambridge, MA: MIT Press.

21. Gallese, V. (2006) Intentional attunement: A neurophysiological perspective on social cognition and its disruption in autism. *Brain Research, 1079,* 15–24.

22. See Gopnik, A., & Wellman, H. (1992). Why the child's theory of mind really *is* a theory. *Mind and Language, 7,* 145–171 for the view that the transition from infancy to childhood is one of an increasing understanding of representations. Many others, such as Josef Perner, see the development as a transition from a behaviourist understanding to a mentalist one. Perner, J. (1991). *Understanding the representational mind.* Cambridge, MA: MIT Press.

23. Gergely, G. (2002). The development of understanding of self and agency. In U. Goswami (Ed.), *Blackwell's handbook of childhood cognitive development* (pp. 26–46). Malden, MA: Blackwell.

24. Thompson, E. (2001). Empathy and consciousness. *Journal of Consciousness Studies, 8*(5–7), 1–32.

3. Engaging Minds

1. The term is frequently mentioned in philosophical discussions about people such as Buber and is implicit in the writings of Trevarthen and others on intersubjectivity since the 1970s. The first explicit use of the term appears to have been in 1989 by John Shotter, though in a slightly different context at the time. Shotter, J. (1989). Social accountability and the social construction of the You. In J. Shotter & K. Gergen (Eds.), *Texts of Identity* (pp. 133–151). Thousand Oaks, CA: Sage Publications. In the context of the "theory of mind" debate, the term appears in 1996: Gomez, J.C. (1996). Second person intentional relations and the evolution of social understanding. *Behavioral and Brain Sciences 19*(1), 129–130; and Reddy, V. (1996). Omitting the second person in social understanding. *Behavioral and Brain Sciences, 19*(1), 140–141. Both are reacting to Barresi and Moore's first-person versus third-person postulation of the problem of other minds in a different way. More recently, it has entered psychological

discourse explicitly in the writings of philosophers in psychology: Gallagher, S. (2001). The practice of mind: Theory, simulation or interaction? In E. Thompson (Ed.), *Between ourselves: Second-person issues in the study of consciousness* (pp. 83–108). Charlottesville, VA: Imprint Academic; and see Reddy, V. (2003). On being an object of attention: Implications for self-other-consciousness. *Trends in Cognitive Science, 7*(9), 397–402.

2. Buber, M. (1958). *I and Thou.* London: Continuum. Bakhtin, M. (1981). *The dialogic imagination.* Austin: University of Texas Press. Macmurray, J. (1961/1991). *Persons in relation.* London: Faber and Faber.

3. Dreyfus, H. L. (1995). *Being in the world: A commentary on Heidegger's "Being and Time," Division 1.* Cambridge, MA: MIT Press.

4. Barresi, J., & Moore, C. (1996). Intentional relations and social understanding. *Behavioural and Brain Sciences, 19*(1), 107–154. The authors suggest that a concept—the intentional schema—develops in humans around the end of the first year and allows the two to be bridged.

5. Lee, D. N. (1993). Body-environment coupling. In U. Neisser (Ed.), *The perceived self: Ecological and interpersonal sources of knowledge* (pp. 43–67). New York: Cambridge University Press.

6. Shotter, J. (1989). Social accountability and the social construction of the You.

7. Ivana Markova contrasts the Cartesian idea of separation of knower from known with the Hegelian idea of a spiral. Markova, I. (1982). *Paradigms, thought and language.* Chichester: John Wiley.

8. For discussion of greater complexity of infant behaviour with adults than when alone and for a model of expanding dyadic states of consciousness, see Tronick, E. (2005). Why is connection with others so critical? In J. Nadel & D. Muir (Eds.), *Emotional development* (pp. 293–315). Oxford: Oxford University Press. Bullowa, M. (1979). Prelinguistic communication: a field for scientific research. In M. Bullowa (Ed.), *Before speech: The beginning of interpersonal communication* (pp. 1–62). Cambridge: Cambridge University Press.

9. Leavens, D.A., Hopkins, W.D., & Bard, K.A. (2005). Understanding the point of chimpanzee pointing: Epigenesis and ecological validity. *Current Directions in Psychological Science, 14,* 185–189. Bard, K. A., Myowa-Yamakoshi, M., Toonaga, M., Tanaka, M., Costall, A., & Matsuzawa, T. (2005). Group differences in the mutual gaze of chimpanzees *(Pan troglodytes). Developmental Psychology, 41,* 616–624.

10. Forster, E.M. (1936). Notes on the English character. *Abinger Harvest.* London: Edward Arnold.

11. David Bakan discusses Brentano's argument at the beginnings of experimental psychology (in 1874), stating that psychology should be empirical rather than experimental. The experiment "was too far removed from experience to be able to tell us much that was significant. The very distinction—let alone the comparison—between the empirical and the experimental is one which many psychologists today find hard to understand. In the culture of contemporary psychology the words are used synonymously" (p. xii). Bakan, D. (1967). *On method: Towards a reconstruction of psychological investigation.* San Francisco: Jossey-Bass.

12. The phenomenologists Ludwig Binswanger, Eugene Minkowski, and H. C. Ruemke are the key proponents of this "method." See Lanzoni, S. (2006). Diagnosing with feeling: The clinical assessment of schizophrenia in early twentieth-century European psychiatry. In F. B. Alberti (Ed.), *Emotions, medicine and disease, 1750–1950*. New York: Palgrave.

13. Hobson. R. P. (2002). *The cradle of thought* (pp. 11–14). London: Macmillan.

14. Rifelj, C. de D. (1992). *Reading the other: Novels and the problem of other minds.* Ann Arbor: University of Michigan Press.

15. Buber, M. (1937/2004). *I and Thou* (p. 21). London: Continuum.

16. Brazelton, T. B. (1986). The development of newborn behavior. In F. Faulkner & J. M. Tanner (Eds.), *Human growth: A comprehensive treatise,* vol. 2 (pp. 519–540). New York: Plenum Press. Bergson, H. L. (1911). *Laughter: An essay on the meaning of the comic.* New York: Macmillan.

17. Bateson, W. (1908). *The method and scope of genetics* (p. 19). Cambridge: Cambridge University Press.

18. Keller, E. F. (1983). *A feeling for the organism: The life and work of Barbara McClintock.* New York: W. H. Freeman and Company.

19. Byrne, R. W. (1997). What's the use of anecdotes? Attempts to distinguish psychological mechanisms in primate tactical deception. In R. W. Mitchell, N. S. Thompson, & L. Miles (Eds.), *Anthropomorphism, anecdotes and animals: The emperor's new clothes?* (pp. 134–150). Lincoln: University of Nebraska Press.

20. Piaget, J. (1951/1972). *Play, dreams and imitation in childhood* (p. 94). London: Routledge.

21. Dewey, J. (1916/1961). *Democracy and education.* New York: Macmillan. Reprinted in McDermott, J. (Ed.). (1973). *The philosophy of John Dewey: The lived experience* (p. 502). New York: Capricorn Books.

22. "No more fiendish punishment could be devised, were such a thing physically possible, than that one should be turned loose in society and remain absolutely unnoticed by all members thereof. If no one turned round when we entered, answered when we spoke, or minded what we did, but if every person we met 'cut us dead,' and acted as if we were non-existing things, a kind of rage and impotent despair would ere long well up in us, from which the cruellest body tortures would be a relief; for these would make us feel that, however bad might be our plight, we had not sunk to such depths as to be unworthy of attention at all." James, W. (1890). *The principles of psychology,* vol. 2 (pp. 293–294). New York: Holt.

23. Frederickson, B. (2002). Positive emotions. In C. R. Snyder & S. J. Lopez (Eds.), *Handbook of positive psychology* (pp. 120–134). New York: Oxford University Press.

4. Making Contact

1. Friedman, M. (1955). *Martin Buber: The life of dialogue* (4th ed.) (p. 70). London: Routledge.

2. An approach to intervention called "Intensive Interaction" was introduced by Geraint Ephraim: Ephraim, G. W. E. (1979). Developmental processes in mental

handicap: A generative structure approach. Unpublished Ph.D. thesis, Brunel University. The approach was further developed for adults by Phoebe Caldwell and independently researched in France with children with autism by Jacqueline Nadel: Caldwell, P. (2002). *Learning the language*. Brighton: Pavilion Publishing. Nadel, J., & Fontaine, A. (1989). Communicating by imitation: A developmental and comparative approach to transitory social competence. In B. H. Schneider, G. Attili, J. Nadel, & R.P. Weissberg (Eds.), *Social competence in developmental perspective* (pp. 131–144). New York: Kluwer Academic/Plenum Publishers. Nadel, J., & Peze, A. (1993). Immediate imitation as a basis for primary communication in toddlers and autistic children. In J. Nadel & L. Camioni (Eds.), *New perspectives in early communicative development* (pp. 139–156). London: Routledge.

3. Darwin, C. (1905). *The voyage of the "Beagle"* (p. 202). London: Amalgamated Press.

4. J. Nadel, personal communication, April 1999.

5. Myowa-Yamakoshi, M., Tomonaga, M., Tanaka, M., & Matsuzawa, T. (2004). Imitation in neonatal chimpanzees *(Pan troglodytes). Developmental Science,* 7(4), 437–422. Bard, K. (2007). Neonatal imitation in chimpanzees *(Pan troglodytes)* tested with two paradigms. *Animal Cognition, 10,* 233–242. Ferrari, P. F., Visalberghi, E., Paukner, A., Fogassi, L., Ruggiero, A., & Suomi, S.J. (2006). Neonatal imitation in rhesus macaques. *PLoS Biology,* 4(9), 1501–1508.

6. O. Maratos, personal communications, September 1999 and March 2007. Maratos, O. (1982). Trends in the development of imitation in early infancy. In T. Bever (Ed.), *Regressions in mental development: Basic phenomena and theories* (pp. 81–101). Hillsdale, NJ: Lawrence Erlbaum Associates.

7. Nadel, J., & Butterworth, G. (1999). *Imitation in infancy.* New York: Cambridge University Press. They suggest several reasons for the neglect (and occasional denigration) of imitation as a phenomenon worthy of serious psychological interest.

8. Quoted in Edwards, D. (1994). Imitation and artifice in apes, humans and machines. *American Behavioral Scientist,* 37(6), 754–771.

9. Darwin, C. (1905). *The voyage of the "Beagle"* (pp. 202–203).

10. Byrne, R.W. (1999). Object manipulation and skill organization in the complex food preparation of mountain gorillas. In S.T. Parker, R.W. Mitchell, & H.L. Miles (Eds.), *The mentalities of gorillas and orangutans: Comparative perspectives* (pp. 147–159). New York: Cambridge University Press. Whiten, A., & Ham, R. (1992). On the nature and evolution of imitation in the animal kingdom: Reappraisal of a century of research. In P.J. Slater, J. Rosenblatt, C. Beer, & M. Milinski (Eds.), *Advances in the study of behaviour* (pp. 239–283). New York: Academic Press. Heyes, C. (2001). Causes and consequences of imitation. *Trends in Cognitive Sciences, 6,* 253–261.

11. Van der Meer, A.L.H., Van der Weel, F.R., & Lee, D.N. (1995). The functional significance of arm movements in neonates. *Science,* 267(5198), 693–695.

12. De Vries, J.I.P., Visser, G.H.A., & Prechtl, H.F.R. (1985). The emergence of fetal behaviour: II. Quantitative aspects. *Early Human Development, 12,* 99–129.

13. Jacobson, S. (1979). Matching behaviour in the young infant. *Child Development, 50*(2), 425–430.

14. Anisfeld, M. (1996). Only tongue protrusion modelling is matched by neonates. *Developmental Review, 16,* 149–161.

15. Kugiumutzakis, G. (1999). Genesis and development of early infant mimesis to facial and vocal models. In J. Nadel & G. Butterworth (Eds.), *Imitation in infancy* (pp. 36–59). Cambridge: Cambridge University Press. Kugiumutzakis, G. (1998). Neonatal imitation in the intersubjective companion space. In S. Braten (Ed.), *Intersubjective communication and emotion in early ontogeny* (pp. 63–88). Cambridge: Cambridge University Press. Bard, K.A. (2007). Neonatal imitation in chimpanzees. Bard, K.A., & Russell, C.L. (1999). Evolutionary foundations of imitation: Social cognitive and developmental aspects of imitative processes in non-human primates. In J. Nadel & G. Butterworth (Eds.), *Imitation in infancy* (pp. 89–123). Cambridge: Cambridge University Press.

16. Fontaine, R. (1984). Imitative skills between birth and six months. *Infant Behavior and Development, 7*(3), 323–333. Myowa, M. (2006). Imitation of facial gestures by an infant chimpanzee. *Primates, 37*(2), 207–213.

17. Thelen, E., & Fisher, D.M. (1982). Newborn stepping: An explanation for a "disappearing" reflex. *Developmental Psychology, 18*(5), 760–775.

18. Kugiumutzakis, G. (1993). Intersubjective vocal imitation in early mother-infant interaction. In J. Nadel & L. Camaioni (Eds.), *New perspectives in early communicative development* (pp. 23–47). London: Routledge.

19. Heimann, M., & Ullstadius, E. (1999). Neonatal imitation and imitation among children with autism and Down's syndrome. In J. Nadel & G. Butterworh (Eds.), *Imitation in infancy* (pp. 235–253). Cambridge: Cambridge University Press.

20. Butterworth, G. (1999). Neonatal imitation: Existence, mechanisms and motives. In J. Nadel & G. Butterworth (Eds.), *Imitation in infancy* (pp. 63–88). New York: Cambridge University Press.

21. Vinter, A. (1986). The role of movement in eliciting early imitations. *Child Development, 57,* 66–71.

22. Jacobson, S. (1979). Matching behaviour in the young infant.

23. Meltzoff, A., & Moore, M.K. (1989). Imitation in newborn infants: Exploring the range of gestures imitated and the underlying mechanisms. *Developmental Psychology, 25,* 954–962.

24. Meltzoff, M., & Moore, M.K. (1994). Imitation, memory and the representation of persons. *Infant Behaviour and Development, 17,* 83–99.

25. Nagy, E., & Molnar, P. (2004). Homo imitans or homo provocans? The phenomenon of neonatal imitation. *Infant Behaviour and Development, 27,* 57–63.

26. Kugiumutzakis, G. (1999). Genesis and development of early infant mimesis to facial and vocal models.

27. Heimann, M. (2002). Notes on individual differences and the assumed elusiveness of neonatal imitation. In A.N. Meltzoff & W. Prinz (Eds.), *The imitative mind: Development, evolution and brain bases* (pp. 74–84). Cambridge: Cambridge University Press.

28. Kugiumutzakis, G. (1999). Genesis and development of early infant mimesis to facial and vocal models.

29. Meltzoff, M., & Moore, M.K. (1994). Imitation, memory and the representation of persons.

30. Jones, S. (1996). Imitation or exploration? Young infants' matching of adults' oral gestures. *Child Development, 67*(5), 1952–1969.

31. Ramachandran, V.S. (2000). Mirror neurons and imitation learning as the driving force behind "the great leap forward" in human evolution. http://www .edge.org.3rd_culture (accessed November 28, 2006).

32. Rizzolatti, G., & Arbib, M. (1998). Language within our grasp. *Trends in Neurosciences, 21*(5), 188–194.

33. Decety, J., & Chaminade, T. (2003). Neural correlates of feeling sympathy. *Neuropsychologia, 41*, 127–138.

34. Fadiga, L., Craighero, L., Buccino, G., & Rizzolatti, G. (2002). Speech listening specifically modulates the excitability of tongue muscles: A TMS study. *European Journal of Neuroscience, 15*, 399–402. Fadiga, L., Fogassi, L., Pavesi, G., & Rizzolatti, G. (1995). Motor facilitation during action observation: A magnetic stimulation study. *Journal of Neurophysiology, 73*, 2608–2611. Hari, R., Forss, N., Avikainen, S., Kirveskari, E., Salenius, S., & Rizzolatti, G. (1998). Activation of human primary motor cortex during action observation: A neuromagnetic study. *Proceedings of the National Academy of Sciences USA, 95*, 15061–15065. Cochin, S., Barthelemy, C., Roux, S., & Martineau, J. (1999). Observation and execution of movement: Similarities demonstrated by quantified elecetroencephalography. *European Journal of Neuroscience, 11*, 1839–1842.

35. Conceptualising imitation as a series of independent acts rather than as an ongoing overlapping process is itself problematic. See also Rizzolatti, G., & Arbib, M. (1998). Language within our grasp.

36. Meltzoff, A.N., & Moore, M.K. (1998). Infant intersubjectivity: Broadening the dialogue to include imitation, identity and intention. In S. Braten (Ed.), *Intersubjective communication and emotion in early ontogeny* (pp. 47–62). New York: Cambridge University Press. Meltzoff, A.N. (2002). Elements of a developmental theory of imitation. In A.N. Meltzoff & W. Prinz (Eds.), *The imitative mind: Development, evolution, and brain bases* (pp. 19–41). New York: Cambridge University Press.

37. Gallese, V. (2006). Intentional attunement: A neurophysiological perspective on social cognition and its disruption in autism. *Brain Research, 1079*, 15–24.

38. Decety, J. (2002). Is there such a thing as functional equivalence between imagined, observed, and executed action? In A.N. Meltzoff & W. Prinz (Eds.), *The imitative mind* (pp. 291–310). New York: Cambridge University Press.

39. See also Butterworth, G. (1999). Neonatal imitation: Existence, mechanisms and motives. In J. Nadel & G. Butterworth (Eds.), *Imitation in infancy* (pp. 63–88). New York: Cambridge University Press. See also Merleau-Ponty, M. (2002). *Phenomenology of perception*. London: Routledge. Merleau-Ponty saw imitation as a direct response to the other's intentions (not just bodily movements).

40. Bundell, K. (2002). *Infants, action, meaning, others.* Unpublished manuscript.

41. See Zeedyk, M.S., & Heimann, M. (2006). Imitation and socio-emotional processes: Implications for communicative development and interventions. *Infant and Child Development, 15*(3), 219–222.

42. Bruner, J., & Kalmar, D.A. (1998). Narrative and meta-narrative in the construction of Self. In M.D. Ferrari & R.J. Sternberg (Eds.), *Self-awareness: Its nature and development* (pp. 308–331). New York: Guilford Press.

43. Quoted in Taussig, M. (1993). *Mimesis and alterity: A particular history of the senses* (p. 76). New York: Routledge.

44. Taussig, M. (1993). *Mimesis and alterity: A particular history of the senses* (p. 77).

45. Kugiumutzakis, G., Kokkinaki, T., Makrodimitraki, M., & Vitalaki, E. (2004). Emotions in early mimesis. In J. Nadel & D. Muir (Eds.), *Emotional development* (pp. 161–182). Oxford: Oxford University Press.

46. O'Neill, M., & Zeedyk, S. (2006). Spontaneous imitation in the social interactions of young people with developmental delay and their adult carers. *Infant and Child Development, 15,* 283–295. Caldwell, P. (2006). Speaking the other's language: Imitation as a gateway to relationship. *Infant and Child Development, 15*(3), 275–282.

47. Farroni, T., Csibra, G., Simion, F., & Johnson, M.H. (2002). Eye contact detection in humans from birth. *Proceedings for the Natural Academy of Sciences, 99*(14), 9602–9605.

48. Brazelton, T.B. (1986). The development of newborn behavior. In F. Faulkner & J.M. Tanner (Eds.), *Human growth: A comprehensive treatise,* vol. 2 (pp. 519–540). New York: Plenum Press.

49. Zeedyk, S. (2006). From intersubjectivity to subjectivity: The transformative roles of emotional intimacy and imitation. *Infant and Child Development, 15,* 321–344. Nadel, J. (2002). Imitation and imitation recognition: Functional use in preverbal infants and nonverbal children with autism. In A. Meltzoff & W. Prinz (Eds.), *The imitative mind: Development, evolution and brain bases* (pp. 42–62). Cambridge: Cambridge University Press.

5. Opening Conversations

1. Tagore, R. (1894/1985). Broken song. In *Rabindranath Tagore: Selected poems* (p. 55). London: Penguin.

2. Dewey, J. (1925). *Experience and nature: The Paul Carus lectures* (p. 135). Peru, IL: Open Court Publishing.

3. Emde, R.N., & Robinson, J. (1979). The first two months: Recent research in developmental psychobiology and the changing view of the newborn. In J. Noshpitz (Ed.), *Basic handbook of child psychiatry* (pp. 72–105). New York: Basic Books. Stern, D.N. (1977). *The first relationship: Infant and mother.* Cambridge, MA: Harvard University Press. Trevarthen, C. (1974). Conversations with a two-month-old. *New Scientist, 2,* 230–235.

4. Reddy, V., & Bundell, K. (1986). Unpublished diaries.

5. For a description of this history see Trevarthen, C. (1998). The concept and foundations of intersubjectivity. In S. Braten (Ed.), *Intersubjective communication and emotion in early ontogeny* (pp. 15–46). Cambridge: Cambridge University Press.

6. Stern, D.N. (1971). A micro-analysis of mother-infant interaction: Behaviors regulating social contact between a mother and her three-and-a-half-month-old twins. *Journal of the American Academy of Child Psychiatry, 10,* 501–517. Stern, D.N. (1974). The goal and structure of mother-infant play. *Journal of the American Academy of Child Psychiatry, 13,* 402–421. Papousek, H. (1967). Experimental studies of appetitional behavior in human newborns and infants. In H.W. Stevenson, E.H. Hess, & H.L. Rheingold (Eds.), *Early behavior: Comparative and developmental approaches* (pp. 249–277). New York: John Wiley.

7. The term *intersubjectivity* comes from Juergen Habermas' writings in sociopolitical philosophy and was first imported into psychology in 1974 by Joann Ryan: Ryan, J. (1974). Early language development: Towards a communicational analysis. In M. Richards (Ed.), *The integration of a child into a social world* (pp. 185–213). Cambridge: Cambridge University Press. It was then used by Trevarthen (provocatively because of its Marxist overtones). In essence, it refers to a relation between two subjects rather than objects, an inter-mental relation. Trevarthen was initially virtually alone in claiming the "innateness" of intersubjectivity as well as its presence at 2 months. For a change of position, see Stern, D. (2002). *The interpersonal world of the infant* (2nd ed.). New York: Basic Books.

8. Markova, I. (1982). *Paradigms, thought and language.* Chichester: John Wiley.

9. Experiments comparing the social versus private contexts for communication testify to the salience and persistence of this issue: Franco, F., Perucchini, P., & Butterworth, G. (1992). Pointing for an age-mate in 1 to 2 year-olds. Paper presented at the Sixth European Conference on Developmental Psychology, Seville, September. Delgado, B., Gomez, J.C., & Sarria, E. (in press). Private pointing and private speech: Developing parallelisms. In A. Winsler, C. Fernyhough, & I. Montero (Eds.), *Private speech, executive functioning and the development of verbal self-regulation.* Cambridge: Cambridge University Press. Legerstee, M. (1992). A review of the animate-inanimate distinction in infancy: Implications for models of social and cognitive knowing. *Early Development and Parenting, 1,* 59–67.

10. Kaye, K. (1982). *The mental and social life of babies.* London: Methuen. Collis, G.M., & Schaffer, H.R. (1975). Synchronisation of visual attention in mother-infant pairs. *Journal of Child Psychology and Psychiatry, 16*(4), 315–320.

11. First described in Trevarthen, C. (1977). Descriptive analyses of infant communication behavior. In H.R. Schaffer (Ed.), *Studies in mother-infant interaction: The Loch Lomond symposium* (pp. 227–270). London: Academic Press. See review by Tronick, E.Z. (2003). Things still to be done on the still-face effect. *Infancy, 4*(4), 475–482.

12. Reddy, V., & Bundell, K. (1986). Unpublished diaries.

13. Lynne Murray found one infant who strangely seemed happier during the still-face condition; this infant's mother was later discovered to be seriously

psychologically disturbed: Murray, L. (1980). *The sensitivities and expressive capacities of young infants in communication with their mothers.* Ph.D. thesis, University of Edinburgh. Tiffany Field found that infants of depressed mothers did not show any differences in cardiac measures in the still-face condition: Field, T. (1984). Early interactions between infants and their postpartum depressed mothers. *Infant Behaviour and Development, 7,* 527–532.

14. Murray, L. (1980). *The sensitivities and expressive capacities of young infants in communication with their mothers.* Murray, L., & Trevarthen, C. (1985). Emotional regulation of interactions between two-month-olds and their mothers. In T. Field & N. Fox (Eds.), *Social perception in infants* (pp. 101–125). Norwood, NJ: Ablex. Murray, L., & Trevarthen, C. (1986). The infant's role in mother-infant communication. *Journal of Child Language, 13,* 15–29. Nadel, J., Carchon, I., Kervella, C., Marcelli, D., & Reserbat-Plantey, D. (1999). Expectancies for social contingency in 2-month-olds. *Developmental Science, 2*(2), 164–173.

15. Rochat, P., Neisser, U., & Marian, V. (1998). Are young infants sensitive to interpersonal contingency? *Infant Behavior and Development, 21*(2), 355–366.

16. Nadel, J., Carchon, I., Kervella, C., Marcelli, D., & Reserbat-Plantey, D. (1999). Expectancies for social contingency in 2-month-olds.

17. Tronick, E. (1989). Emotions and emotional communication in infants. *American Psychologist, 44*(2), 112–119. Gianino, A., & Tronick, E. Z. (1988). The mutual regulation model: The infant's self and interactive regulation coping and defense. In T. Field, P. McCabe, & N. Schneiderman (Eds.), *Stress and coping* (pp. 47–68). Hillsdale, NJ: Lawrence Erlbaum Associates.

18. Gergely, G. (2003). The development of understanding of self and agency. In U. Goswami (Ed.), *Blackwell's handbook of childhood cognitive development* (pp. 26–46). Malden, MA: Blackwell. Gergely, G., & Watson, J. (1996). Early socio-emotional development: Contingency perception and the social bio-feedback model. In P Rochat (Ed.), *Early social cognition: Understanding others in the first months of life* (pp. 101–136). Mahwah, NJ: Lawrence Erlbaum Associates. Gergely, G. (2004). The role of contingency detection in early affect-regulative interactions. *Social Development, 13,* 468–488.

19. Field, T. M., Woodson, R. W., Greenberg, R., & Cohen, C. (1982). Discrimination and imitation of facial expressions by neonates. *Science, 218,* 179–181. Lindy, B., & Field, T. (1996). Newborns of mothers with depressive symptoms are less expressive. *Infant Behaviour and Development, 19,* 419–424.

20. Dondi, M., Simion, F., & Caltran., G. (1999). Can newborns discriminate between their own cry and the cry of another newborn infant? *Developmental Psychology, 2,* 418–426.

21. Nelson, C. A., & Horowitz, F. D. (1983). The perception of facial expressions and stimulus motion by two- and five-month-old infants using holographic stimuli. *Child Development, 54,* 868–877.

22. Izard, C., & Malatesta, C. Z. (1987). Perspectives on emotional development 1: Differential emotions theory of early emotional development. In J. Osofsky (Ed.), *Handbook of infant development* (pp. 494–554). Chichester, U.K.: John Wiley.

23. Haviland, J.M., & Lelwica, M. (1987). The induced affect response: 10-week-old infants' responses to three emotion expressions. *Developmental Psychology, 23*(1), 97–104.

24. Hamilton, M.S. (1990). Maternal depressive affect: Its effect on infant affective regulation. *Dissertation Abstracts International, 50*(9-B), 3919.

25. Hatzinikolaou, K. (2002). *The development of empathy and sympathy in the first year.* Ph.D. thesis, University of Reading, U.K.

26. See also discussion about the joint creation of meaning in Adamson, L.B. (1995). *Communication development during infancy.* Boulder, CO: Westview Press.

27. Legerstee, M., & Varghese, J. (2001). The role of maternal affect mirroring on social expectancies in three-month-old infants. *Child Development, 72*(5), 1301–1313.

28. Markova, G., & Legerstee, M. (2006). Contingency, imitation and affect sharing: Foundations of infants' social awareness. *Developmental Psychology, 42*(1), 132–141.

29. Cohn, J.F., & Tronick, E.Z. (1983). Three-month-old infants' reaction to simulated maternal depression. *Child Development, 54*, 185–193.

30. Field, T. (1990). *Infancy.* Cambridge, MA: Harvard University Press.

31. Malloch, S., Črnčec, R., Bradley, B., Adam, B., Dodds, C., Barnett, B., & Tam, P. (under review). Infant social behaviour in peer-only trios and the impact of post-natal depression.

32. Gergely, G. (2004). The role of contingency detection in early affect-regulative interactions.

33. Tronick, E. Why is connection with others so critical? The formation of dyadic states of consciousness and the expansion of individuals' states of consciousness: Coherence governed selection and the co-creation of meaning out of messy meaning making. In J. Nadel & D. Muir (Eds.), *Emotional development* (pp. 293–316). Oxford: Oxford University Press.

34. Panksepp, J., & Smith-Pasqualini, M. (2005). The search for the fundamental brain/mind sources of affective experience. In J. Nadel & D. Muir (Eds.), *Emotional development: Recent research advances* (pp. 5–30). New York: Oxford University Press.

35. Fridlund, A. (1994). *Human facial expression: An evolutionary view.* San Diego, CA: Academic Press.

36. Kirschenbaum, H., & Henderson, V.L. (Eds.). (1989). *Carl Rogers: Dialogues* (chapter 3, p. 57). Boston: Houghton Mifflin.

37. Stern, D. (2004). *The present moment in psychotherapy and everyday life.* New York: W.W. Norton & Co.

38. Stern, D. (2004). *The present moment in psychotherapy and everyday life.*

39. Smuts, B. (2001). Encounters with animal minds. *Journal of Consciousness Studies, 8*, 5–7, 293–309.

40. Tomasello, M. (1999). Having intentions, understanding intentions, and understanding communicative intentions. In P.D. Zelazo, A.W. Astington, & D.R. Olson (Eds.), *Developing theories of intention* (pp. 63–75). Mahwah, NJ: Lawrence Erlbaum Associates.

41. Shotter, J. (1998). Agency and identity: A relational approach. In A. Campbell & S. Muncer (Eds.), *The social child* (pp. 271–291). Hove, U.K.: Psychology Press.

Fogel, A. (1993). *Developing through relationships: The origins of communication, self and culture* (p. 19). Chicago: University of Chicago Press.

42. Fogel, A. (1993) *Developing through relationships: The origins of communication, self and culture* (p. 3).

43. *King Lear*, Act 1, Scene 1.

6. Experiencing Attention

1. Merleau-Ponty, M. (1961). *The phenomenology of perception* (p. 351). London: Routledge.

2. James, W. (1890). *The principles of psychology*, vol. 2 (pp. 293–294). New York: Holt.

3. Posner, M.I., & Cohen, Y. (1984). Components of visual orienting. In H. Bouma & D. Bouwhuis (Eds.), *Attention and performance X* (pp. 531–554). Hillsdale, NJ: Lawrence Erlbaum Associates.

4. Neisser, U., & Becklen, R. (1975). Selective looking: Attending to visually specified events. *Cognitive Psychology, 7,* 480–494. Simons, D.J., & Chabris, C.F. (1999). Gorillas in our midst: Sustained inattentional blindness for dynamic events. *Perception, 28,* 1059–1074.

5. Duncan, J. (1984). Selective attention and the organisation of visual information. *Journal of Experimental Psychology: General, 113,* 501–517. Egly, R., Driver, J., & Rafal, R.D. (1994). Shifting visual attention between objects and locations: Evidence from normal and parietal lesion subjects. *Journal of Experimental Psychology: General, 123,* 161–177.

6. Scholl, B. (2001). Objects and attention: The state of the art. *Cognition, 80,* 1–46.

7. Gibson, J.J., & Pick, A.D. (1963). Perception of another person's looking behaviour. *American Journal of Psychology, 76,* 386–394.

8. Butterworth, G., & Jarrett, N. (1991). What minds have in common is space: Spatial mechanisms serving joint visual attention in infancy. *British Journal of Developmental Psychology, 9*(1), 55–72.

9. Amano, S., Kezuka, E., & Yamamoto, A. (2003). Infant shifting attention from an adult's face to an adult's hand: A precursor of joint attention. *Infant Behaviour and Development, 205,* 1–17.

10. Bates, E., Camaioni, L., & Volterra, V. (1976). Sensorimotor performatives. In E. Bates, *Language and context: The acquisition of pragmatics* (pp. 49–71). New York: Academic Press.

11. Butterworth, G., & Jarrett, N. (1991). What minds have in common is space: Spatial mechanisms serving joint visual attention in infancy.

12. Butterworth, G. & Jarrett, N. (1991) What minds have in common is space: Spatial mechanisms serving joint visual attention in infancy. Franco, F. (2005). Infant pointing: Harlequin, servant of two masters. In N. Eilan, C. Hoerl, T. McCormack, & J. Roessler (Eds.), *Joint attention: Communication and other minds* (pp. 129–164). Oxford: Oxford University Press.

13. Song of Solomon, 6:5, King James Bible.

14. When someone else looks at you (and you look at them), it is a funny situation in which neither of you is looking at the same object! But we are trying to understand the infant's awareness of the other's attention, not what the infant understands about having a common object of attention. The triadicity involved in joining attention on a common external object is therefore not the central issue for us—it is the awareness of attention which is key. The triadicity is merely one amongst many tools to establish it.

15. Gale, A., Spratt, G., Chapman, A.J., & Smallbone, A. (1975). EEG correlates of eye contact and interpersonal distance. *Biological Psychology, 3*(4), 237–245. Kampe, K.K., Frith, C.D., Dolan, R.J., & Frith, U. (2001). Reward value of attractiveness and gaze. *Nature,* 413(6856), 589. Mutual gaze in adults, especially if the other's face is perceived to be attractive, leads to activation of the right anterior cingulate and the central striatum.

16. Striano, T., Kopp, F., Grossman, T., & Reid, V.M. (2006). Eye contact influences neural processing of emotional expressions in 4-month-old infants. *Social Cognitive and Affective Neuroscience, 1*(2), 87–94.

17. Farroni, T., Csibra, G., Simion, F., & Johnson, M.H. (2002). Eye contact detection in humans from birth. *Proceedings for the Natural Academy of Sciences, 99*(14), 9602–9605. Farroni, T., Johnson, M.H., & Gergely, C. (2004). Mechanism of eye gaze perception during infancy. *Journal of Cognitive Neuroscience,* 16, 1320–1326. Farroni, T., Mansfield, E.M., Lai, C., & Johnson, M.H. (2003). Infants perceiving and acting on the eyes: Tests of an evolutionary hypothesis. *Journal of Experimental Child Psychology, 85*(3), 199–212. See also Hains, S.M.J., & Muir, D.W. (1996). Infant sensitivity to adult eye direction. *Child Development, 67,* 1940–1951, showing that mutual gaze leads infants to more communicative exchanges.

18. Reddy, V., & Bundell, K. (1986). Unpublished diaries.

19. Brazelton, T.B. (1986). The development of newborn behavior. In F. Faulkner & J.M. Tanner (Eds.), *Human growth: A comprehensive treatise,* vol. 2 (pp. 519–540). New York: Plenum Press. For a difficulty in disengaging from any object of attention in children with autism, see also Leekam, S.R., Lopez, B., & Moore, C. (2000). Attention and joint attention in pre-school children with autism. *Developmental Psychology, 36,* 261–273. Fletcher-Watson, S., Leekam, S.R., Turner, M., & Moxon, L. (2006). Do people with autism spectrum disorders have normal selection for attention? Evidence from change blindness. *British Journal of Psychology, 97*(4), 537–554.

20. Reddy, V., & Bundell, K. (1986). Unpublished diaries.

21. Brazelton, T.B. (1986). The development of newborn behavior. Stern, D.N. (1977). *The first relationship: Infant and mother.* Cambridge, MA: Harvard University Press.

22. Reddy, V. (2000). Coyness in early infancy. *Developmental Science, 3*(2), 186–192. Videos from study.

23. Reddy, V. (2000). Coyness in early infancy. Reddy, V. (2001). Positively shy! Patterns of continuity and change in the development of expressions of shyness,

bashfulness and embarrassment. In R. Crozier & L. Aldon (Eds.), *International handbook of social anxiety* (pp. 77–99). Chichester, U.K.: John Wiley.

24. Adamson, L., & Bakeman, R. (1991). The development of shared attention during infancy. In R. Vasta (Ed.), *Annals of child development*, vol. 8 (pp. 1–41). London: Jessica Kingsley Publishers.

25. Atkinson, J., Hood, B., Wattam-Bell, J., Anker, S., & Tricklebank, J. (1988). Development of orientation discrimination in infancy. *Perception, 17,* 587–595.

26. Caron, A., Caron, R., Roberts, J., & Brooks, R. (1997). Infant sensitivity to deviations in dynamic facial-vocal displays: The role of eye regard. *Developmental Psychology, 33*(5), 802–813. Farroni, T., et al. (2003). Infants perceiving and acting on the eyes: Tests of an evolutionary hypothesis.

27. D'Entremont, B., Hains, S.M.J., & Muir, D. (1997). A demonstration of gaze following in 3- to 6-month-olds. *Infant Behavior and Development, 20,* 569–572. Hains, S., & Muir, D. (1996). Infant sensitivity to eye direction. *Child Development, 67,* 1940–1951. Muir, D., & Hains, S.M.J. (1999). Young infants' perception of adult intentionality. In P. Rochat (Ed.), *Early social cognition: Understanding others in the first months of life* (pp. 155–188). Mahwah, NJ: Lawrence Erlbaum Associates.

28. Reddy, V. (1991). Playing with others' expectations: Teasing and mucking about in the first year. In A. Whiten (Ed.), *Natural theories of mind* (pp. 143–158). Oxford: Blackwell.

29. Reddy, V. (1998). *Person-directed play. Humour and teasing in infants and young children.* Report on Grant No. R000235481 received from the Economic and Social Research Council, U.K. Transcripts from study, names changed.

30. The relationship between these two variables was strong, but not when developmental age was controlled for. This suggests that whatever link there is does not support a modular explanation. Unpublished data from Reddy, V. (1998). *Person-directed play: Humour and teasing in infants and young children.*

31. Baron-Cohen, S., Allen, J., & Gilberg, C. (1992). Can autism be detected at 18 months? The needle, the haystack and the CHAT. *British Journal of Psychiatry, 161,* 839–843.

32. Reddy, V., Williams, E., & Vaughan, A. (2002). Sharing humour and laughter in autism and Down's syndrome. *British Journal of Psychology, 93,* 219–242.

33. Perner, J (1991) *Understanding the representational mind.* Cambridge, MA: MIT Press.

34. Nadel, J., & Tremblay-Leveau, H. (1999). Early perception of social contingencies and interpersonal intentionality: Dyadic and triadic paradigms. In P. Rochat (Ed.), *Early social cognition: Understanding others in the first months of life* (pp. 189–212). Mahwah, NJ: Lawrence Erlbaum Associates.

35. Fivaz-Depeursinge, E., & Corboz-Warnery, A. (1999). *The primary triangle: A developmental systems view of mothers, fathers and infants.* New York: Basic Books.

36. Adamson, L., & Bakeman, R. (1991). The development of shared attention during infancy. In R. Vasta (Ed.), *Annals of child development*, vol. 8 (pp. 1–41). London: Jessica Kingsley Publishers.

37. Reddy, V. (1998). *Person-directed play.* Transcripts from study.
38. Leavens, D.A., & Todd, B.K. (2002). Audience effects on infant communication. Unpublished raw data.
39. See also Reddy, V. (2003). On being an object of attention: Implications for self-other-consciousness. *Trends in Cognitive Sciences, 7*(9), 397–402; and Reddy, V. (2007). Experiencing the social: A second-person approach. In U. Mueller, J. Carpendale, N. Budwig, & B. Sokol (Eds.), *Social life and social knowledge: Toward a process account of development.* Mahwah, NJ: Lawrence Erlbaum Associates.
40. Farroni, T., et al. (2003). Infants perceiving and acting on the eyes: Tests of an evolutionary hypothesis.
41. Grandin, T. (1988). Teaching tips from a recovered autistic. *Focus on Autistic Behaviour, 3*(1), 8.

7. Feeling Self-Conscious

1. Buber, M. (1937/2004). *I and Thou* (p. 11). London: Continuum.
2. Merleau-Ponty, M. (1962/2003). *The phenomenology of perception* (pp. 371–383). London: Routledge.
3. Montaigne, M. de. (1575/1991). *The complete essays,* trans. M.A. Screech (p. 380). London: Penguin. More recently, Ulrich Neisser has made this point in Neisser, U. (1993). *The perceived self: Ecological and interpersonal sources of self-knowledge.* New York: Cambridge University Press.
4. Jackson, M. (1998). *Minima Ethnographica: Intersubjectivity and the anthropopological project.* Chicago: University of Chicago Press.
5. Neisser, U. (1993). *The perceived self: Ecological and interpersonal sources of self-knowledge.*
6. James, W. (1891). *The principles of psychology* (chapter 10). New York: Holt.
7. Sheets-Johnstone, M. (1990). *The roots of thinking* (p. 371). Philadelphia: Temple University Press.
8. Von Hoftsten, C. (1982). Eye-hand coordination in the newborn. *Developmental Psychology, 18*(3), 450–446. Von Hoftsten, C. (1993). Studying the development of goal directed behaviour. In A.F. Kalverboer, B. Hopkins, & R. Geuze (Eds.), *Motor development in early and later childhood: Longitudinal approaches* (pp. 109–124). New York: Cambridge University Press.
9. Martin, G.B., & Clark, R.D. (1982). Distress crying in neonates: Species and peer specificity. *Developmental Psychology, 18,* 3–9. Sagi, A., & Hoffman, M.L. (1976). Empathic distress in the newborn. *Developmental Psychology, 12*(2), 175–176.
10. Van der Meer, A.L.H., Van der Weel, F.R., & Lee, D.N. (1995). The functional significance of arm movements in neonates. *Science, 267*(5198), 693–695.
11. Rochat, P., & Striano, T. (1999). Emerging self-exploration by 2-month-olds. *Developmental Science, 2*(2), 206–218.
12. Stern, D. (1985). *The interpersonal world of the infant.* New York: Basic Books.
13. Rochat, P., & Hespos, S.J. (1997). Differential rooting response by neonates: Evidence for an early sense of self. *Early Development and Parenting, 6*(3–4), 105–112.

14. Piontelli, A. (2002). *Twins: From foetus to child*. London: Routledge.

15. Buss, A.H. (1980). *Self-consciousness and social anxiety*. San Francisco: Freeman. Buss, A.H. (1986). A theory of shyness. In W.H. Jones, J.M. Cheek, & S.R. Briggs (Eds.), *Shyness: Perspectives on research and treatment* (pp. 39–46). New York: Plenum Press. Lewis, M., Sullivan, M.W., Stanger, C., & Weiss, M. (1989). Self development and self-conscious emotions. *Child Development, 60*(1), 146–156. Gallup, G.G. (1977). Absence of self-recognition in a monkey *(Macaca fascicularis)* following prolonged exposure to a mirror. *Developmental Psychobiology, 10*(3), 281–284.

16. Lewis, M. (1999). Social cognition and the self. In P. Rochat (Ed.), *Early social cognition: Understanding others in the first months of life* (pp. 81–98). Mahwah, NJ: Lawrence Erlbaum Associates.

17. Draghi-Lorenz, R. (2001). *Non-basic emotions in infants*. Ph.D. thesis, University of Portsmouth. Hart, S. (2002). Jealousy in 6 month-old infants. *Infancy, 3*(3), 395–402.

18. Amsterdam, B. (1972). Mirror self-image reactions before age two. *Developmental Psychobiology, 5*(4), 297–305. Amsterdam, B., & Greenberg, L.M. (1977). Self-conscious behaviour of infants. *Developmental Psychobiology, 10*(1), 1–6. Lewis, M., & Brooks-Gunn, J. (1979). *Social cognition and the acquisition of self*. New York: Plenum. Lewis, M., et al. (1989). Self development and self-conscious emotions. Bretherton, I., & Ainsworth, M. (1974). Responses of one-year-olds to a stranger in a strange situation. In M. Lewis & L.A. Rosenblum (Eds.), *The origins of fear* (pp. 131–164). New York: John Wiley. Ricard, M., & Decarie, T.G. (1993). Distance maintaining in infants' reaction to an adult stranger. *Social Development, 2*(2), 145–164. Stifter, C.A., & Moyer, D. (1991). The regulation of positive affect: Gaze aversion during mother-infant interaction. *Infant Behaviour and Development, 14*(1), 111–123.

19. Lewis, M. (1995). Embarrassment: The emotion of self-exposure and evaluation. In J.P. Tangney & K.W. Fischer (Eds.), *Self-conscious emotions: The psychology of shame, guilt, pride and embarrassment* (pp. 199–218). New York: Guilford Press. For a discussion of the distinction between these kinds of shyness see Reddy, V. (2001). Positively shy! Developmental continuities in the expression of shyness, coyness, and embarrassment. In R.W. Crozier & L.E. Alden (Eds.), *International handbook of social anxiety: Concepts, research and interventions relating to the self and shyness* (pp. 77–99). New York: John Wiley.

20. Amsterdam, B. (1972). Mirror self-image reactions before age two. Amsterdam, B., & Greenberg, L.M. (1977). Self-conscious behaviour of infants.

21. Lewis, M., et al. (1989). Self development and self-conscious emotions.

22. Asendorpf, J.B. (1990). The expression of shyness and embarrassment. In W.R. Crozier (Ed.), *Shyness and embarrassment* (pp. 87–118). Cambridge: Cambridge University Press. Keltner, D. (1995). Signs of appeasement: Evidence for the distinct displays of embarrassment, amusement and shame. *Journal of Personality and Social Psychology, 68*(3), 441–454.

23. Asendorpf, J.B. (1990). The expression of shyness and embarrassment.

24. Buss, A.H. (1986). *Social behaviour and personality*. Hillsdale, NJ: Lawrence Erlbaum Associates. Lewis, M., et al. (1989). Self development and self-conscious emotions.

25. Buss, A. (1980). *Self-consciousness and social anxiety*. San Francisco: Freeman. Leary, M.R., Britt, T.W., & Cutlip, W.D. (1992). Social blushing. *Psychological Bulletin, 112*(3), 446–460. Keltner, D., & Anderson, C. (2000). Saving face for Darwin: The functions and uses of embarrassment. *Current Directions in Psychological Science, 9*(6), 187–192.

26. Shotter, J. (1998). Agency and identity: A relational approach. In A. Campbell & S. Muncer (Eds.), *The social child* (pp. 271–291). Hove, U.K.: Psychology Press.

27. Eibl-Eibesfeldt, I. (1989). *Human ethology*. Hawthorne, NY: Aldine de Gruyter.

28. Lewis, M. (1995). Embarrassment: The emotion of self-exposure and evaluation. Izard, C.E., & Hyson, M.C. (1986). Shyness as a discrete emotion. In W.H. Jones, J.M. Cheek, & S.R. Briggs (Eds.), *Shyness: Perspectives on research and treatment* (pp. 147–160). New York: Plenum Press.

29. Argyle, M., & Dean, J. (1965). Eye-contact, distance and affiliation. *Sociometry, 28,* 289–304.

30. Amsterdam, B., & Greenberg, L.M. (1977). Self-conscious behaviour of infants. Bretherton, I., & Ainsworth, M. (1974). Responses of one-year-olds to a stranger in a strange situation. Young, G., & Decarie, T.G. (1977). An ethology-based catalogue of facial/vocal behaviour in infancy. *Animal Behaviour, 25*(1), 95–107. The infant smiles discussed here were closer to Young and Decarie's description of coy smiles, involving narrowed eyelids and open-mouth smiles, rather than shy smiles with normal eyes and close-mouth smiles.

31. Oster, H. (2005). The repertoire of infant facial expressions: An ontogenetic perspective. In J. Nadel & D. Muir (Eds.), *Emotional development* (pp. 261–292). Oxford: Oxford University Press.

32. Keltner, D. (1995). Signs of appeasement: Evidence for the distinctive displays of embarrassment, amusement and shame. Amsterdam, B.K., & Morton, L. (1980). Consciousness of self and painful self-consciousness. *Psychoanalytic Study of the Child, 35,* 67–83.

33. A few psychologists have noticed and described "showing off" in the first year, notably, Elizabeth Bates and her colleagues in Italy and the United States, and Colwyn Trevarthen and Penny Hubley, both in the 1970s. Bates, E., Benigni, L., Bretherton, I., Camaioni, L., & Volterra, V. (1979). *The emergence of symbols: Cognition and communication in infancy.* New York: Academic Press. Trevarthen, C., & Hubley, P. (1978). Secondary intersubjectivity: Confidence, confiding and acts of meaning in the first year. In A. Lock (Ed.), *Action, gesture and symbol* (pp. 183–229). London: Academic Press.

34. Reddy, V. (1998). *Person-directed play: Humour and teasing in infants and young children.* Report on Grant No. R000235481 received from the Economic and Social Research Council, U.K. Transcripts from study, names changed.

35. Reddy, V. (1991). Playing with others' expectations: Teasing and mucking about in the first year. In A. Whiten (Ed.), *Natural theories of mind* (pp. 143–158). Oxford: Blackwell.

36. Reddy, V. (1998). *Person-directed play*. Transcripts from study.

37. Reddy, V. (1998). *Person-directed play*. Transcripts from study.

38. Reddy, V. Williams, E., & Lang, B. (under submission). Engaging with the self in a mirror: Preschool children with autism and with Down syndrome.

39. Reddy, V. Williams, E., & Lang, B. (under submission). Engaging with the self in a mirror: Preschool children with autism and with Down syndrome.

40. Reddy, V. Williams, E., & Lang, B. (under submission). Engaging with the self in a mirror: Preschool children with autism and with Down syndrome.

41. Chidambi, G. (2003). Autism and self-conscious emotions. Unpublished Ph.D. thesis, University of London, University College. See also Hobson, R.P., Chidambi, G., Lee, A., & Meyer, J. (2006). Foundations for self-awareness: An exploration through autism. *Monographs of the Society for Research in Child Development, 71*(2), 1–188.

42. Hobson, R.P. (1990). On the origins of self and the case of autism. *Development and Psychopathology, 2*(2), 163–181.

43. White, B.L. (1971). *Human infants: Experience and psychological development*. Englewood Cliffs, NJ: Prentice-Hall. Kopp, C.B. (2002) The co-developments of attention and emotion regulation. *Infancy, 3*(2), 199–208.

44. See Draghi-Lorenz, R., Reddy, V., & Costall, A. (2001). Re-thinking the development of "non-basic" emotions: A critical review of existing theories. *Developmental Review, 21*(3), 263–304.

45. James, W. (1905). *Textbook of psychology* (p. 467). London: Macmillan and Co.

46. Amodeo, J., & Wentworth, K. (1986). *Being intimate: A guide to successful relationships* (p. 95). London: Arkana.

47. For a critical review of theories in this area, see Draghi-Lorenz, R., et al. (2001). Re-thinking the development of "non-basic" emotions: A critical review of existing theories.

48. Bahrick, L.E., Moss, L., & Fadil, C. (1996). Development of visual self-recognition in infancy. *Ecological Psychology, 8*(3), 189–208. Van der Meer, A.L.H., et al. (1995). The functional significance of arm movements in neonates.

49. Stern, D. (1985). *The interpersonal world of the infant*. New York: Basic Books. Neisser, U. (1997). The roots of self-knowledge: Perceiving Self, It and Thou. In J.G. Snodgrass & R.L. Thompson (Eds.), *The self across psychology: Self-recognition, self-awareness and the self-concept*, vol. 818 (pp. 18–33). New York: Annals of the New York Academy of Sciences. Butterworth, G. (1995). The self as an object of consciousness in infancy. In P. Rochat (Ed.), *The self in infancy: Theory and research* (pp. 35–51). Amsterdam: Elsevier. Lewis, M. (1999). Social cognition and the self.

50. See also Neisser, U. (1993). *The perceived self: Ecological and interpersonal sources of self-knowledge*. Fogel, A. (1993). *Developing through relationships*. Chicago: University of Chicago Press. Butterworth, G. (1995). The self as an object of consciousness in infancy.

8. Playing with Intentions

1. Asch, S. (1952). *Social psychology* (pp. 157–161). Oxford: Prentice-Hall.
2. Reddy, V. (1991). Playing with others' expectations: Teasing and mucking about in the first year. In A. Whiten (Ed.), *Natural theories of mind* (pp. 143–158). Oxford: Blackwell.
3. Sacks, O. (1996). *An anthropologist on Mars.* Toronto: Vintage Books.
4. For a discussion of different approaches to intentionality and of the particular difficulty of explaining development given a focus on goal-directedness, see Zeedyk, M. S. (1996). Developmental accounts of intentionality: Towards integration. *Developmental Review, 16,* 416–461.
5. Olson, D. R., Astington, J. W., & Zelazo, P. W. (1999). Introduction: Actions, intention and attributions. In P. D. Zelazo, J. W. Astington, & D. R. Olson (Eds.), *Developing theories of intention: Social understanding and self-control* (pp. 1–13). Mahwah, NJ: Lawrence Erlbaum Associates.
6. Astington, J. (1991). Intention in the child's theory of mind. In D. Frye & C. Moore (Eds.), *Children's theories of mind: Mental states and social understanding* (pp. 157–172). Hillsdale, NJ: Lawrence Erlbaum Associates.
7. Vedeler, D. (1994). Infant intentionality as object-directedness: A method for observation. *Scandinavian Journal of Psychology, 35*(4), 343–366.
8. Woodward, A. (1998). Infants selectively encode the goal object of an actor's reach. *Cognition, 69,* 1–34. Woodward, A. (1999). Infants' ability to distinguish between purposeful and non-purposeful behaviours. *Infant Behaviour and Development, 22*(2), 145–160. Woodward, A. (2003). Infants' developing understanding of the link between looker and object. *Developmental Science, 6*(3), 297–311. Woodward, A. L., & Somerville, J. A. (2000). Twelve-month-olds interpret action in context. *Psychological Science, 11*(1), 73–77.
9. Heider, F. (1959). Thing and medium. *Psychological Issues, 1*(3), 4–6.
10. Newtson, D. (1993). The dynamics of action and interaction. In L. B. Smith & E. Thelen (Eds.), *A dynamic systems approach to development: Applications* (pp. 241–264). Cambridge, MA: Bradford Books/MIT Press.
11. Baldwin, D. (2001). Infants parse dynamic action. *Child Development, 72*(3), 708–717. Baldwin, D., & Baird, J. A. (2001). Discerning intentions in dynamic human action. *Trends in Cognitive Sciences, 5*(4), 171–178. Brand, R. J., Baldwin, D. A., & Ashburn. L. A. (2002). Evidence for "motionese": Modifications in mothers' infant-directed action. *Developmental Science, 5*(1), 72–83.
12. Michotte, A. (1963). *The perception of causality.* Oxford: Basic Books.
13. Heider, F., & Simmel, M. (1944). An experimental study of apparent behavior. *American Journal of Psychology, 57,* 243–259.
14. Johansson, G. (1973). Visual perception of biological motion and a model for its analysis. *Perception and Psychophysics, 14*(2), 201–211. Moore, D. G., Hobson, R. P., & Lee, A. (1997). Components of person-perception: An investigation with autistic, non-autistic retarded and typically developing children and adolescents. *British Journal of Developmental Psychology, 15*(4), 401–423.

15. Premack, D. (1991). The infant's theory of self-propelled objects. In D. Frye & C. Moore (Eds.), *Children's theories of mind: Mental states and social understanding* (pp. 39–48). Hillsdale, NJ: Lawrence Erlbaum Associates.

16. Runeson, S. (1994). Perception of biological motion: The KSD Principle and the implications of a distal versus proximal approach. In G. Jansson, S.S. Bergsson, & W. Epstein (Eds.), *Perceiving events and objects* (pp. 383–405). Hillsdale, NJ: Lawrence Erlbaum Associates.

17. Tomasello, M., Carpenter, M., Call, J., Behne, T., & Moll, H. (2005). Understanding and sharing intentions: The origins of cultural cognition. *Behavioral and Brain Sciences, 28*, 675–735.

18. Michotte, A., Thines, G., Costall, A., & Butterworth, G. (1991). *Michotte's experimental phenomenology of perception*. Hillsdale, NJ: Lawrence Erlbaum Associates. For recent writings on the topic see Hobson, P. (2007). On being moved in thought and feeling: An approach to autism. In C. Nieto, J.M. Perez, P.M. Gonzalez, & M. Llorente Comi (Eds.), *New developments in autism: The future is today* (pp. 139–154). London: Jessica Kingsley Publishers; and Braten, S. (Ed.). (2007). *On being moved: From mirror neurons to empathy*. Amsterdam: John Benjamins Publishing Company.

19. Becchio, C., & Bertone, C. (2004). Wittgenstein running: Neural mechanisms of collective intentionality and we-mode. *Consciousness and Cognition, 13*(1), 123–133.

20. Legerstee, M. (1991). The role of people and objects in early imitation. *Journal of Experimental Child Psychology, 51*, 423–433.

21. Hobson, R.P., & Lee, A. (1999). Imitation and identification in autism. *Journal of Child Psychology and Psychiatry, 40*(4), 649–659.

22. See Lord, C. (1993). The complexity of social behaviour in autism. In S. Baron-Cohen, H. Tager-Flusberg, & D. Cohen (Eds.), *Understanding other minds: Perspectives from autism* (pp. 292–316). New York: Oxford University Press.

23. Warneken, F., Chen, F., & Tomasello, M. (2006). Altruistic helping in human infants and young chimpanzees. *Child Development, 77*, 640–663.

24. Klin, A., Volkmar, F.R., & Sparrow, S. (1992). Autistic social dysfunction: Some limitations of the theory of mind hypothesis. *Journal of Child Psychology & Psychiatry, 33*, 861–876.

25. Lord, C. (1993). The complexity of social behaviour in autism.

26. Dreyfus, H.L. (1995). *Being in the world: A commentary on Heidegger's "Being and Time," Division 1.* Cambridge, MA: MIT Press.

27. Reddy, V. (1998). *Person-directed play: Humour and teasing in infants and young children.* Report on Grant No. R000235481 received from the Economic and Social Research Council, U.K. Videos from study, names changed.

28. Behne, T., Carpenter, M., Call, J., & Tomasello, M. (2005). Unwilling versus unable: Infants' understanding of intentional action. *Developmental Psychology, 41*(2), 328–337.

29. Phillips, W., Baron-Cohen, S., & Rutter, M. (1992). The role of eye contact in goal detection: Evidence from normal infants and children with autism or mental handicap. *Development and Psychopathology, 4*(3), 375–382.

30. Kohler, W. (1925). *The mentality of apes.* London: Kegan Paul. Adang, O. (1984). Teasing in young chimpanzees. *Behaviour, 88* (1–2), 98–122. Groos, K. (1901/1976). The play of man: Teasing and love-play. In J. Bruner, A. Jolly, & K. Sylva (Eds.), *Play: Its role in development and evolution* (pp. 244–261). Harmondsworth, U.K.: Penguin.

31. Reddy, V. (1991). Playing with others' expectations: Teasing and mucking about in the first year.

32. Reddy, V. (1998). *Person-directed play.* Transcripts from study.

33. Reddy, V. (1991). Playing with others' expectations: Teasing and mucking about in the first year.

34. Reddy, V., Williams, E., & Vaughan, A. (2002). Sharing humour and laughter in autism and Down's syndrome. *British Journal of Psychology, 93,* 219–242. Heerey, E., Capps, L., Keltner, D., & Kring, A. (2005). Teasing: Lessons from children with autism. *Journal of Abnormal Child Psychology, 33*(1), 55–68.

35. Brand, R.J., et al. (2002). Evidence for "motionese": Modifications in mothers' infant-directed action.

36. Ratner, N., & Bruner, J. (1978). Games, social exchange and the acquisition of language. *Journal of Child Language, 5*(3), 391–401.

37. Winograd, T., & Flores, F. (1986). *Understanding computers and cognition.* Norwood, NJ: Ablex. Williams, E. (2004). Who really needs a theory of mind. *Theory and Psychology, 17,* 704–724.

38. Tomasello, M., Carpenter, M., Call, J., Behne, T., & Moll, H (2005). Understanding and sharing intentions: The origins of cultural cognition.

39. Gergely, G. (2003). The development of teleological versus mentalising observational learning strategies in infancy. *Bulletin of the Meninger Clinic, 67*(2), 113–131.

40. Baldwin, D., & Baird, J.A. (2001). Discerning intentions in dynamic human action.

41. Woodward, A. (1998). Infants selectively encode the goal object of an actor's reach. Woodward, A. (1999). Infants' ability to distinguish between purposeful and non-purposeful behaviours. Woodward, A. (2003). Infants' developing understanding of the link between looker and subject. Woodward, A.L., & Somerville, J.A. (2000). Twelve-month-olds interpret action in context.

9. Sharing Funniness

1. Eco, U. (1986). *Travels in hyperreality.* San Diego: Harvest.

2. Berlyne, D.E. (1960). *Conflict, arousal and curiosity.* New York: McGraw-Hill. Berlyne, D.E. (1972). Humor and its kin. In J.H. Goldstein & P. McGhee (Eds.), *The psychology of humor* (pp. 43–60). Oxford: Academic Press. Koestler, A. (1964). *The act of creation.* New York: Dell. Shultz, T.R. (1976). A cognitive-developmental analysis of humour. In A.J. Chapman & H.C. Foot (Eds.), *Humour and laughter: Theory, research and applications* (pp. 11–36). New York: John Wiley. McGhee, P. (1979). *Humour: Its origin and development.* San Francisco:

W.H. Freeman Co. McGhee, P. (1980). Development of the sense of humour in childhood: A longitudinal study. In P.E. McGhee & A.J. Chapman (Eds.), *Children's humour* (pp. 213–236). New York: John Wiley.

3. Bergson, H. (1913). *Laughter: An essay on the meaning of the comic.* London: Macmillan.

4. Chapman, A.J., & Chapman, W.A. (1974). Responsiveness to humor: Its dependency upon a companion's humorous smiling and laughter. *The Journal of Psychology, 55,* 245–252. Fridlund, A. (2001). Sociality of solitary smiling: Potentiation by an implicit audience. In W.G. Parrott (Ed.), *Emotions in social psychology: Essential readings* (pp. 265–280). New York: Psychology Press. Hermann, C. (1989). *The tongue snatchers.* Lincoln: University of Nebraska Press.

5. Shultz, T.R. (1976). A cognitive-developmental analysis of humour. However, see also Pien, D., & Rothbart, M.K. (1976). Incongruity and resolution in children's humor: A re-examination. *Child Development, 47*(4), 966–971.

6. McGhee, P. (1979). *Humour: Its origin and development.* McGhee, P. (1980). Development of the sense of humour in childhood: A longitudinal study.

7. Pien, D., & Rothbart, M.K. (1976). Incongruity and resolution in children's humor: A re-examination.

8. Neruda, P. (1952). *The Captain's verses.* New York: New Directions Books.

9. Berlyne, D.E. (1972). Humor and its kin.

10. Chevalier-Skolnikoff, S. (1986). An exploration of the ontogeny of deception in human beings and nonhuman primates. In R.W. Mitchell & N.S. Thompson (Eds.), *Deception: Perspectives on human and nonhuman deceit* (pp. 205–220). Albany, NY: SUNY Press. Panksepp, J., & Burgdorf, J. (1999). Laughing rats? Playful tickling arouses high frequency ultrasonic chirping in young rodents. In S. Hameroff, D. Chalmers, & A. Kazniak (Eds.), *Toward a science of consciousness III* (pp. 124–136). Cambridge, MA: MIT Press.

11. Provine, R.R. (1993). Laughter punctuates speech: Linguistic, social and gender contexts of laughter. *Ethology, 95,* 291–298. Provine, R.R. (1996). Laughter. *American Scientist, 84,* 38–45.

12. Cited in Darwin, C. (1872/1998). *The expression of the emotions in man and animals* (3rd ed.) (p. 195). London: HarperCollins.

13. Berlyne, D.E. (1972). Humor and its kin.

14. Fogel, A., Dickson, K.L., Hsu, H-C., Messinger, D., Nelson-Goens, G.C., & Nwokah, E. (1997). Communication of smiling and laughter in mother-infant play: Research on emotion from a dynamic systems perspective. In K.C. Barrett (Ed.), *The communication of emotion: Current research from diverse perspectives* (pp. 5–24). San Francisco: Jossey-Bass.

15. Sroufe, L.A., & Wunsch, J.P. (1972). The development of laughter in the first year of life. *Child Development, 43,* 1326–1344.

16. Reddy, V. (1998). *Person-directed play: Humour and teasing in infants and young children.* Report on Grant No. R000235481 received from the Economic and Social Research Council, U.K. Transcripts from study, names changed.

17. Reddy, V., Williams, E., & Vaughan, A. (2002). Sharing humour and laughter in autism and Down's syndrome. *British Journal of Psychology, 93*(2), 219–242.
18. Berlyne, D.E. (1972). Humor and its kin. Gibson, J.J. (1979). *The ecological approach to visual perception* (p. 127). Boston: Houghton Mifflin.
19. See Darwin, C. (1872/1998). *The expression of the emotions in man and animals* (pp. 209–210).
20. See also Ambrose, A. (1963). The age of onset of ambivalence in early infancy: Indications from the study of laughing. *Journal of Child Psychology and Psychiatry, 4*(3–4), 167–181.
21. Reddy, V. (1998). *Person-directed play*. Transcripts from study.
22. Fogel, A., et al. (1997). Communication of smiling and laughter in mother-infant play: Research on emotion from a dynamic systems perspective.
23. Reddy, V., et al. (2002). Sharing humour and laughter in autism and Down's syndrome.
24. Reddy, V. (1998). *Person-directed play*. Transcripts from study.
25. Freud, S. (1960). *Jokes and their relation to the unconscious* (pp. 194–195). New York: W.W. Norton.
26. Reddy, V. (1991). Playing with others' expectations: Teasing and mucking about in the first year. In A. Whiten (Ed.), *Natural theories of mind* (pp. 143–158). Oxford: Blackwell.
27. Reddy, V. (2001). Infant clowning: The interpersonal creation of humour in infancy. *Enfance, 3*, 247–256.
28. Reddy, V. (1998). *Person-directed play*. Transcripts from study.
29. Reddy, V. (1998). *Person-directed play*. Transcripts from study.
30. Reddy, V. (1998). *Person-directed play*. Transcripts from study.
31. Nakano, S., & Kanaya, Y. (1993). The effects of mothers' teasing: Do Japanese infants read their mothers' play intention in teasing? *Early Development and Parenting, 2*, 7–17.
32. Adang, O. (1984). Teasing in young chimpanzees. *Behaviour, 88*(1–2), 98–122.
33. Loudon, J. (1970). Teasing and socialisation in Tristan da Cunha. In P. Mayer (Ed.), *Socialisation: The approach from social anthropology* (pp. 193–332). London: Tavistock.
34. Huizinga, J. (1950). *Homo ludens: A study of the play-element in culture*. Oxford: Roy.

10. Faking in Communication

1. Eco, U. (1976). *Theory of semiotics*. Bloomington: Indiana University Press.
2. Whiten, A., & Byrne, R. (1988). Tactical deception in primates. *Behavioral and Brain Sciences, 11*, 233–273. Byrne, R.W., & Corp, N. (2004). Neocortex size predicts deception rate in primates. *Philosophical Transactions of the Royal Society of London B, 362*(1480), 621–637. Byrne, R.W., & Whiten, A. (1990). Tactical de-

ception in primates: The 1990 database. *Primate Report, 27,* 1–101. Byrne, R.W., & Whiten, A. (1992). Cognitive evolution in primates: Evidence from tactical deception. *Man, 27,* 609–627. Humphrey, N. (1976/1988). The social function of intellect. Reprinted in R. Byrne & A. Whiten (Eds.), *Machiavellian intelligence* (pp. 13–26). Oxford: Clarendon Press.

3. Perner, J., Leekam, S., & Wimmer, H. (1987). 3-year-olds' difficulty with false belief: The case for conceptual deficit. *British Journal of Developmental Psychology, 5,* 125–137.

4. Leudar, I., & Costall, A. (2004). On the persistence of the "problem of other minds" in psychology: Chomsky, Grice and theory of mind. *Theory and Psychology, 14*(5), 601–622. See also Fogel, A. (1993). *Developing through relationships: Origins of communication, self and culture* (p. 19). Chicago: University of Chicago Press.

5. Liszkowski, U., Carpenter, M., Henning, A., Striano, T., & Tomasello, M. (2004). Twelve-month-olds point to share attention and interest. *Developmental Science, 7*(3), 297–307. Legerstee, M., & Barillas, Y. (2003). Sharing attention and pointing to objects at 12 months: Is the intentional stance implied? *Cognitive Development, 18,* 91–110.

6. Golinkoff, R.M. (1986). "I beg your pardon?" The preverbal negotiation of failed messages. *Journal of Child Language, 13,* 455–476. Golinkoff, R.M. (1993). When is communication a "meeting of minds"? *Journal of Child Language, 20,* 199–207. See also Rodriguez, C. (2007). God's eye does not look at signs: Early development and semiotics. *Infancia y Aprendizaje, 30*(3), 343–374.

7. Baldwin, D. (1994). Early understanding of referential intent and attentional focus: Evidence from language and emotion. In C. Lewis & P. Mitchell (Eds.), *Children's early understanding of mind: Its origins and development* (pp. 133–156). Hillsdale, NJ: Lawrence Erlbaum Associates.

8. This is in contradiction to Piaget's prediction that language during the period from 18 months to 4 years is "preconceptual" and "aiming at success rather than truth." See Pea's landmark study: Pea, R.D. (1982). Origins of verbal logic: Spontaneous denials by two- and three year-olds. *Journal of Child Language, 9,* 597–626. And the revision of Pea's methodology using questions rather than statements, yielding earlier success: Hummer, P., Wimmer, H., & Antes, G. (1993). On the origins of denial negation. *Journal of Child Language, 20,* 607–618. See also Sharpe, D., Eakin, L., Saragovi, C., & Macnamara, J. (1996). Resolving apparent contradictions: Adults' and preschoolers' ability to cope with non-classical negation. *Journal of Child Language, 23,* 675–691.

9. Reddy, V., & Simone, L. (1995). Acting on attention: Towards an understanding of knowing in infancy. Paper presented at the Annual Conference of the Developmental Section of the British Psychological Society, Strathclyde. Tomasello, M., & Haberl, K. (2003). Understanding attention: 12- and 18-month-olds know what is new for other persons. *Developmental Psychology, 39*(5), 906–912.

10. O'Neill, D. (1996). Two-year-old children's sensitivity to a parent's knowledge state when making requests. *Child Development, 67,* 659–677.

11. Newton, P. (1994). *An investigation into the cognitive prerequisites for deception.* Unpublished Ph.D. thesis, University of Portsmouth.

12. Olson, D. (1988). On the origins of beliefs and other intentional states in children. In J.W. Astington, P.L. Harris, & D.R. Olson (Eds.), *Developing theories of mind* (pp. 414–426). Cambridge: Cambridge University Press.

13. Wilson, A.E., Smith, M.D., & Ross, H.S. (2003). The nature and effects of young children's lies. *Social Development, 12*(1), 21–45.

14. The term was first used by Clara and William Stern in the early 1900s: Stern, C., & Stern, W. (1909). *Mongraphien uner die seelische Entwicklung das kindes 2. Band: Erinnerung, Aussage und luge in der ersten Kindheit.* Leipzig: Barth. The term was then used by Piaget in the middle of the last century: Piaget, J. (1932/1977). *The moral judgement of the child.* Harmondsworth, U.K.: Penguin Books; and then more or less consistently by "theory-theorists."

15. Perner, J., & Sodian, B. (1991). The development of deception in children. *British Journal of Developmental Psychology, 9,* 173–188. Sodian, B. (1993). The theory of mind deficit in autism: Evidence from deception. In S. Baron-Cohen, H. Tager-Flusberg, & D.J. Cohen (Eds.), *Understanding other minds: Perspectives from autism.* Oxford: Oxford University Press. Sodian, B. (1994). Early deception and the conceptual continuity claim. In C. Lewis & P. Mitchell (Eds.), *Children's early understanding of mind: Origins and development* (pp. 385–401). Hove, U.K.: Lawrence Erlbaum Asociates. Sodian, B., Taylor, C., Harris, P.L., & Perner, J. (1991). Early deception and the child's theory of mind: False trails and genuine markers. *Child Development, 62,* 468–483.

16. All of the examples presented in this section are from Newton, P. (1994). *An investigation into the cognitive prerequisites for deception.* See also Newton, P., Reddy, V., & Bull, R. (2000). Children's everyday deception and performance on false-belief tasks. *British Journal of Developmental Psychology, 18,* 297–317.

17. Perner, J. (1991). *Understanding the representational mind.* Cambridge, MA: MIT Press.

18. Premack, D. (1988). "Does the chimpanzee have a theory of mind" revisited. In R. Byrne & A. Whiten (Eds.), *Machiavellian intelligence: Social expertise and the evolution of intellect in monkeys, apes and human* (p. 162). New York: Clarendon Press. Ristau, C. (1991). Before mindreading: Attention, purposes and deception in birds? In A. Whiten (Ed.), *Natural theories of mind* (pp. 209–222). Oxford: Blackwell.

19. Byrne, R.W., & Whiten, A. (1990). Tactical deception in primates: The 1990 database.

20. Reddy, V. (2007). Getting back to the rough ground: Deception and social living. *Philosophical Transactions of the Royal Society of London B, 362*(1480), 621–637. Uses data from Dunn, J. (1988). *The beginnings of social understanding.* Oxford: Basil Blackwell; Reddy, V. (1991). Playing with others' expectations: Teasing and mucking about in the first year. In A. Whiten (Ed.), *Natural theories of mind*

(pp. 143–158). Oxford: Blackwell; and Reddy, V. (1998). *Person-directed play: Humour and teasing in infants and young children.* Report on Grant No. R000235481 received from the Economic and Social Research Council, U.K. Transcripts from study, names changed.

21. Reddy, V. (1991). Playing with others' expectations: Teasing and mucking about in the first year.
22. Reddy, V. (2007). Getting back to the rough ground: Deception and social living.
23. Reported in Dunn, J. (1988). *The beginnings of social understanding.*
24. Reddy, V. (1998). *Person-directed play.* Transcripts from study.
25. Reddy, V. (1991). Playing with others' expectations: Teasing and mucking about in the first year.
26. Reddy, V. (1998). *Person-directed play.* Transcripts from study.
27. Reddy, V. (1998). *Person-directed play.* Transcripts from study.
28. Reddy, V. (1998). *Person-directed play.* Transcripts from study.
29. Onishi, K., & Baillargeon, R. (2005). Do 15-month-old infants understand false beliefs? *Science, 308,* 214–216. Song, H.J. (2006). Infants' reasoning about others' misperceptions and false beliefs. Paper presented at the Fifteenth International Conference on Infant Studies, Kyoto, Japan.
30. However, for an argument about domain specific learning in this mechanism, see Leslie, A.M., German, T.P., & Polizzi, P. (2005). Belief-desire reasoning as a process of selection. *Cognitive Psychology, 50*(1), 45–85.

11. Other Minds and Other Cultures

1. Eliot, T.S. (1974). *Collected poems 1909–1962* (*East Coker V,* pp. 202–203). London: Faber and Faber.
2. Geertz, C. (1993). *The interpretation of cultures.* London: Fontana.
3. Carruthers, M. (1992). *Why humans have cultures.* New York: Oxford University Press.

Index

Active intermodal matching (AIM), 57
Adamson, L., 112, 250n26, 253n24
Address, 27–28, 30, 32, 39, 47
Affective attunement, 80, 92
Affective awareness, 116
Affective centres of gravity, 81
Affective communication, 82
Affective core, 77
Affective engagement, 22–23, 78, 80, 145
Affective experience, 119, 181
Affective mirroring, 79–80
Affective responses (or reactions), 30, 79,
  80, 114, 115, 144, 146–147, 232, 234
Affective self-consciousness. *See* Self-
  conscious affect; Self-conscious emo-
  tions
Affective synchrony, 77
Affective tension, 145
Affect sharing, 111–112, 113
Affordances, 58, 197–199; affectively
  toned affordances, 180; shared afford-
  ances, 213
Ambiguity, 113, 193, 195, 197
Amsterdam, B., 130, 136
Anisfeld, M., 50
Argument from analogy, 18–21, 24, 46,
  57
Aristotle, 191
Attribution, 20–21, 25, 57, 69–70, 77–78,
  152, 153, 181
Autism, 34, 42, 233; and imitation, 44, 62,
  64, 244n2; and attention, 103, 109–110,
  118; and self-consciousness, 140–142,
  146–147; and intentions, 151, 158, 166,

167–168, 169–170, 171, 174–175, 180;
  and humour, 192, 196–198, 202–203,
  204, 208–209, 210; and deception, 216,
  221
Awareness of emotion, 6, 24, 41, 78, 79,
  81, 140, 151

Baillargeon, R., 229
Bakhtin, M., 28, 32, 232
Baldwin, D., 157, 177
Baldwin, J.M., 153
Bates, E., 91, 97, 108, 256n33
Bateson, M.C., 68
Bateson, W., 36
Behaviourism, 10–11, 56, 69, 181,
  241n22. *See also* Cognitivism
Bergson, H., 185, 186–187, 209
Berlyne, D., 197
Blushing, 126, 128
Body: as separate from the mind, 2–5,
  8–11, 14, 18, 23, 92, 239n2 (chap. 2); as
  intentional, 14–15, 152, 162; similarity
  to others, 20–21, 45–46, 85; potential
  for action, 59; sharing of, 61; as a tool,
  86; orientation of, 105; body parts as ob-
  jects, 106–110, 114, 117, 227; distinct
  awareness of, 123, 125; whole body,
  133, 134, 142; constraints or kinematics
  of, 154, 157; involvement of, 162–163,
  167, 179, 180; as common ground, 236
"Body babbling," 57
Body schema, 20. *See also* Active intermodal matching; "Body babbling"
Bravado, 219–220, 221

Brazelton, T.B., 64, 68

Bruner, J., 68, 94, 176

Buber, M., 28, 34–35, 43, 64, 82, 86, 119, 120, 233

Bumblebees, 2–3

Bundell, K., 58–59

Butterworth, G., 51, 96

Byrne, R.W., 37, 224, 226

Bystander, 7, 24, 25, 119, 146. *See also* Observing, versus participating; Spectator

Caldwell, P., 44, 64

Chidambi, G., 141

Chimpanzees, 31, 46, 50, 61, 159, 191, 212

Chomsky, N., 181

Clowning, 84, 108–110, 115, 204–209, 214

Cognitivism, 10–11, 69, 85. *See also* Behaviourism

Communication: communicative intentions, 85–88; paradox of, 87–88; as a representational act, 88–89

Compliance, 127, 159–160, 168–169, 173–174, 210. *See also* Non-compliance

Concealment: of minds, 16; of vitality contours, 81; of the self, 127; deceptive, 215, 224–225, 228

Context: and action, 14; theoretical context, 23; and thought, 24; and observations, 37; interactive context, 62, 228; and imitation, 63; and expressions, 79; and culture, 117; and coy reactions, 132, 133, 142, 148; and intentions, 152, 154, 160–162, 163, 177, 180, 181; and teasing, 175; and laughter, 192, 193, 194, 198, 199, 202, 203; of play, 194, 198; and deception, 221, 222, 223, 225, 230; and pretending, 227, 228

Coyness, 39, 115, 126, 129–145. *See also* Embarrassment; Shyness

Culture, 2, 5, 13, 16–17, 24, 33, 36, 44, 81, 117, 133, 159, 168, 180, 183, 187, 206, 213–214, 235–236; and experts, 5; and sayings about mind, 13; and privacy, 16–17; culture-centrism, 24; and methods, 33, 36, 242n11; and making

contact, 44, 60; drawing infants into, 81; and objects of attention, 117; and shyness, 133; and intentions, 151, 159, 168, 180; and humour, 183, 187, 206, 213–214, 235–236

Darwin, C., 14, 44, 47, 61, 128, 193, 199

Deception, 13, 17, 40, 215–216, 218–219; verbal, 219–224; non-verbal, 224–229; development of, 229–231

Decety, J., 58

Denials, 217, 222–223, 263n8

Descartes, R., 8–11, 12, 14, 19, 21, 23, 24, 29, 30, 48, 81, 90, 147, 235, 239n2 (chap. 2), 242n7. *See also* Dualism

Detachment, 5, 24, 32–39, 90, 142, 143, 209, 232–233

Dewey, J., 38, 66

Directedness: of attention, 40, 92, 94, 100–101, 106, 113, 116, 121, 126, 144, 214; of actions/intentions, 55, 126, 152, 153, 154, 155–157, 160, 162–165, 167–168, 173, 176, 179, 180, 181; of communicative intentions, 85–86; of laughter, 203

Dis-embedding, 4, 92. *See also* Embedding

Disembodiment, 4–5, 9–12, 14–15, 18

Disengagement, 28, 33, 34–36, 38, 50, 84, 102, 183, 209–210, 213, 215, 232, 252n19

Distance, 28, 33, 35, 115, 144, 154, 168, 169, 179, 209

Distracting, 215, 224–226, 228, 231

Donaldson, M., 18

Dostoevsky, F., 34

Down syndrome, 117, 140, 174, 192

Dualism: mind-body, 8, 86–87; mind-behaviour, 8–11, 14, 23, 48, 69, 78, 81, 86–87; adualism (of self and other), 123–125

Dyad, 61, 81, 114, 140, 231

Dyadic engagements, 81, 105, 112, 227

Dyadic expansion, 81

Dyadic interaction, 83, 111, 117

Dyadic states of consciousness, 84

Eibl-Eibesfeldt, I., 133

Embarrassment, 90, 126, 128–145, 148, 191. *See also* Coyness; Shyness

Embedding, 3–5, 29, 69, 81, 122, 145, 192, 200, 201, 233. *See also* Dis-embedding

Emotional attunement and reciprocity, 57, 71, 72, 78, 86

Emotional engagement, 4, 5, 6, 24, 26, 27, 30, 33, 39, 40, 41, 80–81, 118, 125, 230–231, 233, 235, 236

Emotional responses, 21, 27, 30, 31, 34, 80–81; and mentality, 27, 30, 41, 81, 233; to attention, 90, 91, 92, 100, 101–103, 106, 109, 117–118; in teasing, 174; to actions, 179, 180

Emotion and communication, 68, 71, 78–82, 84, 86

Emotion and humour, 184–185, 186, 187, 191, 196, 206

Emotion and neonatal imitation, 59, 63

Emotion tied to perception and proprioception, 26, 30, 100, 117, 153, 230

Engagement, 1–6, 7, 13, 15, 16, 18, 20, 21, 22–23, 24, 25, 26–42, 232–236; and imitation, 43, 49, 60, 63, 64; in early dialogue, 70, 71, 72–85, 86, 88; with attention, 90–94, 99–100, 102, 105, 109, 110–112, 114, 115, 117–118; in self-consciousness, 120, 122, 125–126, 130, 131, 136, 139, 140, 143–147, 148–149; with intentions, 150, 152, 153, 154, 160, 161–164, 168, 169, 170, 172, 174–175, 176–182; in humour, 183–184, 186, 190–192, 193, 199–203, 205–206, 208–214; in deceiving, 215–216, 219, 221, 225, 227, 229–231

Expectation, 74, 84, 151, 155, 159–160, 168, 171, 184, 189, 192, 199, 200, 210, 214, 220, 221

Experts, 5, 11

Expression: in relation to mentality, 14; directed to the self, 27, 30; awareness of, 41, 72; imitation of, 47, 60, 62; responses to, 78–82, 84; of coyness, 130, 132–134; change in form with age, 134;

and context, 161; odd facial expressions in clowning, 206, 207; meanings of expressions in pretending, 227–228

Faking, 215, 224–229; laughing, 192, 200, 203, 207; coughing, 207; actions and expressions, 219, 224, 226; crying, 226

False belief, 216, 218, 221, 229

Farroni, T., 63, 252n17

First person, 7, 18, 19–21, 24–25, 232, 233, 235, 240–241n17, 241n1; and imitation, 46, 57; and attention, 90, 99; and self-consciousness, 125; and intention, 153, 163, 180

First-person experience, 8, 19, 29–30, 125, 153, 163, 180, 233

First-person information, 8

First-person method, 33, 34

Fivaz-Depeursinge, E., 111–112

Fogel, A., 87, 192

Freud, S., 123, 204

Frijda, N., 17

Gallese, V., 21, 57

Gap, 4, 7–25, 26, 29–31, 45, 46, 54, 55–58, 61, 233

Genuine attending, 96

Genuine communication, 68, 85, 86

Genuine crying, 226

Genuine deception, 216, 222

Genuine dialogue, 28, 82

Genuine engagement, 16, 34, 169, 176, 177–178

Genuine expressions, 134

Genuine identification, 48

Genuine imitation, 48–49

Genuine laughs, 191, 192

Genuine play, 213

Genuine skills, 86

Genuine turn-taking, 74

Gergely, G., 77–78, 81

Gestalt psychologists, 29, 93

Gibson, J.J., 29, 197

Giving: objects, 114, 115, 127, 150, 161–162, 171; information, 217–218, 224, 229

Golinkoff, R.M., 171, 217
Grandin, T., 151

Hegel, G.W.F., 32, 64, 82, 233, 242n7
Heidegger, M., 29, 170
Heimann, M., 51, 53
Hermeneutic background, 59–60
Hermeneutic circle, 88
Hobson, R.P., 34, 144, 148, 162, 166
Hubley, P., 71, 168, 256n33
Huizinga, J., 213

"Idea of me," 128, 143, 148
Inaccessibility: of minds, 11–12; of cultures, 235. *See also* Privacy
Incongruity, 184–185, 188, 193–195
Inflexibility, and deception, 219, 221–224
Inflexible reflexes, 52
Informing, 216–217, 224, 229
Innate releasing mechanism (IRM), 49, 50–51
Intentional schema, 152, 242n4
Intersubjectivity, 23, 66, 68–71, 77, 88, 111, 168, 241n1
Intimacy, 4, 13, 28, 34, 65, 122, 133, 134, 147, 212, 213
Invisibility of minds, 8, 11–12. *See also* Inaccessibility; Privacy
Itakura, S., 165
I-Thou (or *I-You*), 28, 34, 57, 63, 86, 119, 120, 184, 233, 241n1
Izard, C., 144, 148

James, W., 39, 90, 121–122, 147, 232, 243n22
Joint attention, 40, 86, 97, 103, 109, 111

Keltner, D., 132, 136
Koestler, A., 185
Kugiumutzakis, G., 51, 53–54, 56, 61, 63

Lanzoni, S., 34
Leary, M., 133
Leavens, D., 113
Legerstee, M., 79–80
Leslie, A., 229, 265n30

Lewis, M., 128–129, 130, 132, 133, 143
"Like-me" representations, 20–21, 59, 126
Literature, and other minds, 34
Lord, C., 169

Macmurray, J., 1, 28
Malinowski, V., 33
Maratos, O., 46
Matching, 55, 57, 58, 80, 124, 128
McClintock, B., 36, 38
McGhee, P., 189
Mead, G.H., 69
Meltzoff, A.N., 47, 50, 52, 54, 56, 57, 59, 60, 165
Merleau-Ponty, M., 14, 61, 90, 120
Mesquita, B., 17
Michotte, A., 159, 162
Mill, J.S., 19
Mirror: reactions to self in, 102–103, 123, 130, 131, 136, 140–142; self-recognition, 128–129, 140, 142, 146
Mirroring, 62, 79–80
Mirror neurones, 14, 55–56, 59
Miscommunication, 76–77
Mis-expectedness in humour, 189, 210, 213
Mis-understanding, 171, 209, 214
Moore, C., 96
Moore, K., 50, 52, 57, 59
Motherese, 76, 177
Motionese, 177
Motor attunement, 56
Murray, L., 73, 75, 248–249n13
Mutual attention, 100, 101, 105, 116–117, 118, 119
Mutual contact, 16
Mutual gaze, 35, 44, 132, 133, 134, 233
Mutuality: in engagement, 32, 83; in imitation, 56, 61, 63; of explanation, 61; in intentions, 175, 182; in humour, 209, 211, 213
Mutual motor attunement, 56
Mutual recognition, 67, 82, 85
Mutual regulation, 78
Mutual responsiveness, 35
Mutual teasing, 178

Mutual understanding, 63, 213, 214
Mutual visibility of selves, 127

Nadel, J., 62, 64, 76, 111
Nagy, E., 53, 56, 59, 61, 177
Nakano, S., 211
Newton, P., 218–224
Non-compliance, 159, 168, 172–174, 175, 207, 210
Nwokah, E., 192

Objective self-consciousness or self-awareness, 121, 125, 148
Objects: person treated as object, 28; of attention (and object-based views of attention), 29, 49, 71, 90, 91–118, 126, 129, 140, 143, 144, 146, 147, 148, 234; *Thou* as object, 35; intentional or mental object, 85–86; self as object, 121, 122, 125–126, 128–129, 132, 133, 140–141, 142, 143, 144, 146, 148, 234; of intention (and object-directed views of intention), 152–154, 155–156, 157, 159, 161, 164, 165, 167–168, 172–173; humorous, 184; and pretending, 227–228
Observing, versus participating, 1, 6–7, 11, 14, 19, 21–25, 26–34, 36–39, 81, 92, 94, 97, 98, 120, 153, 162, 163, 181, 193, 205, 232–236
Olson, D., 153, 239n5
Onishi, K., 229
Openness, 28, 41, 67, 82–84, 162, 179, 230, 234, 235
Oster, H., 134
Other minds: problem of, 8–14, 24–25, 48, 239n2 (chap. 2), 240n16, 241n1; first- and third-person solutions to, 18–23, 232, 240n17; second-person solutions to, 26, 29–30, 32–34, 40–42, 232–236; humour and, 213; and other cultures, 235–236

Papousek, H., 68, 73, 75
Papousek, M., 73, 75
Paradox: of thought, 38; of skill, 47; of communication, 87–88; engagement in humour, 209, 214; of deception, 215

Parsimony, 23, 229
Participant. *See* Bystander
Participation, 7, 42, 68, 74, 83, 151, 162–163, 168, 186, 209, 212, 233–236
Perception: of mind, 4, 11, 14, 15, 16, 23, 26, 57; of similarity, 20–21; in engagement, 29–31, 32, 33, 39, 152, 153; of action, 58, 61; of attending, 63, 86, 94, 97, 101, 126, 144; of emotion, 72, 79–81, 86, 144, 145, 146, 177; of intentions, 153–165, 168–169, 175–176, 179–180; of funniness, 185, 187, 192, 195, 205; of deceivedness, 230
Perner, J., 221
Piaget, J., 8, 24, 36–37, 45–47, 50, 68, 69, 108, 123, 224
Playfulness, 84, 102, 135, 139, 150, 164, 172, 176–177, 178, 179–180, 186, 189, 198, 210, 212, 218, 227–228, 234
Positive affective core, 77
Positive attention, 117–118, 127, 136, 139, 142, 144
Positive emotions, 41, 63, 236
Positive evaluation, 132–133, 140
Positive events in triadic interactions, 112
Positive reactions to shyness and embarrassment, 136
Positive shyness, 130–132, 133, 144, 145, 147
Praecox feeling, 34
Premack, D., 222
Pretending, 139, 158, 168, 189, 198, 203, 210, 215, 224–228, 229
Privacy: and mind, 4, 9, 12–13, 14, 15–18; and communication, 20, 87–88, 248n9; privacy regulation, 133; of meanings, 235
Privileged access to the self, 19–21, 23
Proprioception, 8, 20, 29–31, 46, 57, 100, 117, 153, 230
Proto-conversations, 66, 68, 91
Proto-declarative pointing, 91, 104, 109, 208, 217
Proto-humour, 193
Proto-imperative pointing, 91
Proto-informative pointing, 217

Proto-interrogatives, 217
Proust, M., 34
Provocation, 53, 56, 59, 61, 104, 172–173, 175, 177–178, 210–211
Pseudo-communication, 68, 73, 77, 85, 88–89. *See also* Genuine communication; Genuine dialogue; Genuine turn-taking
Pseudo-deception, 218–219, 224. *See also* Genuine deception
Pseudo-imitation, 68. *See also* Genuine imitation
Pseudo-skills, 10. *See also* Genuine skills

Ratner, N., 176
Recognition: of mind, 11, 22, 66, 110, 208; of self-other similarity, 20, 25, 27, 30, 50, 55, 57, 58, 163, 233; of self-other difference, 25, 123; as a person/of a consciousness, 27, 28, 40, 66, 67, 69, 82–85, 89, 232; of acts, 72, 199, 211; awareness of, 233
Reflex: imitation as, 3, 46, 49, 51–55; neonatal, 50–51; self-conscious reactions, 143, 144; versus intentional actions, 158–159, 168
Relation, 1–5, 9, 27–29, 32–39, 43, 45, 64, 69, 78, 81–84, 86, 119, 121–126, 132, 143–149, 154–157, 174, 183–184, 198–199, 209, 212–214, 230, 233
Relevance, 29, 38, 58–59, 67, 78, 81–82, 155, 233
Repair of miscommunication, 76–77
Responses to others' emotions, 32, 78–79, 80–81, 125, 158, 206, 208, 230, 233
Ristau, C., 222
Rizzolatti, G., 55, 56
Rodriguez, C., 217
Rommetveit, R., 69
Rothbart, M., 189, 198
Routine, 61, 169–170, 173, 180, 197, 209
Ryle, G., 14

Scholl, B., 94
Secondary emotions, 128, 144, 148
Secondary intersubjectivity, 71, 168
Second person, 2, 7, 26–32, 39–40, 57, 83, 232–236; and attention, 90, 98, 100, 113–114, 118; and self-consciousness, 121, 125, 142; and intention, 153, 162, 165, 180; and humour, 184, 189, 213; and deception, 216, 230
Second-person address, 27
Second-person experience, 162, 165, 180, 230
Second-person method, 32–34, 50
Second-person voice, 28
Self: understanding through engagement with others, 16, 32, 90, 99, 125–126, 145–147; understanding others through reference to, 18–21, 23, 24–25, 153; recognition of similarity to other, 24–25, 45–46, 50, 54, 55, 57, 58, 163, 233; in relation to the world, 29–31, 43, 125, 149, 234; as separate from other, 30, 55, 56, 57; recognition of difference from other, 57, 123; self-other relevance, 59; as object, 98, 100–105, 114, 115, 116–118, 121, 133, 144, 155, 157, 162, 163, 167, 234; acts as objects, 106–110, 112, 115, 116, 144; boundaries of, 121–122, 123–125; plurality of, 122; fluidity of, 122; self-other adualism, 123–125; visibility to others, 126–128; reducing the visibility of, 129–136, 140–142; heightening the visibility of, 136–142
Self-comforting, 76–77, 79
Self-conscious affect, 39, 40, 125, 126, 129, 142, 144, 146–147, 232, 234
Self-conscious emotions, 120, 126–132, 138–139, 141–144, 147–148. *See also* Self-conscious affect
Self-recognition. *See* Mirror: self-recognition
Self-synchrony, 71, 72
Sheets-Johnstone, M., 123
Shotter, J., 30, 33, 87
Showing off, 108–110, 115, 120, 126–127, 136–140, 143–145, 147, 148, 256n33
Shultz, T., 183, 188, 193
Shyness, 120, 126–127, 129–145, 147
Simulation, 20, 25, 38, 80, 99, 232, 233

Simulation theory, 8, 18, 20. *See also* Argument from analogy
Smith, A., 163
Solitary smiles and laughs, 101, 202
Spectator, 7, 25, 28, 94, 232–233. *See also* Bystander; Observing, versus participating
"Spotlight" theory of attention, 92–94
Stern, D., 4, 68, 74, 81, 83–84, 125
Subjective self-awareness, 125
Subjectivity, 20, 23, 69, 121, 125

Tactical deception, 224–226
Taussig, M., 62
Teasing, 1, 2, 36, 39, 40, 84, 108, 127, 130, 141, 158, 164, 172–179, 186, 199, 209, 210–212, 214, 227
Theory-theory, or theory of mind theory, 8, 18, 22–25, 46, 216–218, 221, 224, 229
Third person, 7, 18, 21–24, 25, 26–27, 30, 232, 233, 235, 241n1; and imitation, 48, 50; and conversation, 81; and attention, 90; and self-consciousness, 125, 129, 142; and intentions, 152, 153, 180; and humour, 184, 208, 213; and deceptive communication, 216
Third-person address (and voice), 27–28
Third-person information, 8
Third-person interactions, 39
Third-person methods, 32, 33–34, 50
Third-person perception, 29, 153

Thou (and *I-Thou*), 28, 32, 34–35, 43, 86, 119, 120, 233
Tomasello, M., 85–86, 99, 161, 167, 170
Touched (being), 38, 74, 147
Trevarthen, C., 60, 68, 71–73, 78, 81, 137, 139
Triadic deceptions, 227
Triadic interaction, 71, 105, 111–112, 117, 140, 252n14
Tronick, E., 73, 74, 76, 78, 81, 84

Uncertainty, 12–13
Unexpected attention, 132–134
Unexpectedness: in conversation, 83, 126, 176, 183, 212, 230; in humour, 185, 189, 212. *See also* Mis-expectedness in humour
Unexpected sensations, 113, 170

Van der Meer, A., 49, 124
Vygotsky, L., 69, 116

Wallon, H., 45, 137
Warnekken, F., 167
Wellman, H., 156
Whiten, A., 224, 226
Wilson, A., 218, 222, 223
Wittgenstein, L., 19–20, 63, 88, 163, 164
Woodward, A., 99, 156, 157, 158, 168

Zazzo, R., 45, 68
Zeedyk, S., 64